Education, Unemployment and the Future of Work

A.G. WATTS

Open University Press

Milton Keynes

Open University Press
A division of
Open University Educational Enterprises Limited
12 Cofferidge Close
Stony Stratford
Milton Keynes, MK11 1BY, England

First published 1983
Reprinted 1984

British Library Cataloguing in Publication Data

Watts, A.G.
   Education, unemployment and the future of work.
   1. Unemployment—Great Britain   2. Education—Great Britain
   I. Title
   331.13'77'0941   HD5765.A6

   ISBN 0-335-10411-8

Text design by W.A.P.

Typeset by Quadset Origination. Milton Keynes
Printed in Great Britain by J. W. Arrowsmith Ltd., Bristol BS3 2NT

Contents

Preface

Unemployment is not an educational problem. It is essentially due to economic forces, and political responses to those forces. It is however a problem *for* education, since it challenges many of the basic assumptions built into the structure of our educational system.

Over the past few years I have had many discussions with teachers and others about unemployment. For most of them, it has clearly been a deeply perplexing issue. They feel that they should respond to it, but they are uncertain how they can do so. They suspect that many of the responses being made at the moment are misconceived, but they find it difficult to mount cogent arguments for alternatives. They also sense that the growth in unemployment may signify a profound and enduring change that is taking place in our society, but they are uncertain about the nature of this change and about its implications for education.

I share many of these doubts and uncertainties. My main reason for writing this book has been to try to explore critically the mass of confused and conflicting ideas which surround the issue of unemployment and its educational implications. I hope that the book may help teachers and others to clarify their own ideas, and to design responses which are soundly based, creative, and intellectually honest.

The book's origins go back to 1976. In that year I was invited to be rapporteur at an Anglo-American conference on 'Young People in Contemporary Industrial Society' organized by the Ditchley Foundation (see Watts, 1977a). The conference accepted that unemployment was a long-term structural problem, which had major implications for youth policies. It had some influence on the policy discussions that subsequently led to the launching of the Youth Opportunities Programme. At a personal level, it challenged many of my assumptions about work and employment, and enabled me to clarify some of my confusions. I remember the strong physical sense of head-ache as I travelled home, my brain reeling from the intellectual intensity of the experience.

Around the same time, I carried out a small project for the Inner London Education Authority on the implications of unemployment for careers education. It was careers teachers and careers officers who in the 1970s carried the main initial brunt of responding to unemployment in schools. The project enabled me to work with a group of teachers in identifying what responses were possible, and what their assumptions and implications were. (see Watts, 1978) I later extended this work with a paper on careers education and the informal economies. (Watts, 1981)

Over the ensuing years, I have been invited to talk to many groups of people about unemployment. Gradually, I noticed that the audiences increasingly included not just careers teachers but head teachers and others with broader curricular and policy responsibilities. Moreover, my involvement in various projects carried out at the National Institute for Careers Education and Counselling (NICEC) made me aware that many of the same issues were being discussed within Manpower Services Commission programmes, in youth and community work, and in further, higher and adult education.

An approach from the Open University Press stimulated me to re-think and extend my previous work, and to place it in a broader framework. This book is the result. At the same time, a small grant from the Schools Council Industry Project enabled me to prepare the case studies which form the basis of chapter three.

I would like to acknowledge the help which both John Skelton (Open University Press) and Ian Jamieson (SCIP) have given me, as well as the hospitality and co-operation of the staff and pupils of the three schools covered in the case studies. I have also benefited from helpful critical comments on drafts from various friends and colleagues, including Anthony Adams, Peter Daws, Robin Guthrie, Ron Heisler, Eddy Knasel, Bill Law, Janet Morley, Elliot Stern, George Walker, and my brother Paul Watts. Gwyneth Neal-Freeman has typed countless drafts with her usual skill and patience. Other colleagues at NICEC and its two sponsoring bodies (CRAC and The Hatfield Polytechnic) have influenced in more indirect ways the ideas and views expressed in this book, as have many other people with whom I have worked over the last few years. Any strengths the book may have owe much to them; the faults and limitations are mine.

Tony Watts
June 1983

Acknowledgements

The author and publisher would like to thank the following for permission to reproduce copyright material:

The Political Quarterly for a passage from Jeremy Seabrook's 'Unemployment Now and in the 1930s' which appeared in Volume 52 No. 1, January-March 1981, and which was later reprinted in the author's book entitled *Unemployment* (Quartet, 1982); Blond and Briggs, for a passage from E.F. Schumacher's *Small is Beautiful* (1973); George Allen and Unwin (Publishers) Ltd. for a passage from W.H. Beveridge, *Full Employment in a Free Society* (1944); the Association for Adult and Continuing Education for two extracts from their evidence to the inquiry by ACACE into Education for Unemployed Adults, which was published in the *NATFHE Journal*, Volume 7 No. 3, April-May 1982, under the title 'More than an Alternative to Work'; the Controller of Her Majesty's Stationery Office for the extract from the Central Policy Review Staff's *Education, Training and Industrial Performance* (1980), and for the extract from the *Employment Gazette*, Volume 91 No. 4, April 1983; *Past and Present* for the various extracts from E.P. Thompson's article 'Time, Work-Discipline and Industrial Capitalism' in No. 38, 1967; Macmillan Publishers Ltd. for a passage from 'Economic Possibilities for our Grandchildren' in *Essays in Persuasion* (1931), by J.M. Keynes.

Part I

EDUCATION AND UNEMPLOYMENT

CHAPTER ONE

Education and Employment: the Traditional Bonds

'Education for unemployment'?

To approach educational aims from the concept of unemployment seems, on the surface, a peculiarly barren undertaking. 'Unemployment' is an essentially negative concept. It is defined not in terms of any positive attributes of its own, but simply in terms of the *absence* of employment. How can one approach education – which by definition is concerned with growth and development – from such a negative standpoint? As one Newcastle-upon-Tyne headmaster put it:

> I hope we shall never "educate for unemployment", which is a contradiction in terms and a sort of defeatist realism we can do without. (quoted in Watts, 1978, p. 233)

Much the same view was expressed by John Tomlinson, then Chairman of the Schools Council, in evidence to a House of Commons Select Committee:

> We utterly refute the notion that we should in the schools train children for unemployment. This is not what we are for, any more than we specifically train them for particular employment. What we are here to do is to release the maximum of their human capacities so that whatever life they may face, they can cope with it to the maximum of their capacity. That is all the schools can do. (quoted in House of Commons Education, Science and Arts Committee, 1981, para 7.42)

The Select Committee, while acknowledging that 'very regrettably, the prospect of the continuing unemployment of large numbers of school leavers is a situation which the schools must recognize', agreed that 'these new circumstances do not, in our view, require wholly new conceptions of the proper role of schools; it is rather that they underline the inadequacies and distortions of existing practice'. (*ibid*, para 7.43)

It is these assumptions that will be explored in this book. The notion of 'educating/training for unemployment', defined in an extreme sense, is unacceptable to most people. It is normally, however, left undefined. The danger is that posing the issue in this polarized way encourages the assumption that schools and other educational institutions can largely ignore the issue of unemployment and can properly retain their existing frameworks of assumptions and practices. This disregards the extent to which these assumptions and practices are based on the concept of *employment*. A consideration of the traditional bonds between education and employment is accordingly an essential starting point for our explorations, and will provide the theme of the rest of this opening chapter.

Ideals and realities

Education has of course much loftier ideals than those of preparation for employment. At its best, it is concerned with the development of the individual's full range of abilities and aptitudes, with the cultivation of spiritual and moral values, with the nurturing of imagination and sensibility, with the transmission and reinterpretation of culture. Indeed, there is a strong tradition within education which derides the instrumental or utilitarian, and which regards vocational matters as being improper educational concerns. As Peterson (1975) puts it:

> Education is, by tradition and in theory, a leisure activity. The word school is etymologically associated with leisure and the belief that "study" and "scholarship" and "learning" should be undertaken for their own sake and arise from the individual pupil's interest is a cliché of the educational theorist and of the prize-giving address. (p. 93)

Nonetheless, education has a close relationship with the world of work. Societies expect schools to develop in young people the knowledge, attitudes and skills which will enable them to contribute to the economy. Young people and their parents, too, expect schools to help them enter a worthwhile job. In a survey carried out by Morton-Williams and Finch (1968), 87 per cent of 15-year-old school-leavers thought that schools should 'teach you things which will help you to get as good a job or career as possible' (pp. 33-4) and

89 per cent of parents agreed with them. (p. 39) Only 47 per cent of teachers and 28 per cent of heads at that time considered this objective as very important for schools. (p. 42) Teachers frequently, however, find it useful to invoke the claim 'If you work hard, you will get a good job.'

Historically, the vocational connections of education in Britain are strong and pervasive. As Williams (1961) points out, the first English schools, from the late sixth century, had a primarily vocational intention: that of training intending priests and monks to conduct and understand the services of the Church, and to read the Bible and the writings of the Christian Fathers. (p. 127-8) As education grew during the Middle Ages, it 'was organized in general relation to a firm structure of inherited and destined status and condition: the craft apprentices, the future knights, the future clerisy'. (p. 131) This remained true through to the eighteenth century, which was remarkable for the growth of a number of new vocational academies, serving commerce, engineering, the arts, and the armed services (p. 134): in these academies, young people were prepared for the occupation they were to assume and the place in society it implied. The old classical education was still focused towards the old professions for which it had a vocational appropriateness – the church, the law (and later, as it grew, towards the Civil Service).

It was only really during the Industrial Revolution that, as Williams puts it, 'the old humanists muddled the issue by claiming a fundamental distinction between their traditional learning and that of the new disciplines' – notably science and technical education:

> . . . it was from this kind of thinking that there developed the absurd defensive reaction that all real learning was undertaken without thought of practical advantage. In fact, as the educational history shows, the classical linguistic disciplines were primarily vocational, but these particular vocations had acquired a separate traditional dignity, which was refused to vocations now of equal human relevance'. (p. 142)

The result was that élite educational institutions from the Victorian era tended to propagate a particular academic and cultural heritage which was associated with a gentlemanly disdain for vocational application, and particularly for industrial manufacture. The seductive social advantages attached to these strategies helped to produce a 'gentrification of the industrialist', which – it has been influentially argued – has contributed significantly to Britain's economic decline. (Wiener, 1981)

At the same time, however, the Industrial Revolution also saw the gradual extension of schooling from select and usually privileged groups to the mass of the population. Again, vocational motives were present. The new factories required large numbers of skilled and semi-skilled employees. Workers recruited for the land were notoriously ill-adapted to factory disciplines, and the schools were seen as one way in which they could be socialized into such disciplines. The aim was explicitly expressed by William Temple, when advocating in 1770 that poor children should be sent at the age of four to workhouses where they should be employed in manufactures and given two hours' schooling a day:

> 'There is considerable use in their being, somehow or other, constantly employed at least twelve hours a day, whether they earn their living or not; for by these means, we hope that the rising generations will be so habituated to constant employment that it would at length prove agreeable and entertaining to them . . . ' (quoted in Thompson, 1967, p. 84)

Factories required time-discipline, they required obedience, and they required a capacity to engage in rote, repetitive work. The new elementary schools were structured to develop all three, as well as to develop the basic skills of reading and counting that would equip workers to understand and implement simple instructions.

During the nineteenth century, such schooling was extended to all. In 1816 about 58 per cent of children attended a school of some kind for some period; by 1835 the figure had risen to 83 per cent, though the average duration of school attendance was still only one year; by 1851 the average duration had been raised to two years; and in 1870 universal elementary schooling became compulsory. (Williams, 1961, pp. 136-7) The notion of compulsory schooling owed much to the 'public educators', who argued that men had a natural right to be educated, and that any good society depended on governments accepting this principle as their duty. (*ibid*, p. 141) It also owed much to those who argued that a limited education in appropriate attitudes and habits – diligence, thrift, sobriety, deference to superiors, etc. – was necessary for social and political stability. (see Simon, 1960, chapter III) On the whole, it was the links between the concerns of the latter group and the focus of the 'industrial trainers' on the social character required by the industrial work-place which tended to be predominant in determining the content of the elementary school curriculum. They were even more influential on the method of pedagogy, with its emphasis on formal instruction requiring pupils to perform specified tasks within set periods of time determined by their teachers.

The battle between the 'public educators', the 'industrial trainers' and the 'old humanists' – as Williams (*ibid*) terms them – continued through the nineteenth and into the twentieth centuries. Gradually, scientific and technical education became established in the schools and universities, though still subject to the snobberies of the 'old humanists'. Gradually, too, the school-leaving age was raised, partly in response to arguments about the upgrading of the skill requirements of jobs and the need for the country to utilize more fully its human resources and talents. In 1944 secondary education for all was established on a tripartite basis – grammar, technical, and secondary modern. The divisions were intended to be broadly related to likely occupational destinations. Technical schools, designed largely to prepare for technician-level occupations, were never established on any very extensive scale; the grammar schools, however, led clearly to 'white-collar' occupations, while the secondary modern led to 'blue-collar' occupations. (Swift, 1973) The tripartite structure accordingly produced a system of what Turner (1960) termed 'sponsored' mobility, in which students were selected early for their occupational and social level, and thereafter were prepared for this status in terms partly of appropriate skills, but also of appropriate expectations, standards of behaviour, and values.

The rigidities of this system attracted increasing criticism during the 1950s and 1960s. It was pointed out that early selection meant decisions about the level of pupils' occupational destinations were being made prematurely before their abilities and aptitudes were evident, and that this had the effect of reinforcing the advantages stemming from their home background. (Floud *et al.*, 1956) The ideological concern for greater equality of opportunity, together with the demands for a more highly skilled work-force from a then prospering economy, provided a climate in which the decision was made to merge the three forms of school into comprehensive schools catering for the full range of ability. The system of 'sponsored' mobility was accordingly replaced to some extent by a system of 'contest' mobility. This Turner (1960) likened to a race or other sporting event, in which all compete on equal terms for a limited number of prizes, and in which premature judgements on the results of the race are avoided.

In the event, this change was never fully implemented. Some areas continued to maintain selective schooling, in practice and even sometimes in name. The differences between catchment areas meant that comprehensive schools in some areas were very like grammar schools, whereas in others they were virtually indistinguishable from secondary moderns. Again, the retention of rigid streaming in many comprehensive schools permitted curricular divisions to survive institutional integration. Finally, the continued existence of élite forms of education outside the state educational system, in the independent schools, meant that some parents continued to be able to purchase advantageous positions in the 'race'.

The incomplete implementation of the comprehensive school reforms meant that the socialization processes within schools preparing pupils for their levels of occupational destination continued to operate (Ashton and Field, 1976), but that they were increasingly concealed within a curriculum structure and examination system which permitted all pupils to take part in the 'race' instead of prematurely excluding large numbers from it. Whereas in 1961/2 73 per cent of pupils in England and Wales had left school without even attempting a public school-leaving examination (Ministry of Education, 1964, table B), the

growth of comprehensive schools – along with the advent of the CSE, and the
raising of the school-leaving age to 16 – meant that by 1973/4 only 20 per cent
of pupils left school in England without a graded GCE/CSE result, and by
1980/1 this figure had fallen to 11 per cent. (DES, 1982b, table 3) Since the
main prizes were perceived as being associated with 'white-collar' work,
almost all pupils became subjected to a more academic curriculum, with increased emphasis on the acquisition of knowledge and the ability to reproduce
it on paper for the benefit of examination assessors. (Dore, 1976) While the
content of the curriculum thus became less relevant to the occupations which
many pupils would come to perform, its connections with the world of
employment grew no less. Its basic rationale was that it provided a
meritocratic foundation on which selection for occupational destinations
could be based. If secondary schools in particular no longer *prepared* pupils for
particular forms of employment in such an overt and direct way as hitherto,
what they did continued to be influenced and justified by the extent to which
it determined *access* to employment.

The bonds

It will be evident from this brief historical outline that links with employment
have been, and continue to be, a powerful influence on the development of
education in Britain. In broad terms, four functions which educational institutions can play in relation to employment can be distinguished: those of selection, socialization, orientation, and preparation. Each will now be briefly examined in turn.

(1) *Selection.* Over the past century or so, there has been a steady movement
from the ascription of status by birth to the achivement of status through
education. As a result, the educational process has ceased to be concerned
simply with the transmission of skills and values: increasingly it has taken on
the functions of allocating and selecting as well as training individuals for their
adult roles. (Banks, 1976, p. 5) Particular educational qualifications are now
necessary prerequisites for entry to many occupations, and are used in selection
by many employers. The case for credentialism of this kind is partly based on a
utilitarian principle of *efficiency,* recognizing the importance of developing the
society's talents to the full and deploying them to maximum effect, so that the
most able people can find their way into the most important and demanding
jobs. In part, too, it is concerned with *equity,* making it possible for the social
status of individuals to be determined by their talents and their efforts rather
than by the accidents of birth.

It is important to recognize that in practice credentialism seems to satisfy
neither of these principles very satisfactorily. In terms of efficiency, the

relationship between educational qualifications and degree of success in an occupation is often very low. (for American evidence on this, see Hoyt, 1965;
Collins, 1979, pp. 19-20) This may be partly because professional associations,
in the search for reduced supply and increased status, are constantly upgrading
the educational qualifications required for entry (Dore, 1976, pp. 24-8; Watts,
1973b); the same process is used by employers seeking convenient ways of
restricting the number of job applicants to a manageable size. As Berg (1970)
has shown in the USA, this process of meritocratic inflation can proceed to a
point where, far from adding to workers' productivity and satisfaction, it
reduces them because the workers are over-qualified and their skills are not
being utilized. Moreover, many of the attributes which are most important in
determining occupational success – social skills, for example – are not
measured by educational qualifications. Such qualifications are thus often used
as criteria for occupational entry not because they are relevant but because
they are administratively convenient and publicly defensible.

Their defensibility is largely due to the appearance they give of being
socially equitable. But here, too, there is room for scepticism. Bourdieu and
Passeron (1977) argue that schools trade in exclusive forms of 'cultural capital'
based on the symbols, language forms, structure and meanings of bourgeois
culture, and that students with access to such cultural capital – primarily
through their families – do well in school because educational achievement is
measured in terms of the skills and knowledge which the cultural capital
provides. Certainly it is the case that upper-middle-class children born in the
period 1930-49 were three times as likely as lower-middle-class children to
reach a university, and nearly 12 times as likely as lower-working-class
children to do so. (Halsey, 1975, p. 14) Admittedly these differentials were
lower than for children born during the period 1910-29, suggesting some
reduction of social class inequalities of access to educational opportunities.
Westergaard and Resler (1975, pp. 324-6), however, have suggested that this
moderate widening of education as an avenue of ability has been counteracted
by a concomitant contraction of other channels of mobility – notably independent entrepreneurial activity and mid-career promotion up the rungs of
bureaucratic hierarchies – resulting from, among other things, increased attention to educational qualifications in schools and colleges. As a result, they
argue, credentialism and the expansion of educational provision are likely to
have had little or no net impact on social mobility. Even if one does not argue
such an extreme case, it is clear that credentialism does not remove inequalities, and that even if it diminishes them to some extent, it adds apparent
legitimacy to those that remain.

Moreover, the extent of the use made of educational qualifications should
not be exaggerated. As Maguire and Ashton (1981) demonstrate, employers
do not in practice place such emphasis on educational qualifications as schools

often imagine they do. At the higher levels of the occupational hierarchy, qualifications are often necessary but not sufficient: employers use them as a convenient pre-selection device when deciding which applicants to consider more closely, but thereafter pay little attention to them. At the lower occupational levels, qualifications are frequently used simply as crude measures not of cognitive abilities but of such normative qualities as perseverance and capacity for hard work, or are ignored altogether.

Nonetheless, the process of credentialism has had a powerful effect on education. It has increased the demand for education; it has also affected its nature. In surveys conducted in Ireland, Raven (1977) found that the goals to which primacy was attached by pupils, ex-pupils, parents, teachers and employers – for example, the fostering of personal qualities and capabilities like initiative, self-confidence, and the ability to deal with others – received scant attention in schools and, as a result, were poorly attained. Teachers and pupils worked not towards the goals which they believed to be the most important from an educational point of view, but towards goals that could be assessed in a manner acceptable for the award of educational qualifications. The result was to restrict what went on in schools to activities that were narrowly utilitarian and instrumental in scope. The available evidence indicates that much the same is true in Britain.

This process contains many ironic contradictions. Intrinsic educational values are subordinated to the extrinsic need to provide tickets to employment. Yet the content of these 'tickets' has very little direct vocational relevance, and its indirect relevance is much more pertinent to white-collar than to other occupations. The content is controlled not by employers but, ultimately, by the universities. For at each stage of the educational system, the content of the curriculum tends to be determined by the needs not of those who will 'drop out' at that stage, but of those who will go on to the next; and at the apex of this structure stand the universities, which in addition exert a powerful influence on school examination boards. Their control 'protects' the school curriculum from vocational influence, in line with the heritage of Williams' 'old humanists'. The status of subjects tends to be measured by the extent to which they have moved away from utilitarian or pedagogic traditions and have become 'academic'. (Goodson, 1983)

The result is an extension to almost all school pupils of an academic curriculum very like that previously offered only to the few in the grammar schools. This curriculum is experienced by many young people as irrelevant to their immediate and future interests. The notion that the traditional liberal curriculum has some particular intrinsic virtue which work-oriented subjects do not, as a medium through which spiritual, intellectual and aesthetic powers can be developed, is itself open to question. (Peterson, 1975, p. 95) But even if it were true, the chances of achieving these ends with pupils suspicious of such a curriculum are greatly diminished by the examination system, which means that these pupils see the curriculum chiefly as a means of labelling them as failures through an opaque process based on restricted academic criteria. They are aware that the applicability of these criteria outside the educational world is highly disputable, particularly in the non-professional and non-clerical jobs for which many of them are destined. Moreover, although the whole process is justified to them by the supposed need to perform a sorting and preselection function for employers, this service in reality is not as widely used by employers as is commonly supposed; and because of their limited vantage point, pupils tend to underestimate even the extent to which it is used. (see Gray *et al.*, 1983, pp. 136-41)

Thus although the examination system provides an effective motivational spur for some, it is counter-productive for others, and can indeed alienate them permanently from formal learning. It also more generally develops an instrumental attitude to learning and work in which intrinsic motives such as actual enjoyment of working hard are rejected and regarded as socially unacceptable. (Turner, 1983) Indeed, Flude and Parrott (1979, pp. 67-8) consider that 'it is the attitudes and values engendered by public examinations, and the image of education which this adolescent, academic steeplechase provokes in parents, teachers and pupils, which represent the main barrier to the development of recurrent education'.

(2) *Socialization.* The second function which educational institutions can play in relation to employment is that of influencing students' attitudes to the world of work, and to their own function within it, through the formal and informal organization of educational institutions and the social relations within them. In the USA, Bowles and Gintis (1976) have argued that in many key respects the structure and social relations of education accurately reflect and reproduce the structure and social relations of the work-place. Both are organized hierarchically; in both, alienated workers are motivated by extrinsic rewards (examination marks in school, pay at work); and in both, work tasks are fragmented. This 'close correspondence between the social relationships which govern personal interaction in the work place and the social relationships of the educational system' (*ibid*, p. 12) means that schools nurture, within young people of different types, attitudes and behaviour consonant with their likely future levels of participation in the labour force. Those destined for managerial and professional occupations are presented during their educational careers with situations in which they are asked to be autonomous, independent and creative; those destined for the shop-floor are subjected to custodial regimes which stress obedience to rules, passivity and conformity.

In the British context, Ashton and Field (1976) have described how the identities of pupils destined for different occupational levels are established or reinforced by the identities created within their schools. Thus those destined for 'extended careers' – characterized by long training and the continuing prospect of advancement – come to see themselves as possessing superior abilities, to see the successful performance of their allotted school tasks in the light of the long-term rewards associated with the entry into a 'good career', and to understand the importance both of personal advancement and of loyalty to the organization. The importance of 'getting on' and of 'making something of themselves' is also transmitted to those destined for 'short-term careers' – in skilled manual trades, technical occupations, and some forms of clerical and secretarial work – which again are characterized by formal training but which offer little chance of advancement beyond a certain level. Here, though, the organizational structure of the school, including streaming and more informal channelling mechanisms, restricts their access to the certification required for entry to extended careers.

Finally, those destined for 'careerless occupations' – which require little training and offer no prospects of promotion and little or no intrinsic job satisfaction – receive derogatory messages which, as we have seen, teach them to see themselves as 'failures'. Their realization that academic subjects have no rewards to offer them persuades them instead to seek some alternative sources of reward or satisfaction in the here and now – for example, through persistent rule-breaking and 'messing about'. Not only are these young people committed to semi-skilled and unskilled work by their educational experience, but their self-image of being academically inferior, their concern with obtaining extrinsic rewards as immediately as they can, and their desire to leave school as soon as possible, all mean that jobs of this kind have certain attractions. As Willis (1977) points out, this means that the very forms of resistance used within a school counter-culture by alienated groups of working-class boys lead them to make a largely willing entry into unskilled forms of labour, in which they are subsequently trapped – a powerful, even poignant, form of 'self-induction'. They even presage the forms of resistance – skiving etc. – which will enable them to cope with the monotony of such jobs.

Such analyses can evidently be applied too rigidly, to a point where they become mechanistic and deterministic. Clearly there are many respects in which schools do not reproduce the values and social relations of the work-place. Indeed, some influential commentators in recent years have argued that schools do not mirror the world of work well enough, but instead encourage patterns of dependency and immaturity which inhibit the process of transition to adulthood and to employment. (Bazalgette, 1978a; Scharff, 1976; see also chapter two) Clearly, too, the divisions between the groups distinguished by Ashton and Field are not as rigidly marked as the description above might suggest. The movement from a 'sponsored' to a 'contest' system – however incomplete it may have been – means that the forces of socialization have been weakened somewhat, because the point of differentiation has been postponed, and its rigidity relaxed to some extent. Teachers have become more resistant to the notion that they should be performing a 'sorting' function, and adapting pupils to accept low-level jobs which make little use of their potential. Such resistance has indeed proceeded to a point where numbers of employers have grown concerned about the discrepancies between the expectations and attitudes that school-leavers have been encouraged to develop and the demands that will realistically be made of them. (for a useful analysis of these and other differences of view between teachers and employers, see Bridges, 1981) Nonetheless, the changes that have taken place in opening up opportunities within educational institutions are often more apparent than real: for example, secondary school pupils continue to be sifted by teachers in terms of their perceived aptitudes, despite the rhetoric of pupils making their own subject 'choices'. (Woods, 1979, especially chapter 2) The process of socialization into employment remains a strong feature of the educational system – all the stronger because it is often implicit rather than explicit, and hidden even to the teachers who promote it.

(3) *Orientation.* The third function is concerned with deliberate curricular interventions designed to help students to understand the world of employment, and to prepare for the choices and transitions they will have to make on entering it. To some extent it can be seen as an attempt to reinforce the process of socialization where it is not proving sufficiently effective. Alternatively, it can also be seen as being designed to make the process more visible and therefore open to question and deliberation – to make it a learning process rather than merely a conditioning process.

This orientation function has two distinguishable facets. One is *careers education,* which is concerned with helping students to prepare for their individual career choices and transitions. From its traditionally peripheral position within education, based on narrow concepts of information-giving and individual interviewing, careers guidance in the early 1970s increasingly came to be incorporated into the curriculum itself. (Schools Council, 1972; DES, 1973; Watts, 1973a) Many schools and other educational institutions now have curricular programmes focused around four broad aims: 'opportunity awareness', covering awareness of the range of alternatives open in and around the world of work, the demands they make, and the rewards and satisfactions they offer; 'self awareness', covering awareness of the distinct abilities, interest, values, etc. that define the kind of person one is and/or wishes to become; 'decision learning', covering development of decision-making skills; and 'transition learning', covering development of skills to cope with the transition to work and subsequent career transitions. (Law and Watts, 1977) Some schools establish careers education as a separate 'subject';

some integrate it into a broader programme of social and personal education; and some seek to 'infuse' it across the traditional areas of the curriculum. A survey conducted in 1975-8 by Her Majesty's Inspectorate (DES, 1979a, p. 230) found that half of secondary schools had a programme of this kind in the fourth and fifth years for all their pupils, and a further 12-15 per cent a programme for some of their pupils. Careers-education programmes have also been introduced in higher education (Watts, 1977b) and for adults. (Watts, 1980) The notion that careers-education programmes can help people to participate actively in the decisions that determine their lives has been questioned by Roberts (1977; 1981), who argues that in reality people's lives are largely determined by the opportunity structure, and that many people have to accept what they can get. This has been disputed by other writers (e.g. Daws, 1977; 1981; Law, 1981a; 1981b), who have argued that there remains sufficient scope for such programmes to have an impact.

The second facet of the orientation function is *learning about work,* as part of social and political education within (in particular) schools. The central concept here is that all school pupils – regardless of when and where they are to work themselves, and as part of the preparation for their role not of *worker* but of *citizen* – should be taught to understand the place of work in society. Various approaches have been developed, including curriculum courses on 'industry' and related topics, and infusion of such topics into traditional subjects across the curriculum. There has also been emphasis on experiential methods, including work experience, work simulation, and the use of 'adults other than teachers' (including employers and trade unionists) in the classroom. (see Jamieson and Lightfoot, 1982; Watts, 1983a)

A particular concern behind many such programmes has been the notion that young people should understand the process of wealth generation in general and the role of manufacturing industry in particular. Discussion of such matters is in principle welcomed not only by the political right but also by the left, so long as it is possible to regard the *status quo* as open to challenge and question. (see e.g. Edgley, 1977) In practice, however, the boundaries set by government statements and the like tend to be narrow, and to avoid any suggestions that the matters under discussion are disputable or politically controversial. Some teachers thus fear that if they engage in such issues, they will be compelled to engage in a form of indoctrination. Accordingly, they sometimes prefer to evade the issues altogether. (Beck, 1981, p. 89) Significantly, the most effective project in this area – the Schools Council Industry Project – has disarmed such suspicions by having the support of the Trades Union Congress as well as the Confederation of British Industry, and has adopted a low-profile approach in which emphasis has been placed not on centrally-produced policy statements and curriculum materials, but on encouraging local curriculum development which is experience-based and in which the teachers' role is shared to a much greater extent than is usual with employers, unionists and other members of the community. (see Jamieson and Lightfoot, 1982)

(4) *Preparation.* The fourth and final function is that of promoting the acquisition of specific skills and knowledge which students will be able to apply in a direct way after entering employment. As we have seen, this function was strongly evident in the practice of education up to the Industrial Revolution, if only in relation to certain occupations. Subsequently it has diminished in prominence, certainly within schools and universities. The general view has come to be that such preparation should properly be left to employers and to other post-school institutions like colleges of further education and polytechnics. It is argued, for example, that introducing significant vocational training into schools would require resources, equipment and expertise which schools rarely possess. It would also run the danger of limiting pupils' occupational horizons prematurely, and – unless great care was taken – it might develop knowledge and skills which would be inappropriate to, or would rapidly become outdated in, a changing labour market. Further, it is pointed out that many of the skills that are most important at work are generic skills like numeracy and literacy: if schools concentrate on these, then they are providing a form of preparation but without closing options unnecessarily.

On the other hand, it is recognized that what the Brunton Report in Scotland felicitously termed the 'vocational impulse' (SED, 1963, p. 24) can be a powerful incentive to learning. Also, unless steps are taken to introduce a wider range of vocational skills into the school curriculum, the effects of schooling may be to establish a bias in favour of the white-collar occupations to which, as was suggested earlier, the academic forms of learning used in schools tend to be most relevant. The result may be to raise aspirations which cannot be met, and to develop attitudes that impede occupational flexibility.

On the whole, however, the tendency until recently has been to limit the extent to which schools have been involved in vocational preparation. The vocational courses set up in many secondary-modern schools in the 1950s to yield the motivational advantages of the 'vocational impulse' largely disappeared with comprehensive reorganization, and teachers became resistant to them, for reasons already mentioned. Even employers tended on the whole to bear out the findings of the Carr Committee (National Joint Advisory Council, 1958, p. 23) that 'the overwhelming majority of industries are of the opinion that education given at school before the minimum school-leaving age is reached should be general rather than vocational in character' and should not engage in offering 'some sort of vocational instruction which industry itself is much better qualified to give'. Trade unions, too, consistently opposed vocational education in schools, on the grounds that it would operate to the disadvantage of working-class children, who would be bound to be pressurized into forms of work which were more appropriate to their social station than to their innate aptitudes and abilities. (Jamieson and Lightfoot, 1982, p. 39) Certainly the evidence from such programmes in the USA indicates that, narrowly defined, they are almost invariably limited to low-attaining students and lower-level occupations, that they restrict access to higher-status and better-paid jobs, and that they accordingly acquire a stigma which limits and in time discredits their appeal. (Grubb and Lazerson, 1981) In short, the irony of vocational-preparation programmes is that they tend to deprive their students of access to what in terms of status and income must be regarded as the *real* vocational prizes.

Concluding comments

It will be evident that there are some tensions and conflicts between the four functions of education in relation to employment, and that the balance between them has shifted over the years. In broad terms, the brief historical outline presented earlier in the chapter can be analysed as a process within which the socialization and preparation functions on the whole were weakened over time, while the selection and orientation functions in general grew stronger.

To understand this, it is helpful to return to Turner's (1960) distinction between 'sponsored' and 'contest' systems of social mobility. In a 'sponsored' system, in which young people are prepared from an early age for their different occupational and social destinations, any selection function will be performed so early that it will not unduly influence the content of the curriculum: instead, the curriculum will be dominated by the socialization and preparation functions, with the orientation function being largely redundant. On the other hand, in a true 'contest' system, in which a common curriculum is offered to all young people and allocation to destinations is postponed until towards the end of the process, the curriculum will tend to be dominated by the demands of the selection function: there will thus be little or no room for the preparation function except in the most general sense, and the socialization function will be sufficiently weakened that there will be demands for it to be bolstered (or further undermined?) by a more deliberate orientation function.

Of course, Britain has never had a true 'contest' system of social mobility. Nonetheless, the three decades following the Second World War saw a significant shift of will in that direction, and as a result the examination system came to dominate the work of secondary schools. Within a growing economy capable of offering employment of some kind to all who wanted it, it had some credibility. The number of prizes seemed sufficient to sustain motivation on the part of a sufficient number of pupils, and there was something to offer even to the losers. In the 1970s and 1980s, however, the economic climate changed drastically, and growing unemployment threatened to undermine the rules of the race. It is to the growth of unemployment, and its impact on the traditional bonds between education and employment, that we turn in chapter two.

Summary

Chapter one has introduced the controversial notion of 'education for unemployment', and has pointed out that wholesale opposition to it tends to disregard the extent of the existing bonds between education and employment. A brief historical outline has indicated the strong vocational influences on the development of education in Britain. Four main bonds have been distinguished. The first is the *selection* function of using educational qualifications in selection for employment. The second is the *socialization* function of influencing in indirect ways students' attitudes to the world of work, and to their own function within it. The third is the *orientation* function of making deliberate curricular interventions designed to help students to understand the world of employment, and to prepare for the choices and transitions they will have to make on entering it. And the fourth is the *preparation* function of developing specific skills and knowledge which students will be able to apply in a direct way after entering employment. It has been argued that the selection and orientation functions have increased in importance, while the socialization and preparation functions have to some extent been weakened, as efforts have been made to delay the point at which students are sorted according to their different occupational and social destinations.

CHAPTER TWO

Unemployment and the Tightening of the Bonds

The growth of unemployment

The two decades following the Second World War were periods of remarkably full employment in Britain. Between 1948 and 1966, unemployment averaged 1.7 per cent, and was almost entirely 'frictional' in nature (i.e. due to workers having fairly short intervals in moving between jobs); for much of the period, the number of long-term unemployed was negligible. (Deacon, 1981, p. 67) The unemployment rate was lower even than the 'irreducible minimum' of 3 per cent envisaged by Beveridge (1944, pp. 126-8) in his report on *Full Employment in a Free Society*.

From 1966, however, unemployment levels began to rise. They did so irregularly, in a cycle which corresponded to the economic cycle of recession and recovery. At each recession, though, the peak of unemployment was higher than in previous ones; and each recovery period had a low point of unemployment higher than the previous recovery. From under half a million officially regarded as unemployed in the mid-1960s, the figure rose to over a million in 1975, to over two million in 1980, and to three million in 1983. Meanwhile, the number of vacancies remained very low, so that by March 1983 there were 24 people unemployed for each vacancy (figure 2.1).

Figure 2.1   Unemployment and vacancies: United Kingdom 1965-83

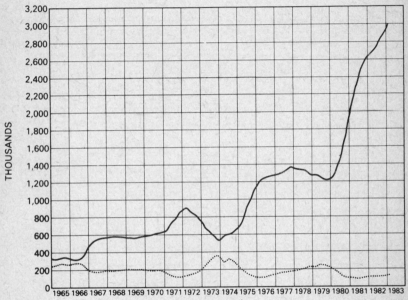

Three-month moving average: seasonally adjusted.

—— Unemployed excluding
school leavers
········ Vacancies at Jobcentres*

*Vacancies at Jobcentres are only about a third of total vacancies.

Source: Department of Employment (1983c, table C1)

It is arguable that these official figures have systematically underestimated the true extent of unemployment. They exclude unemployed school-leavers, of whom in March 1983 there were 112,200 (Department of Employment, 1983c, table 2.1). They also exclude those who register for full-time work but

do not claim benefit: from November 1982 these were dropped from the
official figures, and at the point of transition – in October 1982 – they
amounted to 236,000. (MSC, 1982b, p. 6) Moreover, the 1981 Labour Force
Survey showed that almost one-fifth of those actively seeking work were not
registered as unemployed (OPCS, 1982b, table 4.14): most of these were
married women and others who had no entitlement to benefit. In addition,
there are 'discouraged workers' not entitled to benefit who are available for
and would like work, but are not actively seeking it because they have given
up hope of finding it, and accordingly do not regard themselves as
'unemployed'. (see Joshi, 1981) On the basis of a MORI poll, Kellner (1981)
estimated that these 'discouraged workers' would have raised the total of
unregistered unemployed to one million: it seems likely that this figure will
have increased since then. Even this takes no account of three other groups hit
by unemployment: those on short-time working, of whom in February 1983
there were 138,000 (Department of Employment, 1983c, table 1.11); those
who are 'temporarily stopped' (i.e. ready to resume working but available for
benefit on the day the count is taken), of whom in March 1983 there were
19,225 (*ibid*, table 2.14); and in particular those on government job-creation
and work-experience schemes of various kinds, of whom in January 1983
there were 360,000 who would otherwise have been claiming benefit.
(Department of Employment Press Notice, 31 March 1983) If all these are
added up, the 'true' number of unemployed could be argued to have been
nearing five million at the beginning of 1983.

It is important to point out that a fair proportion of the unemployed is not a
'stagnant pool' but a 'flow'. This means that unemployment directly affects a
far higher proportion of the population than the figures indicate. An
Observer/NOP poll (Taylor, 1982) estimated that, even within conventional
definitions, one in four of Britain's workers – about six million people – had
been unemployed at some point during the preceding 12 months. At the same
time, however, the number of long-term unemployed has been increasing
rapidly. By January 1983, over one million (34 per cent of the unemployed)
had been without employment for more than a year, and of these, 480,000 (15
per cent) and 190,000 (6 per cent) had experienced more than two and three
years' continuous unemployment respectively. (MSC, 1983, p. 4) Moreover,
the fact that many people experience recurrent patterns of unemployment
means that these figures, based upon the duration of single spells of
unemployment, underestimate its impact. In an MSC follow-up study, only
64 per cent of those who had found jobs 10 months after being unemployed
were still in employment after a further 10 months. (*ibid*, p. 5)

Young people have been particularly hard-hit by the rise in
unemployment. In the early 1960s, the unemployment rate among the under-
20s was roughly the same as the overall rate – in 1966 it was 1.4 per cent in

both cases. But from then, the relative position of young people grew steadily worse. (Mukherjee, 1974, p. 28) Between 1972 and 1977, school-leaver unemployment rose by 120 per cent, compared with 45 per cent among the working population as a whole. (Rees and Gregory, 1981, p. 7) From 1977, the scale of school-leaver unemployment was contained somewhat by 'special measures', and notably by diverting many unemployed young people on to the Youth Opportunities Programme for temporary periods. Without such measures, the Manpower Services Commission estimated in 1981 that for those aged under 18, unemployment rates for the first quarter of the year (the low point in the annual cycle of youth unemployment) would have been 17 per cent in 1980 and probably 48 per cent in 1982 and 54 per cent in 1984; the proportions at the peak of the cycle in the second quarter would have been 32 per cent, 63 per cent and 67 per cent respectively. (quoted in *Unemployment Unit Bulletin*, No. 1, 1981) Even when YOP is excluded from consideration, 33 per cent of all 16/17-year-olds available for work in July 1982 were registered as unemployed, and by October 1982 this had only fallen to 28 per cent (as compared with a figure for all ages of 13.5 per cent). (MSC, 1982b, p. 3) Moreover, a survey by Roberts *et al.* (1981, p. 18) found that many unemployed young people aged 16-20 failed to register: the proportion varied between 10-14 per cent in areas of the Midlands and North-West and 40-48 per cent in areas of London.

The development of the Youth Opportunities Programme into the Youth Training Scheme is likely to reduce these figures, since YTS is designed as a 12-month programme rather than as normally a six-month one, and does not have to be preceded, as YOP usually did, by a period on the dole. Furthermore, the extent of youth unemployment should be eased somewhat by demographic factors, since there is due to be a decline of 30 per cent in the numbers of school-leavers between 1981/2 and 1992/3. (DES, 1983)

It seems probable, however, that young people will continue to be particularly badly affected by unemployment. Already there is growing concern not just for the under-18 age group, but also for the 18-19 group (for whom the unemployment rate in October 1982 was 27.8 per cent) and for the 20-24 group (for whom it was 20.1 per cent). (MSC, 1982b, p. 3) Hitherto, the duration of unemployment among young people has been reasonably short. This has meant that the figures at any one time have understated – to an even greater extent than for other groups – the number affected by unemployment, but that its durational impact on the young people concerned has on the whole been less than on other unemployed people. One 1977 survey in Scotland, for instance, found that about half the young people who were employed at the time of the survey had experienced unemployment since leaving school, but that more than half of those who were unemployed at the time of the survey had previously held a job. (Gray *et al.*, 1983, p. 153)

Between 1980 and 1982, however, the rate of long-term unemployment (i.e. those unemployed for more than a year) grew faster among the 18-24 age group than among any other group, and by 1982 it was higher among this group than among any other group apart from those over 60. (MSC, 1982a, p. 42)

Impact on education

What impact has the massive increase of unemployment in general, and of youth unemployment in particular, had on educational institutions? It is of course difficult to disentangle one particular element from the variety of other influences on education during this period. Nonetheless, it seems clear that unemployment has had a significant effect on education in at least three identifiable respects.

First, for school-leavers and their parents it has represented a challenge to the legitimacy of schooling. (Finn, 1982, p. 52) In the 1960s, education was 'sold' to the public as opening doors to better occupational opportunities. Access to examination qualifications, and the advantages they offered, were, as we saw in chapter one, used increasingly as the incentive to persuade adolescent pupils to attend, to behave well, and to work hard in school. With rising unemployment, however, the promises upon which this normative structure was based have become increasingly difficult to deliver. The claim to be offering access to opportunities has begun to ring more and more hollow not only to those who still leave school without any qualifications at all, but also to those who acquire qualifications but then find that they have little or no value on the labour market. The result was considered sufficiently important to be stressed by Pope John Paul II during his visit to Britain in 1982:

> Nowadays, as we have been made only too aware, the possession of a certificate does not bring automatic employment. Indeed, this harsh reality has brought about not only deep frustration among young people, many of whom have worked so hard, but also a sense of malaise in the education system itself. (quoted in *Times Educational Supplement*, 4 June 1982)

A survey in the Vauxhall area of Liverpool suggested that many youngsters 'switched off from school because they quite realistically saw it as a waste of time'. (Ridley, 1981, p. 23)

Second, there began in the mid-1970s to be increasing suggestions – usually implicit, but sometimes explicit – that the growth of youth unemployment had to some extent been *caused* by the deficiencies of schools. Various people – including some politicians and sections of the press – argued that young people were failing to find jobs because their schools had not enabled them to acquire the skills and attitudes which would have made them employable. In historical terms, as an explanation of the rise in youth unemployment, this accusation was nonsense: there was no evidence that educational standards were significantly lower, or less congruent with the needs of employers, than they had been in the period of relatively full employment immediately preceding the rise in unemployment. Clearly youth unemployment resulted essentially from economic forces and political responses to those forces – including, notably, a deficiency of aggregate demand in the economy, a government reluctance to boost demand, and redundancy legislation and trade-union bargaining power which tended to favour those already in jobs at the expense of those entering employment for the first time, as well as deeper structural factors which will be discussed in chapter five. Nonetheless, scapegoats were wanted, and the educational system was a convenient candidate, made the more superficially plausible by the undermining of the promises embedded in the examination system.

Third, and less cynically, education has been seen as an instrument with which to *respond* to the problem of youth unemployment. There have been widespread fears that, if jobs could not be found for young people, this might result in crime, delinquency, riots and threats to the social fabric. (Mungham, 1982) Attention has therefore been focused on ways of keeping unemployed young people off the streets, preferably within some form of education and/or training framework which will maintain and develop their employability, so that if jobs become available, the young people will be equipped to take them. This could be linked with the fact that delayed entry into the labour force – along with the economies in training costs effected by many employers in response to their increasing preoccupation at a time of recession with short-term survival rather than longer-term growth and development – has meant that there is now more need for the educational system to develop the skills and attitudes which previously developed reasonably naturally after entry to employment.

The 'Great Debate' and its aftermath

The first and third of these factors were in close attendance when in 1976 the second factor came into sharp prominence with the launching of the so-called 'Great Debate' on education by the then Prime Minister, James Callaghan. In a widely-reported speech at Ruskin College, Oxford, he expressed his concern about the need to improve relátions between industry and education. He said he was troubled to find industry complaining that new recruits from schools lacked the basic skills required for some jobs, and was further troubled to discover that the best-trained students from universities and polytechnics had no intention of joining industry: there was 'a need for a more technological emphasis in science teaching that will lead towards practical applications in industry, rather than towards academic standards' (sic). At the same time, he was concerned about the standards of school-leavers and about the effects of modern informal teaching methods. While schools clearly should not aim simply to produce technically efficient robots, he said, there was no virtue in producing socially well-adjusted members of society who were unemployed because they lacked skills. (*The Times,* 19 October 1976)

Callaghan's speech was followed by a series of conferences and reports. (notably DES, 1977a; 1977b; 1979a; 1979b; 1980a; 1980b; 1981; Schools Council, 1981) As the 'Great Debate' developed, it became clear that the attack on education had a number of strands to it. (for useful accounts, see Centre for Contemporary Cultural Studies, 1981, chapter 10; Finn, 1982; Jamieson and Lightfoot, 1982, pp. 13 ff) These can be fruitfully linked to the different functions of education in relation to employment which were distinguished in chapter one: selection, socialization, orientation (covering both careers education and learning about work), and preparation.

One set of strands was focused around the notion that schools discouraged their pupils from entering a career in industry. Sometimes this criticism referred to manufacturing industry in general; sometimes more specifically to careers in engineering and technology. On some occasions it referred to the notion that *not enough* young people were being encouraged to enter the careers in question; on others to the notion that not enough of the *most able* young people were being so encouraged. In each case, however, the underlying notion was that teachers were part of a 'benign circle' in which teachers influenced able pupils to move into the liberal professions or into pure science, from which the next generation of teachers merged to continue the process; by contrast the less able pupils were part of a 'vicious circle' whereby those who did not do well on the 'academic' criteria of success valued in schools found themselves in industry, conscious of their inferior status and anxious that their children should avoid their fate. (Jamieson and Lightfoot, 1982, pp. 16-18) One of the responses that was sought was the improvement of careers education in schools. If career choices were left to the hidden curriculum of the school, they would continue to show an 'academic' and 'anti-industrial' bias. Deliberate and positive efforts needed to be made to present a fuller range of career options.

This argument was often loosely linked with another one, which was that – as the discussion document produced by the DES (1977a) for the 'Great Debate' put it – 'pupils leave school with little or no understanding of the workings, or importance, of the wealth-producing sector of our economy'. (p. 12) Behind this lay the view that an important source of Britain's economic problems was the unfavourable attitudes held towards industry by large sections of the population. This antipathy stemmed from a deep vein of cultural influences, including pseudo-aristocratic snobberies and rural nostalgia. (Wiener, 1981) Education was seen as one of the sources of these influences: it was also seen as a means through which they could be mollified or corrected. (Jamieson and Lightfoot, 1982, p. 15) Accordingly it was suggested that teachers should be given greater experience, knowledge and understanding of trade and industry, and that 'young people need to reach maturity with a basic understanding of the economy and its activities, especially manufacturing industry, which are necessary for the creation of Britain's economic wealth'. (DES, 1977b, p. 35) Such arguments tended to make no allowance for any critical views of the structure of the world of work: their concern was with inculcating a particular set of 'right' interpretations and attitudes.

Interestingly, the balance between these two facets of the 'orientation' function – careers education and learning about work – shifted somewhat as the debate proceeded. In the original DES discussion paper for the debate, careers education and guidance was regarded as one of the five 'fixed points in the curriculum' in, particularly, the fourth and fifth years of secondary school. (DES, 1977a, p. 4) In later documents, however, careers education came to be dropped from the 'common core' of the curriculum, and to be included alongside learning about work as one of several aspects of preparation for adult life which all secondary schools should build into their curriculum in some way or other. (DES, 1980a, p. 8; 1980b, p. 18; 1981, p. 18) Moreover, the emphasis of government-supported and industry-supported development work tended to be shifted in the direction of learning about work: the Schools Council Industry Project, which explicitly distanced itself from careers education (Jamieson and Lightfoot, 1982, p. 7), became the largest Schools Council project; and the various industry liaison projects launched or developed in the late 1970s (Cooper, 1981) tended on the whole to include a stronger concern with inculcating positive social attitudes to industry than with helping pupils to prepare for their career choices. It seems that as unemployment grew, particularly in the manufacturing sector, it became evident that the rationale for a form of careers education biased towards the needs of industry had diminished in credibility. Although it continued to be formally affirmed, it accordingly came to be given less prominence than the need to ensure that all young people – whether destined for employment or unemployment – should have a proper understanding of the extent to which their livelihood and the country's prosperity depended on 'industry' (a term which was rarely subjected to clear definition).

A third argument in the 'Great Debate' was that schools no longer adequately socialized young people into the attitudes and values that would prepare them for the work-place – punctuality, willingness to carry out orders, etc. Yet, as Finn (1982, p. 51) points out, 'young workers' commitment to work has always been problematic as they have not yet acquired long term family and domestic responsibilities', and their 'restlessness and readiness to change jobs . . . have persistently been highlighted'. In Finn's view, what changed in the 1970s was not young people's attitudes, but the availability of alternative labour in the form of adult workers who *did* have long-term commitments. Nonetheless, many critics attributed the change to developments within schools. As a report from the MSC (1975) expressed it:

> In recent years the social environment in a number of schools, with more emphasis on personal development and less on formal instruction, has been diverging from that still encountered in most work situations, where the need to achieve results in conformity with defined standards and to do so within fixed time limits calls for different patterns of behaviour. (p. 15)

This neatly linked Callaghan's concern about informal teaching methods to the general critique. It suggested that schools should abandon their 'progressive' tendencies and should reassert a disciplined approach to learning which would both – so this argument ran – improve 'standards' and socialize young people more effectively into the disciplines of the work-place. At times, however, the argument moved in rather different directions: some employers, for instance, complained that they required more initiative and responsibility from their employees than schools seemed to develop, and contrasted the emphasis on collaborative teamwork in many work-places with the emphasis on competition and individual achievement within schools. This seemed to be an argument for teaching to be not more but less formal.

The final 'Great Debate' argument relevant to our present concerns was that schools not only failed to socialize young people for work, but also failed to equip them adequately with the skills they needed if they were to be useful to an employer. Too many school-leavers were illiterate and innumerate; more generally, too much of what was learned in schools was 'academic' in nature and took insufficient account of application in the 'real world'. This argument did not always lead directly to the notion that there should be a stronger vocational-preparation element within the curriculum. But it opened up what had hitherto been regarded as the 'secret garden' of the curriculum to the arbitration of employers and others, and it developed a climate in which vocationally-oriented courses developed by agencies like the City and Guilds of London Institute, the Business Education Council and the Technician Education Council began to be offered in schools – some of them pre-16. These bodies were eventually invited to join a consortium to design a new qualification for those staying on for a year after the minimum leaving age (DES, 1982a), based not on an extension of the traditional subject-based curriculum as recommended by the Keohane Report (DES, 1979c), but on principles of broadly-based vocational preparation that had been initially developed for colleges of further education by the FEU (1979). Such principles attempted to exploit the 'vocational impulse', but to avoid the dangers of narrow vocational specialization by focusing on generic occupational skills that were not limited to restricted occupational areas, yet nonetheless could be explicitly linked in due course to jobs available in local labour markets. (see Townsend and Devereux, 1981) Broadly similar ideas were put forward when in 1983 the government launched an experimental Technical and Vocational Education Initiative – under the aegis, significantly, not of the education authorities but of the Manpower Services Commission – to develop an integrated vocational-preparation curriculum for particular groups of pupils to extend from the age of 14 to the age of 18.

It is thus evident that the 'Great Debate' and its aftermath had the effect of increasing pressure for more attention to be paid by schools to their functions of orientation, socialization, and preparation for employment. Implicitly, too, they represented a challenge to the fourth, selection function: a questioning of the extent to which school success could be held to predict work success, and how far the selection function should be permitted to dominate the curriculum. Yet this particular challenge was rarely articulated. Moreover, it was deflected and confused by the extent to which the concern for 'standards' tended – despite Callaghan's remarks quoted earlier – to outweigh the pressure for vocational reform in the more élite reaches of the educational system (Oxbridge, the public schools, GCE syllabi, etc.), by the way in which such 'standards' became even more strongly associated with performance in public examinations, and by the continued proclivity of employers to use such measures in selection.

The conflict between what employers explicitly demanded of education, and the signals implicit in the way they selected employees, was pointed out by the Central Policy Review Staff (1980):

> This paradox seems to arise because for most employers general intelligence and ability are more important than particular knowledge or skills. Educational certificates are indicators both of specific knowledge and skills and of general ability level. Employers will give preference to the qualifications which attract the ablest candidates even if they would have preferred them to study something else. This then is fed back, perversely, to students as a message that the most popular course is the one best rewarded. The best students continue to choose that course and an enormous bias is created towards preserving the status quo. (p. 5)

This critique of industry's 'double talk' was later developed with great clarity by a British Petroleum manager (Marsden, 1983):

At interviews graduate recruiters look for critical reasoning, communication skills and commercial awareness, while recruiters of operatives stress attitudes like versatility, initiative, pride in the job, getting on with others, good timekeeping and loyalty to the team. At meetings all over the country employers are telling teachers that there should be more emphasis on the basic skills (e.g. communication and practical numeracy) and how to apply them in a variety of situations, teamwork, problem solving (without the answer in the back of the book), economic and business understanding and so on ... Unwittingly, however, while urging through its words these changes in schools, industry by its actual deeds is encouraging the maintenance of the poor curriculum design and teaching practices which prevent the changes from taking place ... The message received by schools ... is that whatever employers say they want in their recruits the initial hurdle requires examination passes ... Naturally parents and children demand that schools gear their teaching to the achievement of as many passes for their pupils as possible. Headteachers, hardpressed for numbers in times of falling rolls, will stress examination results and their classroom teachers will follow suit, quite happily as it is what they are used to and an easy excuse to teach what they have always done without much regard for relevance. Exam results become the main objective of the school and the obvious external measure of educational success ... The result of this in a time of severe recession is, of course, for stipulated exam requirements to be raised, exam results to be stressed by schools and parents even more, employers to over-recruit people with higher "academic" attainment than required and for the school curriculum to become less and less relevant for more and more pupils. (pp. 4-5)

As a result of this line of thought, increasing interest began to be shown in the early 1980s in ways of reducing the pressure on schools' selection function, or at least of broadening the range of tools which schools could use in response to such pressure. Increasing attention began to be paid, in particular, to developing methods of profiling which would enable a wider range of attributes and achievements to be recorded in a more flexible way that would not exert such a narrow control on the curriculum. (Balogh, 1982; Goacher, 1983)

On the whole, though, the effect of the 'Great Debate' and its aftermath was to tighten still further the bonds between education and employment. Indeed, the Centre for Contemporary Cultural Studies (1981, p. 225) declared that the government's Green Paper produced for the debate (DES, 1977b) 'formally set the seal on the school-work bond as the rationale for schooling: the subordination of schooling to the requirements of industry was complete'. This is an exaggerated judgement: all the official 'Great Debate' documents continued to voice wider educational goals. But certainly the needs of employment were now given greater prominence, and other views of the purposes of education were increasingly narrowed to those which were considered to be congruent with rather than offering a challenge to those needs.

The 'Great Debate' had a further effect, which was to articulate and crystallize a massive change in public attitudes to education. Whereas in the 1960s it had been confidently assumed – in line with the human-capital theorists (see especially Becker, 1964) – that the expansion of education contributed to economic growth, this view had now 'been transformed into the view that many aspects of the education system actively inhibited the profitability and growth of industry'. (Finn, 1982, p. 46) This paved the way for, and provided a legitimation of, the cuts in educational expenditure introduced by the government in the later 1970s and early 1980s. (Ginsburg *et al.*, 1979) It also meant that when during the 1970s pressure built up for big new programmes to keep unemployed youngsters off the streets, control of these programmes was consistently given not to the education system but to the Manpower Services Commission.

MSC youth programmes

Reference was made earlier in the chapter to the fact that the third of the main effects of unemployment on education has been that education has been seen as an instrument for responding to the problem of youth unemployment – not least simply through performing the custodial or 'warehousing' function of keeping the unemployed occupied. In principle, this could have been implemented through a further raising of the minimum school-leaving age, or the new programmes could have been led by the colleges of further education: early discussions of a 'youth opportunity guarantee' (see Watts, 1977a) envisaged schemes run by consortia led by the local education authorities. (Jackson, 1983) In practice, however, this was not done. Certainly local education authorities and their colleges have played a substantial role in the programmes that have emerged, but it has been a clearly subordinate role.

There are two main reasons why the controlling role was given to the Manpower Services Commission. One was that it was unfettered by the financial constraints of the education system, and could be directed more closely – and more rapidly – than a locally-controlled service with a strong professional tradition. The other was that it ensured that the programmes could be closely tied to the needs of the labour market. The essential remit of the Manpower Services Commission was to ensure that the economy's manpower needs were met. Its control ensured that the bonds between the youth programmes and employment would be as tight as possible.

The origin of the programmes was the public concern during the 1970s that the rising levels and duration of youth unemployment might make young people unemployable, eroding both their will and their capacity to work. It was also feared, as was mentioned earlier, that it might make them more susceptible to the influence of extreme political groups and to other forms of social disorder. The government was preoccupied with the battle against inflation, and was unwilling to adopt the Keynesian approach of reducing unemployment by encouraging a vigorous expansion of demand. It accordingly sought ways of occupying young people which would provide them with the disciplines of work and yet would not interfere with macro-economic policies. As Sir Richard O'Brien, then Chairman of the MSC, put it:

> They provide a means whereby we can pursue industrial efficiency and competitiveness without individuals suffering unacceptably, and so becoming casualties of, or perhaps enemies to the society which by failing to give them a chance to work has rejected them. (quoted in Markall and Gregory, 1982, p. 60)

The first such programme was Community Industry, which was introduced in 1972 to provide disadvantaged young people with short-term work in a specially designed but industrially realistic environment, doing jobs which would not otherwise get done and which were regarded as being of value to the community. Many of the same principles underlay the Job Creation Programme (JCP), which was set up in 1975 to create temporary work for a wider range of young people, though with less stress on training and more on the community value of the output. Then in 1976 the Work Experience Programme (WEP) was introduced, encouraging employers to create opportunities for young people to experience work in existing work environments: this involved lower capital costs and overheads, and was less open to attack for setting up a new publicly-financed economy which would interfere with and undermine the 'natural' working of the market economy.

In 1977 the Holland Report (MSC, 1977) recommended that these and the various other measures developed as a response to youth unemployment should be rationalized and merged into an integrated programme. This recommendation was accepted by the government, and the Youth Opportunities Programme (YOP) was launched in 1978. It included short training courses, but chiefly consisted of four forms of work experience: Work Experience on Employers' Premises (WEEP), Training Workshops, Project-Based Work Experience, and Community Service (in 1981 the latter two were merged into Community Projects). On the whole, in the composition of and balance between its elements, it bore a stronger mark of WEP than of JCP, more emphasis being attached to 'experience' and 'training' than to the community value of the products of its participants' work. In 1978/9, one in eight of school-leavers entered YOP; by 1980/1, the proportion had risen to one in three; and by 1981/2 it was one in two, comprising some 369,000 leavers alongside some 184,000 other young people. (MSC, 1982d, p. 14)

In its early days, YOP was 'sold' — both politically and to young people — on the grounds that it would provide a route into employment for its trainees. Priority was increasingly attached to the WEEP part of the programme, a distinctive virtue of which was that it might lead to the sponsoring organization offering the YOP trainee a permanent job. At first, the proportion of entrants to the work-experience elements of YOP who on leaving found a job or did some form of education and training was 75 per cent — sufficiently high for the programme to maintain credibility in this respect. As time went by, however, it dropped markedly, not necessarily because of any deficiencies on the part of YOP, but because of the growing scale of unemployment as a whole. By April/June 1980 the placement rate had fallen to 42 per cent, and although it subsequently rose again, it fell back to 44 per cent in January/March 1981. (MSC, 1982e, p. 7)

As the placement rate dropped, attention turned to attempts to increase the effectiveness of YOP in broader terms, and this led to increasing attention being given to its intrinsic quality as an education and training programme. Despite efforts to increase, for example, the proportion of YOP participants who were offered off-the-job training, only one-third were offered it in 1982. (Greaves *et al.*, 1982, p. 8) For this and other reasons, the decision was taken that as from 1983 YOP should be transmuted into the Youth Training Scheme (YTS), under which all 16-year-olds leaving full-time education (and those 17-year-olds who became unemployed within a year of leaving) would have access to a one-year traineeship including at least three months of off-the-job education and training and a number of mandatory learning elements. Furthermore, it should be designed not as an unemployment programme but as a 'permanent bridge between school and work' (MSC, 1982f, para 1.1) — although, in view of the overall unemployment levels, it was clear that it too would be unable to offer very high chances of leading directly to a job.

What have been the functions of these programmes, and how successful have they been? They certainly perform a number of useful purposes for the government. As Loney (1979) pointed out, they allow it to reduce the official unemployment figures without reflating the economy. They also, as we have seen, enable the government to keep the unemployed in contact with the disciplines of work at low cost, thus not only 'oiling' a reserve army of labour to fill any future labour shortage, but also reducing the socially and politically dangerous effects of allowing large numbers of young people to lose contact with the labour market. Furthermore, they provide a manifest indication of government concern, and yet simultaneously allocate responsibility for unemployment to the work-force rather than to the economic and political system. Even though the Holland Report affirmed very clearly that the causes of unemployment did not lie with the characteristics of the unemployed young people themselves – 'unemployed young people are not failures: they are those whom others have so far failed' (MSC, 1977, p. 33) – nonetheless the implicit purpose of the programme that resulted was to compensate deficiencies in the young people so as to make them more employable. (see e.g. Atkinson *et al.*, 1982) Ironically, this tendency to 'blame the victim' became stronger as the 'training' element of the programmes came to outweigh their 'job-creation' element. (Markall, 1982, p. 92)

On the other hand, Loney (1979) also recognized that 'for the young unemployed even £19.50 per week (the YOP allowance at that time – it has since been raised) may be rather more tangible than a sociological critique of the purpose of YOP'. (p. 238) Certainly many of the YOP trainees have reported favourable attitudes to the programme. Although there was an increase in the early 1980s in the proportion of those offered a place in YOP who turned it down, the rejection rate was still only one in 15 in 1981/2. (*Times Educational Supplement,* 29 January 1982) In a lot of cases the decision to enter YOP was clearly *faute de mieux.* Nonetheless, many of the young people entering the programme in 1978/9 subsequently said they had liked being on it, and that they thought it had increased their chances of getting a job afterwards, had improved their self-confidence, and had helped them in getting on with other people. (Bedeman and Harvey, 1981, pp. 6-7 and 36-7) The figures for subsequent years were somewhat lower, but still showed a satisfaction rate on these criteria of between half and three-quarters. (Bedeman and Courtenay, 1983, pp. 19-20; MSC, 1982e, p. 6) It is important to note, however, that these criteria are not particularly demanding: they suggest that the main value of the scheme represented the provision of experiences which even unskilled jobs would offer. (Raffe, 1981a, p. 218)

Some claims, though, were wider than this. For example, between one-eighth and one-third of trainees said that they had improved their reading, writing, arithmetic and measuring abilities. (Bedeman and Courtenay, 1983, p. 18; MSC, 1982e, p. 6) There were indeed many anecdotal claims that the vocational motivation and more practical environment offered by YOP had led to considerable successes in these and related areas, and contrasts were often drawn with the supposed ineffectiveness of schools and with YOP trainees' reported dissatisfaction with their school experience. (e.g. Singer and Johnson, 1983, p. 17) Although there was no firm evidence of the relative effectiveness of YOP and of schools in developing basic skills, even strong critics of MSC programmes (Short and Taylor, 1982) affirmed that 'in the best of YOP we have seen educational experiment and achievement which is of far greater significance in achieving equality of opportunity in education than comprehensivization ever was'. (p. 30)

On the whole, however, it seems that the impact of YOP was less on technical skills than on normative ones like attitudes, motivation and social competence. There is also some objective evidence – based on studies comparing YOP trainees and non-entrants – that it did have some effect on improving subsequent prospects of employment, if not very markedly (Main and Raffe, 1983); and that it alleviated the detrimental psychological effects of unemployment on psychological well-being (though the detrimental effects returned for those ex-trainees who reverted to being unemployed after YOP). (Stafford, 1982; Banks *et al.*, 1983)

At a broader structural level, there has been considerable speculation about the effects of YOP (and WEEP in particular) on the labour market. At least three hypotheses have been put forward. The first is that it *reduced* the number in 'real' employment because employers used successive groups of work-experience trainees to perform jobs that would otherwise have been done by ordinary employees (the 'substitution' effect). The second is that it had no net effect on 'real' employment but *redistributed* jobs from older workers to young people. The third is that it *increased* the number in 'real' employment because employers, having worked with a youngster and identified his or her potential, took him or her on and if necessary sought increased business to justify it. (Bayly, 1978, p. 21) A survey of WEEP sponsors by IFF (1978) found some evidence of all three effects. On the whole, however, it seems likely that the substitution effect became the strongest of the three: a survey of employers in 1981 estimated that 30 per cent of WEEP places were in place of normal recruits (Barry and O'Connor, 1982, p. 114), and in view of the fact that this was based on information provided by the employers themselves, the real figure could well have been higher.

YOP and YTS have indeed had a considerable effect on the nature of the youth labour market. Along with the Young Workers' Scheme, they have helped to drive down young people's wages: YOP/YTS allowances have been low, and the extension of YTS (under the so-called 'additionality' principle) to some of employers' normal recruits has meant that they have been extended to young people who otherwise would have entered jobs at union-agreed wage-rates. Moreover, depending on one's point of view, YOP/YTS can be seen as undermining, or providing a basis for the reform of, the apprenticeship system. The notion of training focused toward generic skills has been viewed by some as an 'attack on craft barriers' which would mean that 'rapid changes of technical competence demanded by accumulation could be achieved free from the impedance of "old" knowledges (sic) and working-class organization based around them' (Centre for Contemporary Cultural Studies, 1981, p. 238); alternatively it could be seen as a way of ensuring that 'as a result of training, ownership of skills lies with the trainee and not the employer/sponsoring organization'. (Hayes *et al.*, 1982, p. 5)

A related structural effect of YOP/YTS has been to prolong the period of dependency for young people. It seems clear that few school-leavers will henceforth enter the labour market at the age of 16, and that gradually the status of 16/17-year-olds is being altered. The government's original intention when planning YTS was to make it in effect 'compulsory' for statutory-age school-leavers who failed to get a job, by withdrawing the right of 16-year-olds to supplementary benefit. After considerable pressure from a wide variety of interest groups, this proposal was eventually withdrawn. But Norman Tebbit (the Secretary of State for Employment) in announcing the scheme declared explicitly that the government 'still believe that these young people should not be entitled to supplementary benefit in their own right'; although in deference to 'the firmly held and clearly expressed views of those on whom the operation of the scheme depends' they had decided not to withdraw such benefits in 1983, there would in due course be a 'further review' of this matter. (*Hansard*, 21 June 1982, col. 23) The withdrawal in April 1983 of access to accommodation allowances for 16/17-year-olds living at home on supplementary benefit was a further step along this particular road.

The extension of dependency may not stop at 17. Already there are proposals for youth programmes to be extended to run for the two years from 16 to 18, since it is at 18 that a broader range of jobs becomes available to the mature young worker. (Ashton *et al.*, 1982, p. 58) It seems, then, that the questions asked in the early years of the century by the Departmental Committee on Juvenile Education (1917) –

> Can the conception of the juvenile as primarily a little wage-earner be replaced by the conception of the juvenile as primarily the workman and the citizen in training? Can it be established that the educational purpose is to be the dominating one, without as well as within the school doors, during those formative years between 12 and 18? (p. 5)

– may at last be answered in the affirmative. There are benign arguments for such a conception. (see e.g. Rubber and Plastics Processing Industry Training Board, 1978) It means, however, that young people are denied access to adulthood – and the financial independence, status and responsibility it brings – for a longer period. It also means that the resources available for education and training continue to be poured into a 'front-loading' model based on a principle of effective compulsion, rather than into a 'continuing education' model based on a principle of voluntary participation. (see chapter eleven)

What seems to be emerging, then, is a transitional institution between school and employment, based on broadly educational principles in the sense that the prime avowed aim is the learning acquired by the individual rather than his or her immediate economic contribution, but located to a large extent in work-places and focused heavily around learning directly related to vocational criteria. In principle, it permits young people to explore different kinds of work before committing themselves to a particular employer. It also in many cases enables employers to test potential employees in relation to the performance of directly relevant skills and competencies before deciding whether to recruit them.

One structural by-product of this latter point which is relevant to our concerns here is that this process could well remove some of the pressure on schools to perform a selection function in relation to employment. Raffe (1981b, table 3) found in Scotland that school-leavers without YOP had a much better chance of employment if they had sat O-grades, but that among school-leavers who had been on YOP, the employment rates of those who had sat O-grades were similar to the rates of those who had not. Again, O'Connor (1982) found that although qualifications did affect the relative probabilities of securing employment for trainees who had been placed in different parts of YOP, they were least important in WEEP, where they added very little to employment chances: O'Connor argued that 'since a large number of WEEP sponsors recruit trainees from their schemes to their permanent workforces, it is likely that they pay less attention to the academic qualifications of such recruits than they would to the qualifications of those who had not been on their schemes and about whom they knew very little'. (p. 11) This appeared to confirm the finding of an earlier study (Smith, 1980) that YOP participants who succeeded in obtaining permanent jobs from their sponsors did so independently of formal qualifications, while for other participants their educational qualifications continued to affect their subsequent employment opportunities.

The liberating effect of the reduced emphasis on school certification is thus significant, though limited. It is limited still further by the fact that such certificates continue to be important for further and higher education, and for jobs that continue to recruit direct from school. In addition, the certificates may become important in determining access to particular schemes in YTS, in view of the fact that employers are exercising more control over recruitment to YTS than they did to YOP. Nonetheless, YOP and YTS could add to other pressures for reform of the school examination system and for the more widespread adoption in schools of profiling methods – not least as profiling methods are being widely used within YTS itself.

The impact of YTS on schools is indeed likely to be much greater than that of YOP, partly because it is directly 'end-on' to schools, and partly because it is designed not as a temporary but as a permanent programme. This could have the effect of releasing schools more generally from the pressures to which they have been subject from the demands of employment, with schools being able to deflect many of these demands towards YTS. On the other hand, it is argued that many of the attitudes and deficiencies which YTS is called upon to 'correct' or 'make good' have their roots in, or have been exacerbated by, schools. Accordingly, YTS could intensify the vocational pressures on schools, with vocational-preparation ideas and concepts gradually infiltrating the pre-16 curriculum. At present there is considerable duplication, with concepts such as work experience, profiling, and social education/social and life skills being introduced both in schools and in YOP/YTS, with little or no co-ordination. (Watts, 1982)

Concluding comments

It is clear, then, that both in schools and in YOP/YTS the main effect of unemployment has been, paradoxically, to tighten the bonds between education and employment. The same picture could be painted in higher education, where there has been increased pressure for courses to be more vocationally relevant; and in adult and continuing education, where non-vocational courses have been hardest hit by public-expenditure cuts, and increasing emphasis has been placed – for example in the MSC's Open Tech Programme and the DES Pickup Programme – on provision to be attuned more closely to the needs of employers.

The paradox is not, of course, senseless. First, it responds to the anxieties of individuals: when employment is scarce, people are more likely to judge educational provision by vocational criteria, and less likely to apply other criteria in the assurance that they will be able to find a job at the end anyway. Second, it to some extent serves the interests of equity: the more people that can be helped to be employable, the more chance there is that unemployment will be shared around rather than confined to particular hard-core groups of long-term unemployed. (see e.g. Ridley, 1981, p. 24) But there is also a third and more covert rationale, which is that it distracts attention from the political and economic causes of unemployment. It maintains the illusion that there continues to be an adequate world of employment to prepare for. Unemployment is ignored, or is used as a motivational stick to beat students with, or is regarded as a personal problem to be 'treated'.

Yet this kind of response carries with it considerable dangers. It encourages individuals to invest ever more heavily in the desirability of securing employment. It does nothing to prepare them for the possibility that they may not achieve their goal. It accordingly only exacerbates their likely sense of disillusionment if they fail. Yet it also does nothing, on a 'macro' scale, to increase the number who will achieve the goal: at best it increases the chances of some people *at the expense of others*. As a total policy, therefore, it is deficient. For some it leads inevitably to the same kinds of disenchantment that Marris and Rein (1967) graphically described in relation to American projects for deprived young people in the 1960s:

> As each door they opened led nowhere, they were continually adding anterooms in which an appearance of hopeful activity disguised the ultimate frustration. (p. 90)

Moreover, the sense of colluding with a deceit undermines the confidence of those engaged in operating such programmes. Teachers in schools, supervisors in YOP/YTS, begin to doubt the value of what they are doing. The time-honoured phrase 'If you work hard, you will get a good job' freezes on their lips. Yet, often, they are fearful of abandoning it, or of confronting the source of their doubts.

Some, however, are prepared to do so, and to try to find some wider and more adequate way of responding to the issue of unemployment. In chapter three, some examples of practice will be presented, based on three schools that have made determined attempts to respond to the realities of unemployment in the curriculum they offer to their pupils. This will be followed in chapter four by a brief examination of the extent to which similar approaches have been explored in other schools, in YOP/YTS, and in other sectors of education, and by an analysis of the main options and their implications.

Summary

Chapter two has documented the extent of the massive growth in Britain in unemployment in general, and youth unemployment in particular. The impact on education has been threefold. First, it has undermined the promise of employment which has been implicit in the structure of schooling. Second, there have been suggestions that the growth of youth unemployment has to some extent been caused by the deficiencies of schools. Third, education and training has been seen as an instrument with which to respond to youth unemployment. The overall effect has been, paradoxically, to tighten the traditional bonds between education and employment. This has been particularly evident in the 'Great Debate' and its aftermath, and in the advent of the youth programmes run by the Manpower Services Commission. The nature and effects of these developments have been described, and their limitations as responses to unemployment have been identified.

CHAPTER THREE

Wider Curricular Responses in Three Schools

Most of us hope deep down that the crisis will disappear if we only wait long enough – perhaps next summer, soon. We keep telling ourselves that the good old days will return if we just sit still and do no more than we used to in the good old days. It's often difficult – and unpleasant – to face the facts. But if you've been hiding from the truth for long enough, it can sometimes come as a relief to face up a situation.'

Ritt Bjerregaard, Danish Minister of
Social Affairs (quoted in Dauncey, 1983)

The project

With the aid of a small grant from the Schools Council Industry Project, I set out in 1982 to look into what was happening in a small number of schools that seemed to be attempting to respond creatively to the challenge posed by unemployment. I decided at the outset that I would focus primarily on efforts in schools not just to increase pupils' employability, but to tackle the problem in a broader way. Beneath this lay the assumption that efforts focused narrowly towards employability, however valid and *necessary* they might be, were arguably no longer *sufficient*. I noted that examples of broader responses might include:

- making significant attempts to equip pupils to survive psychologically and economically if they experienced periods of unemployment;
- preparation for self-employment etc.;
- programmes of social and political education designed to help pupils to grapple with the causes and implications of unemployment and with changing concepts of work;
- establishing strong links with community initiatives responding to the issue of unemployment.

I placed letters stating my interest in *Education* and in the *Times Educational Supplement*. I received not a single reply from a school. Although many teachers lack time and inclination to respond to the correspondence columns of the educational press, such a total silence was, in my experience, unusual. Did it mean that little was happening? Or that teachers in schools did not want to volunteer to be publicly identified with a project capable of being labelled as being concerned with 'preparation for unemployment'?

I subsequently made a number of informal enquiries among members of Her Majesty's Inspectorate, Local Education Authority advisers, SCIP staff, NICEC colleagues etc., about schools known to them which seemed to be making creative responses to unemployment. On the basis of these enquiries, I followed up contacts with 10 schools, of which I eventually selected three. I visited each of them during the summer and autumn of 1982. I conducted focused but unstructured interviews with the Head and senior management, and with some of the teachers involved with programmes that seemed relevant to unemployment. I also attempted to speak more briefly to a few other teachers and a few pupils, and to sit in on a timetabled session related to unemployment, so as to give me some 'feel' of the range of attitudes in the school and to 'ground' the evidence from the interviews. Written reports were subsequently fed back to the schools for their comments, and the revised versions are used as the source for this chapter.

Such condensed fieldwork inevitably carries dangers of superficiality and omission. It cannot enable one to understand adequately the full complexity of the way a school operates in practice. If however there is a reasonbly specific theme for the enquiry, it can provide a snapshot which – though static and two-dimensional, and based largely on teachers' reports rather than on direct observation – is illuminating and makes the school's experience accessible to others. I hope this is what the small enquiry reported here manages to achieve.

The three schools

The three schools selected were: Madeley Court School in Telford,
Shropshire; City School in Sheffield; and Springfield School in
Middlesbrough. They were selected because of their apparent diversity in two
main respects. First, they were situated in different kinds of areas: Telford is a
new town, Sheffield a hitherto prosperous city with little tradition of
unemployment, and Middlesbrough a town which experienced a boom in the
1960s but nonetheless is in an area with a longer tradition of unemployment.
Second, their responses to unemployment as reported to me in advance
seemed reasonably diverse: Madeley Court had set up a 'Year 2000'
conference and a production-line project involving the whole fourth year;
City School was considering a reform of its school day; Springfield had made
significant responses to unemployment within its social-education programme.

In the event, the similarities between the schools in certain key respects
were at least as important as the differences. First, all three were situated in
areas of very high unemployment, in which school-leavers' chances of
securing conventional paid employment had declined severely within the
previous two or three years. Thus in City School in 1979, only 15 of the 223
summer leavers were unemployed by mid-September; whereas in 1982, 66 out
of the 256 summer leavers were unemployed, and a further 63 were on YOP
or pilot YTS schemes. Again, at Springfield, only 15 (10 per cent) of the 1982
summer leavers got jobs by the end of September (as against 27 in 1981, and
37 in 1980): of the others, 37 per cent had entered YOP schemes, 19 per cent
had gone to sixth-form college or full-time FE, 26 per cent had become
unemployed, 6 per cent were 'unknown' (but likely to be unemployed), and
2 per cent had moved to other areas.

Second, all three were in reasonably homogenous working-class catchment
areas, drawing largely on high-density council housing estates. They had few
pupils likely to enter higher education. Their public examination results were
reasonably modest, though all three claimed that they were good in relation
to the social background of their catchment areas. None had a significant
proportion of pupils from ethnic minorities.

Third, all three schools had strong senior management teams committed to
a high level of staff consultation and participation in decision-making. In each
case, the Head and Deputy/Assistant Heads formed a close-knit team sharing a
strong commitment to the principles of comprehensive education, but also a
concern to reinterpret these principles in response to changing local realities.
They were however concerned to involve other staff actively in this process,
and all saw school-based in-service training as an essential part of effective

organizational development.

Fourth, all three schools attached considerable importance to links with the community. All three had been actively involved in the Schools Council Industry Project (this was not true of most of the other seven schools that were initially contacted, and I was not conscious of it when selecting the three schools). Accordingly, all three had made strong use of 'adults other than teachers' as learning resources – this was particularly well developed in Springfield and to a slightly lesser extent at Madeley Court, but City School too was developing such contacts rapidly. Each of the schools also had well-established and extensive work-experience programmes.

Finally, it is perhaps worth noting that in none of the schools was there a strong and separate careers department that had played a key role in turning the school's attention to ways of responding to unemployment. At Madeley Court, although the Senior Teacher was acknowledged as having responsibility for careers work, there was no careers department as such: the school's philosophy was that *all* teachers should be involved in helping pupils prepare for going out into the world as well as in helping them to pass examinations, and that a strong careers department might inhibit this. At City School, the highly-experienced and well-respected Head of Careers Guidance represented a traditional approach to careers work, with a strong emphasis on occupational information, work experience, contact with local employers, etc., and the responses to unemployment had developed as his work had gradually become more closely integrated with that of a new social and personal education team. Similarly, at Springfield the careers work had until recently been run on a traditional basis, but since the former Head of Careers had left the school it had become increasingly integrated into the work of the social-education team, and it was there that the main innovation related to unemployment was taking place. Thus in all three schools there was a clear trend towards the integration of careers education into some wider framework. How far this was a *cause* or a *result* of the schools' efforts to respond to unemployment is difficult to discern, but it seems likely that it was a bit of both.

These similarities between the schools should not conceal the considerable differences between them. Although all were mixed comprehensive schools, Madeley Court was an 11-18 school, City School 12-18, and Springfield 11-16. City School had previously been a grammar school, and signs of this tradition were still evident; Madeley Court and Springfield were purpose-built comprehensives. City School and Springfield were based in largely urban local authorities in which their problems were widely shared and understood; Madeley Court was located in a shire-county authority which at times found it difficult to understand the problems of a new town. (these tensions subsequently led to the resignation of the headmaster – see *Times*

Educational Supplement, 25 March 1983) There were also of course many other, more subtle differences between the schools.

Nonetheless, the similarities are interesting. Of course, no conclusions can be drawn from such a small sample selected in such an informal way. Even so, it seems plausible to suppose that schools will only make serious efforts to respond to unemployment when it becomes a major rather than a peripheral problem in their area, and where they have both the will and the capacity to cry hard to respond to the realities of life in their surrounding communities. Many schools find it more comfortable to keep such realities at a safe distance: the pressures towards blinkered vision and inertia are strong.

Beyond this, there are some enticing but more tentative questions raised by the similarities. Is it the case, for example, that schools with more heterogeneous intakes – not least in ethnic-minority terms – will find it difficult to respond to unemployment: perhaps because the issue will more readily be seen as (and opposed as) preparing particular and identifiable groups for unemployment? Is it also the case that schools will only make a significant response if there is a strong lead from the senior management in the school, but also a style of management which enables the issues involved to be worked at by at least a substantial proportion of the staff? And is it the case that if unemployment is to be addressed, it requires that careers education be extracted from the separate department into which it is cast in so many schools, and integrated into broader structures within the school? All are interesting hypotheses: none can be confirmed by the present study.

One final caveat is necessary before the material from the three case studies is presented. Because the focus of the present chapter is on responses to unemployment, it does not aim to present a full view of the three schools themselves. It should also not be taken to imply that in these schools unemployment was in any significant sense the starting-point for curriculum development. Many of the schools' educational aims were much wider than employment or unemployment, and some of the practices described below started from elsewhere. The aim of this chapter, however, is to concentrate on the ideas and activities that seemed to have some direct relationship to unemployment, and to present them in a form which teachers etc. in other places may be able to use. Comments are identified in terms of whether they were made by teachers at City School (C), Madeley Court (MC), or Springfield (S): it should not however be inferred that they necessarily represented majority views at their school, or might not equally well have been made in the other schools.

Responses to unemployment

Staff meetings. The concern about the implications of unemployment was the focus of considerable staff discussions within each of the schools. Many of these were informal, or integrated into other discussions within the staff meetings that were part of the normal pattern of the school's life. At Springfield, for example, unemployment frequently came up in the demanding round of staff meetings related to the school's social-education course: these included a weekly lunch-time meeting for administrative matters; a twice-a-term meeting held at the school for planning etc.; and a twice-a-term meeting held in the evening at someone's home with a much more open agenda; as well as the twice-a-term meetings of a working party containing representatives of industry, commerce, trade unions, psychological services, social services, the careers service, etc., that helped to plan and run the course.

At Madeley Court and at City School, staff meetings focused specifically on the issue of unemployment were held for the whole staff. At Madeley Court, the school had adopted the practice about six times a year of closing at 2.10 p.m. and asking the staff to stay until 5 p.m. for an 'in-service discussion'. In 1982, a session was held on unemployment, designed 'to look at what difference it makes if our kids don't get jobs: most of what we used to do assumed that kids *would* get jobs'. A talk on local sport and other recreation provision was followed by small-group discussions. Three questions were presented:

(a) Which *skills* and *knowledge* do all pupils need to learn by the time they are 16 (citizenship, leisure, personal and social development)?
(b) Which skills and knowledge do pupils need to prepare them for being *at* work?
(c) Which skills and knowledge do pupils need to prepare them for being *out of* work?

In each case, the teachers were also asked to discuss how schools should teach the area in question. Finally, they were asked:

What could we do at Madeley Court during the next two years to prepare our pupils better for life when they leave school?

The notes for the groups included quotations from some unemployed people in Telford, identifying the impact of unemployment on income, health, morale, etc. The group discussions were followed by a plenary discussion.

At City School, the issue first arose in a major way at an open staff meeting attended by around three-quarters of the staff, at which a fairly junior but well-regarded home-economics teacher declared that she was working a lot harder than ever before with a particular group of pupils, and yet 'the kids don't want to know'. She felt that she had never before had such an apathetic group to teach, and she asked for help. Her view had been echoed elsewhere, and seemed related to the demoralizing effect that the backwash of youth unemployment was beginning to have within the school. The discussion made a considerable impact on the Head. When a little later he received a note from the LEA's Adviser on Careers Education, offering to come into schools and talk with staff about unemployment, the Head accepted the offer with some alacrity.

The result was three sessions run by the Adviser in consecutive weeks during the autumn term of 1981 on 'Responses to Unemployment'. On each occasion the school closed 45 minutes early, and staff were asked to stay on an extra 45 minutes, so making possible a one-and-a-half-hour session. Each time the Adviser gave a short input, and the rest of the time was spent in small-group discussion and open plenary discussion. Each department was subsequently invited to respond to the issues that had been raised, and this led to a middle-management (heads of department and year tutors) meeting and to publication of the departments' responses. One of the effects was to make the staff as a whole more aware of the extent of unemployment in the area and its effect on young people, and to be more sympathetic to the problems it posed both for pupils and for the school.

Questioning the examination incentive. In many of these meetings, a dominant issue was the one which triggered off the City School meetings: the demoralizing effect on motivation within the school. The same effect was noted, for instance, at Springfield:

> We're finding it more difficult to get kids to work at academic subjects, even able youngsters. (S)

This showed itself clearly in non-attendance at public examinations, which at both City School and Springfield had shot up from virtually nothing to around 30–35 examination entries:

> When you talk to them, they just say to you "Well, there's not much point, we won't get a job anyway, whether we get qualifications or not." (S)

Consequently:

> We can no longer say, "I'm sorry, son, we do this because I say so and the exam syllabus says so and you're going to work for the exam". The old carrot idea has failed now. (S)

The result was that, as the Head of City School put it:

> We have taken on board the need to renegotiate the old deal where the school's job was to provide the ticket to employment and that is why they did their

examinations. We understand why students feel, "Why should I work for examinations if the ticket for which I work is no longer a ticket to a job?" (C)

This did not mean that examinations were generally regarded as no longer being important. Some staff still believed strongly in the motivational force that examinations could produce, and considered that it was not totally dependent on being 'tickets to employment': the pupils benefited from being monitored, and acquired an intrinsic sense of value and confidence from the achievement of qualifications. Moreover, qualifications remained extremely important for some jobs – more important, in fact, in view of the increased competition for jobs (if less sufficient for entry). As the Head of Careers Guidance in City School said:

If you get 5 O-levels, you've got an educational standard and some chance of getting *some* job. Because that's what opens the door, to pull out the one from the hundreds of applicants. (C)

A great many teachers, however, said that they now referred explicitly to this much less than they had previously. They were concerned about the extent to which the sense of value and confidence acquired by some pupils was gained at the expense of others for whom examinations were a symbol of failure and of being devalued: to these now needed to be added those for whom a narrow unquestioning emphasis on examinations might foster aspirations which had little or no chance of being realized. There was also the sense that too strong a claim about the importance of examinations was likely to be challenged by the pupils, and that such a challenge was not easy to refute. The result in all three schools was a strong awareness among the staff that although academic achievement continued to be important, especially for some pupils, it was even less adequate than it had been as a basic rationale for the school's activities.

Increasing employability. One response was to make other efforts to increase employability apart from maximizing examination performance. Even though there might be few jobs available, employment was still so important in the surrounding society that the school would be failing in its responsibility to its pupils if it did not help them to improve their chances of getting the jobs that still existed. To encourage them to think that they had no chance could easily become a self-fulfilling prophecy:

You've got to encourage the kids to have that determination not to give up: to keep applying ... Because as soon as they start giving up, they don't really stand a cat in Hell's chance. (C)

The point here perhaps was that although the school could predict that a fair proportion of pupils would become unemployed, it could not accurately predict which pupils these would be – for evidence on this, see Lavercombe and Fleming (1981) – and even if it could, it arguably had a duty *at an individual level* to try to defeat the predictions. Interestingly, two teachers in two separate schools spoke about the notion of 'preparation for unemployment' as a resignation issue:

> I would resign if I was asked somehow to separate those going to be unemployed from those going to be employed, and to provide something different for them. (C)

> I won't teach for unemployment: if we once start giving in to the concept that none of our kids will get jobs, then we're not going to equip them with what they need in this competitive world . . . If someone walked in and said "Right, social education is about educating for unemployment", then I'd leave. (S)

Neither interpreted this as meaning that schools should not prepare pupils for the *possibility* that they might become unemployed: both were concerned, however, that they should *also* try to maintain and improve the pupils' employability.

At all three schools, it was clear that the work-experience programme was considered an important means of doing this. It had other, wider objectives – experience in working with (and relating to) adults, building confidence and initiative, etc. (for an analysis of the declared and latent objectives attached to work experience in schools, see Watts, 1983a, chapter 1) But at a follow-up session I attended in City School for pupils who had been on work experience, its purpose was discussed almost exclusively in terms of the advantages it offered in securing a job – getting oneself known by an employer, obtaining a good report that could be taken to another employer, etc. Again, Madeley Court's relatively successful job-placement record in relation to other schools in its area was widely attributed to the effects of its work-experience programme:

> Inevitably, a bit of horse-trading goes on. (MC)

Work experience further provided an opportunity to demonstrate to pupils the attitudes and behaviour which were likely to attract or offend potential employers. Efforts were made at each of the schools to improve job-seeking skills through practice in completing job-application forms, mock interviews, etc., and at City School this was built around the work experience, thus establishing a link between classroom exercises and reality. An elaborate programme was developed in which as many as 25 of the 74 teaching staff, plus a few other adults, were involved in conducting interviews (normally lasting five to ten minutes each) for the work-experience placements: they were then encouraged to spend a few minutes 'out of role' to comment on what had happened in the interviews and on the points which the pupils needed to work on for future interviews. Although one of the days chosen for this activity turned out to be a health-service unions' 'day of action' on which normal teaching was suspended, most of the pupils 'responded brilliantly' – turning up, dressing carefully for the occasion, and generally taking it very seriously.

Although work experience was mainly relevant to employment, it could also provide insights into unemployment, particularly through placements at establishments where workers were being laid off or placed on short-time working. At one firm, a City School pupil 'got a lot of stick' because some of the workers were thought he had been taken on in place of one of their mates. At Madeley Court, the concept of work experience was increasingly being integrated with that of community service, with 'work' being defined not just as employment but more broadly as 'corporate activity towards some end'. Whether the integration was accepted by the pupils was however more questionable.

Another way of increasing employability was to encourage pupils to consider a wider range of alternatives:

> We've got to encourage the kids to widen the net . . . So, rather than looking at jobs, I want them to look at groups of jobs, at industries and so on. (C)

There was also, though, some concern about the danger of placing too much value on securing employment:

> When a fifth-year kid gets a job, we congratulate them. What does that do to the kids who don't get jobs? (MC)

Suggesting 'official' alternatives to employment. One reasonably uncontroversial alternative to employment was the possibility of staying in full-time education, either in school or in Further Education. At Springfield, one of the effects of unemployment had been to increase the proportion of pupils going on to sixth-form college. The nearest college was situated in a middle-class area, and 'while it's not all that far away, it's not within the boundaries of our kids' experience'. Accordingly, the school made arrangements for various visits etc. Similar visits to local FE colleges etc. were made at the other two schools.

The 'points' system in secondary schools can mean that if more pupils are persuaded to stay on in schools which have sixth forms, their senior staff will receive higher salaries. It would be surprising if this did not influence, however unconsciously, the guidance which such schools give to their pupils, and make it less impartial. The Head of City School, however, said that he and his colleagues often actively encouraged pupils to go to further education or on YOP/YTS schemes instead:

I've no worries about this school's group total. We're right at the top of group
11. The school has nothing to gain in staff points or Head and Deputy Head
remuneration. I'm profoundly suspicious of some schools' motives – hanging on
to kids in their sixth form at all costs. We don't do that. (C)

At Madeley Court, the fourth-year social studies course included a visit to a
local YOP community project run by a museum in an old tile works. The
visit, which I joined, included a tour of the works and a talk by the scheme
manager in which he explained the aims of the scheme, the nature of the
work, the level of YOP trainees' allowances, the opportunities for day-
release, and the disciplinary procedures. He pointed out that, after allowing
for travelling, most of the YOP trainees were only a little better off than they
would have been on the dole: he thought this was an insufficient incentive,
but he also pointed out the other advantages of joining the scheme. The pupils
on the whole were favourably impressed, partly because they recognized
some of the trainees personally and thought it would be 'a good meeting-
place'. On this particular occasion, however, they were not given any
structured opportunities to talk to the trainees about their experience of the
scheme.

At Springfield, a much more extensive and systematic attempt had been
made to enable YOP trainees to share their experiences with pupils. This was
done within the social-education course, which was taken by all pupils for a
half-day a week during the fourth and fifth years. The course had received
considerable national publicity, largely through its links with SCIP (see
Holmes and Lightfoot, 1981; Jamieson and Lightfoot, 1982, pp. 181-6): one of
its most notable and distinctive features was that it was planned and
implemented by a team of teachers working in co-operation with a working
party containing local representatives of employers, unions, etc. The fifth year
included a 'change and alternatives' module in which, in the Head's words:

A deliberate attempt is made to consider issues that some might view as taboo
areas, e.g. unemployment. (S)

In 1982 the central element of this module was two sessions in consecutive
weeks, in which YOP trainees were invited to come in and share their experience of YOP and of unemployment with small groups of up to 15 pupils:
the small-group approach was considered essential if any genuine sharing of
experience was to take place. Some 40 trainees were brought into the school,
and groups were free to work with them in whatever way they wished. One
group used the task of making a video on 'What It's Like Being 16, 17, 18 in
Middlesbrough in 1982' to provide a basis for talking and sharing:

Eventually we finished up with a very open session where the kids were asking,
"What are you doing wasting your time doing YOP schemes? What you want

is a proper job." Back came the answer, "Well, it's better than sitting at home: you wait till you leave school, you'll know then" . . .

Then the kids said: "The YOP scheme is slave labour". Back came the other side of the coin: "This YOP scheme has given me experience, so now I'm in a better position to get a job than if I'd been loafing." One of my kids came back: "OK, what sort of experience have you got? You say you've got experience. You've washed down doorsteps and gardens: you could have done that for your mother, or you could have gone to your gran's and done it." The YOP kid's reply was: "Ah, but I'm placed in a position of trust: I go shopping for 48 old people: I've got a lot of money in my purse. My supervisor can say, 'I've got a very reliable girl here, a girl who's on time every morning, who does what I tell her, who's got ideas about things, who's outward-going, someone who gets on well with people.' "

So that gave them an opportunity to explore some things, and made an impression on some. It made a definite impression on one of my lads who had been convinced that YOP was a waste of time. (S)

I asked the teacher whether this sort of discussion could have taken place if the YOP trainees had not been present:

Definitely not. Those kids were bringing new dimensions: things I'd never thought of. If I'd told them about the scheme, they'd never have reacted like that. (S)

In the end, the video was made hurriedly in a few minutes at the end of the session. Nonetheless, the teacher considered that a joint task of this kind was important to provide an impetus for the discussion and to break down some of the barriers that inevitably existed at the outset between the pupils and the YOP trainees.

Promoting 'opportunity creation'. The 'change and alternatives' module at Springfield started with pupils being invited within their groups to 'brainstorm' the alternatives open to them on leaving school, and to indicate the ones they would like to pursue. Two groups came up with the idea of exploring co-operatives. The Cleveland Co-operative Development Agency was accordingly invited to come in. They decided to give a tape/slide presentation to all the pupils in one large group, followed by an exercise in which the individual groups were asked to go through the motions of setting up a co-operative to run a newspaper: defining the market, how much to charge for it, where to have it printed, etc. – 'as an example of a group of people working together to try to produce something that others would buy'. A resource pack was provided for the groups to draw upon where relevant.

In previous years, the 'change and alternatives' module had included a focus on self-employment and the setting-up of small businesses. Two approaches were used. The first was based on an 'interests flow chart', in which pupils were asked to think imaginatively but realistically about whether their current interests (no matter how limited) could be developed and extended into the future, eventually asking themselves if they could (a) enjoy making a living from developing a particular interest, and (b) think of ways in which this might become a financial reality. The pupils were asked to scrutinize such possibilities and note any ideas that might limit practical development. These barriers were then explored on a group basis: they included such problems as lack of self-esteem, adult and parent attitudes, financial matters, lack of information, peer attitudes, and time-management. Going back to their own investigation, pupils were asked to think more about the exact nature of their own barriers and how they might be overcome.

The second approach, which followed a few weeks later, was a session in which people who had set up a small business came in and talked to the pupils about how they had done it, noting such issues as finance, accommodation, education and training requirements, legal requirements, and the advantages of running one's own business. Attempts were also made to encourage pupils to return to their own 'interests flow chart' to apply some of the points made in the session; in the following week, pupils were asked to work individually or in small teams either (a) to work out how they could set up a small business, or (b) to find out more information about jobs relating to the personal interest they had identified, and then to share them in a short talk to the rest of their group. Whether this work had actually resulted in any ex-pupils applying the idea of self-employment to their own lives was not known, though one teacher mentioned that two youngsters on a YOP scheme had recently told him that they were considering setting up a painting and decorating business when they left the scheme, and had connected it to identifying this interest in the social-education programme.

Both of these approaches had been dropped for 1982, largely because of lack of time, and because the second approach in particular had not worked too well. The idea of reintroducing it in 1983 in a different form was, however, being explored with the Chairman of the local Small Business Club. In particular, the possibility was being explored of developing a simulation which the pupils could get involved in, and which could provide a basis on which local small businessmen could then share their experiences in the real world.

An extended project of this kind, though affecting fewer pupils, has been set up in various schools under the Young Enterprise scheme (see Bray, 1983), in which small groups of youngsters set up a company and trade for a period. An adaptation of this concept had been set up at City School in the guise of Phoenix Enterprises, a school business venture run mainly by economics fifth-year and sixth-form pupils. At the time of my visit, about 22 pupils were involved, of whom eight acted as a board of directors. They had officially formed a partnership – partly to give them the experience of drawing up their own articles of association – but it had been agreed that it should run on the lines of a joint stock company. A total of 300 shares had been sold, no single person being allowed to buy more than five shares. A block of 30 shares was however sold to the school to give it a substantial stake in the company: in addition, the school was guaranteed 20 per cent of all profits, plus further sums in lieu of rent for equipment borrowed etc. The school could also, through the company's adviser, veto any activity or terminate the venture should this prove necessary.

The aims of the project were to teach the pupils about setting up and running a business, but also to fill in gaps in the school in terms of services – partly the services it 'sold' (e.g. selling cups of tea on parents' evenings), and partly the goods and services that the school's 'profit' from the company enabled it to buy (e.g. chess sets and other games equipment). The scheme differed from a Young Enterprise scheme in that it was based on retailing rather than on manufacturing, because it was felt that the difficulty in a manufacturing project of producing sufficient goods to yield a profit, and the resulting pressures of the production line, would limit the extent of the learning from it. Among the goods currently being retailed were umbrellas, toys, jumpers, hair driers, pen watches, pen/calculator sets, sweat-shirts, toasters, tea-towels, and Christmas and birthday cards. In addition, a bingo evening had been run, and there were plans to set up a video club. The business meeting I briefly attended was an emergency partnership meeting called because a couple of the partners considered that the sales staff were not performing as well as they might: it was proposed that the whole sales department should be restructured to produce more efficient stock control and to reduce delays between orders and purchase.

One of the limitations of this kind of project is that it tends to involve mainly more able pupils: it is also strictly an extra-curricular activity (though no less valid for that). At Madeley Court, on the other hand, a production-line project was set up in 1980 for all fourth-year pupils during a week toward the end of the summer term when the school's normal timetable was suspended. It was based on a large quantity of Melamine pre-cut pieces acquired free from a local factory which had gone bankrupt. Designs were invited; most came from teachers, and in retrospect some teachers felt that more time should have been spent on encouraging and helping pupils to get involved at this stage. The main emphasis, however, was on the production process, with production lines, office work, management, union representatives, catering, sales, etc. The exercise was repeated in 1981, involving most of the fourth year, and with a more diverse range of materials, including the Melamine stock left over from the previous year, but also some metal-casting and small wood artefacts. For 1982, the production-line exercise was based on a smaller group, producing a wider range of products, and with more involvement in decision-making over the production process: each day, the group reviewed what it had done, providing a sense of self-direction.

At the time of my visit, plans were being made to carry a group on throughout 1982/3 for two afternoons a week, and to set up a co-operative to market the products and distribute the proceeds. The group would consist of pupils likely at best to acquire only low-grade CSEs, and the emphasis would be on self-direction within a co-operative model. The co-ordinator believed that educational qualifications were of little use any more for most pupils, and that it was more important to help them to see that they could create work for themselves, rather than being subject to large institutional frameworks outside their control. In particular, they needed to be shown how to recycle materials and join with other people in small units to determine their own work. There was no rigid ideological bias here:

> If it leads to people setting up a company on a capitalist basis, I'll applaud. (MC)

Nonetheless, he considered that the co-operative model, with its emphasis on co-operation and self-determination, was 'technically right' for learning purposes.

Of course, some activities of these kinds have been initiated by schools even at times of relatively full employment. Moreover, self-employment, co-operatives, etc. are unlikely to offer a viable option for more than a small minority of pupils. Nonetheless, they extend the range of options open to pupils, and interest in them has increased in many schools. Moreover, it is arguable that they develop skills and attitudes of self-reliance which may be of more general applicability – not least in the 'informal economies'. (see chapter nine)

Extending 'leisure' activities. Self-reliance could be important in relation to unemployment not only in economic terms but also in terms of psychological survival. Thus four of the possible responses that emerged from the staff meeting on unemployment at Madeley Court were:

(a) Introducing pupils to a wide range of *leisure* activities – not just sport, but also gardening, hiking, camping, bands, dancing, etc. (though some of these required money and equipment).

(b) Encouraging a *sense of personal fulfilment* from initiating, organizing or participating in chosen activities, based on intrinsic satisfaction and not necessarily on success or on eventual utility.

(c) Encouraging pupils to be more *self-directing*, and to develop their initiative, self-discipline, and capacity for sustained effort and for self-analysis: in short, helping them to prepare to survive and grow outside the dependent structures traditionally provided by employment.

(d) Encouraging pupils to work together in autonomous *groups*, capable of developing their own structures independent of teachers: this might include organizing work tasks, events, and leisure activities like discos, boat-building, play-group parties, decorating, basket-ball teams, etc. ('. . . and not always within their chosen friendship groups').

Residential courses were widely recognized as being particularly helpful in this respect: at City School, for instance, trips to the school's Outdoor Pursuits Farm at Hayfield in Derbyshire were considered to be 'more relevant now', since they gave pupils experience in making use of their own time, without the props of their normal environment, and also introduced them to specific activities which they might take up subsequently. In addition, they developed pupils' capacity to relate to others and to work collaboratively with them, and gave them 'confidence'.

Efforts were also being made within the schools to extend pupils' range of leisure activities. At City School, for example, all pupils were introduced in their second year to four musical instruments: a wind instrument, a brass instrument, the guitar, and a string instrument. By using peripatetic teachers, groups were kept to a maximum of 14. In 1982/3 the scheme led to about 50 per cent of pupils wanting to take up instrumental tuition – it was only possible to accommodate about 22 per cent, but this was an unusually high proportion for the school, and very few had subsequently given up. The project started in 1980, before unemployment was seen as a major issue in the area. Nonetheless, the independent learning methods used on the course were held to be relevant:

> They are left to their own devices as to when they practise the instrument, so that when we say, "You must have practised this instrument twice by next Thursday's lesson," it's up to them how they do it . . . So later, if they become unemployed, they'll be more likely to go out of their way to go to the factory and say, "There are no vacancies advertised, but have you got a vacancy?" Or if they're at home, they'll find something to fill their time rather than sit about doing nothing. (C)

There was also the possibility of the pupils actually using their time to continue playing the instrument itself, though:

> One becomes aware that when children in schools have instrument lessons, the vast majority will not touch the instrument once they've left school. (C)

At Springfield, a seven-week leisure module had been introduced into the social-education course. There was a 'brainstorm' in tutor groups of the activities pupils would like to try out; these were then sifted to identify those that it was humanly possible to put on; and the resulting list was given to pupils to select the activities in which they would be most interested. Activities offered in recent years included: orienteering, canoeing, horse-riding, ice-skating, flying, land-yachting, cycling, golf, roller-skating, hiking, keep-fit, swimming, rifle-shooting, bowls, squash, and weight-lifting. For some of these, pupils/parents had to be charged fees; others were offered free. Attention was given in classroom discussion to constraints on leisure activities (costs, etc.), to the local facilities for engaging in them (local societies, physical amenities, etc.), and to the planning required (travel, etc.). There was also discussion of the extent to which such activities might fill the larger amounts of time that people now have on their hands as a result of shorter working hours and of unemployment. The hope was to extend the range of activities that pupils had access to:

> Some of the kids have never even been to a leisure centre, even though there are four or five of them around here. (S)

Three interesting ideas on informing pupils about local leisure facilities emerged from the staff meeting at Madeley Court:

(a) A weekly pupil bulletin to include news, items for sale, etc., and with an emphasis on making the most of the local opportunities for enjoyment and learning. The school might produce it, but the information might be researched by the pupils.
(b) A resource file on local facilities, including those for the unemployed.
(c) A Leavers' Day to include an introduction to local facilities, clubs, political parties, etc., possibly in the form of a convention with stalls, guidebooks, etc.

The latter two could be seen as interesting adaptations of traditional careers information files and careers conventions.

In addition, all three schools had programmes of community service which, it was hoped, would not only 'make the pupils more aware of the needs of the community of which they are a part' but would also 'provide, for some, an introduction to a more lasting experience – if not vocational, voluntary work in the near future'.

The notion of 'education for leisure' as a response to unemployment was regarded with deep suspicion by some of the teachers: it smacked too much of using leisure as an opiate. Nonetheless, one teacher spoke nostalgically of the way in which many unemployed people in the 1930s had been helped to survive by their allotments, their pigeon lofts, and other hobbies. The conflict in dealing with the issue in school was partly related to the paradox of trying to cultivate pupils' capacity to make their own choices about the use of their own time within a structured and involuntary setting. The leisure component of the social-education course at Springfield, for example, was written off by one teacher as being merely 'a nice morning out of school'.

Developing survival skills. In addition to the use of time, other efforts were made to prepare pupils to be able to survive if, despite all efforts to avoid it, they still became unemployed. Examples included budgeting skills, knowledge of benefits to which the unemployed were entitled, and awareness of local centres for the unemployed. At Springfield, one of the social-education groups chose within the 'change and alternatives' module to set up a 'town trail': the pupils were asked to go round the town finding a number of specified agencies with which they might subsequently have dealings, and to collect relevant set pieces of information at each place. The agencies included the careers office and the unemployment benefit office, as well as other places less directly related to unemployment like the local radio station, gas and electricity showrooms, the family planning clinic, the citizens' advice bureau, etc. The group also did some preparatory group work on meeting people in unfamiliar situations.

More generally, attempts were made to help pupils to anticipate what it might be like to be unemployed. In the fifth-year English course at City School, pupils were asked to imagine what form the experience would take: the emphasis was on emotional responses, to complement the more informational emphasis of the social and personal education course. One of the points to emerge was that:

> The girls were sorry for the boys . . . saying it was worse to be unemployed as a boy because boys were more likely to get into trouble . . . A group of girls sitting on a wall would tend to sit and talk, while a group of lads on a wall would start to throw stones or something and get told off. (C)

The discussion of productive ways of using time rather than getting into trouble led into a discussion of things they might do around the home, and this in turn drifted into a discussion of the black economy – ways of making money, and what skills they had. The teacher considered that the issue of unemployment had 'taken off' in this discussion because most pupils were now beginning to have direct family experience of it, especially from brothers and sisters, to draw upon.

More structured access to experience was incorporated into the fourth-year social studies course at Madeley Court, which explored what unemployed people could do about their situation. Use was made of videotaped television programmes showing unemployed young people talking about their experiences. A visit was also made to a local centre for the unemployed where, after talking with the community worker based there, the pupils divided into pairs to interview an unemployed person using the centre (they had previously had classroom discussions about the questions to ask, and the unemployed people had been told about, and agreed to, the visit). In addition, some working people were drawn into the classroom from the community – a policeman, a community worker, a shopkeeper, a publican and a journalist – to talk about the impact which the increase of unemployment locally had on their own work: for example, the publican talked about the way in which it had forced him to take out some slot machines and to offer less expensive bar snacks.

The basis of this kind of work was expressed by teachers at City School as being the need somehow to prepare pupils so that, if they became unemployed and entered the cycle of stages this tended to involve (see Hayes and Nutman, 1981, chapters 2-3), they would 'bottom out' more quickly. Whether an intervention focused on the pupils alone could be very effective in this regard must be open to question. In this respect it is noteworthy that a Madeley Court teacher said that he and other colleagues made deliberate efforts to talk to parents about the realities of the local employment situation. They hoped thereby to prevent the parents from exacerbating their children's difficulties by believing that if the children failed to secure a job this indicated that they were lazy and feckless.

Raising economic and political awareness. The sense that unemployment was not due to individuals' inadequacies but to economic forces, and the political responses to those forces, led some teachers to question the validity of responding at an individual level at all:

> Rather than looking at the curriculum, we should be going down to Downing Street and talking to a few politicians: that's where the problems lie. It's a matter of sharing the work out: that's the only real answer. (C)

This argument could readily lead to the stance that the school should do little or nothing to respond:

> In a way I feel the school is trying to patch up – put a piece of elastoplast over – a rather larger sickness in society. It's up to society as a whole to do something about it . . . I've always taken the view that if we've been right in the past – giving kids a general education and doing our best, particularly in a comprehensive school, for all the kids – then we're on the right lines, and all that is needed is a slight change in emphasis, taking into account the fact that kids can't get jobs. I don't want to see a major upheaval in the school today just because of the effect of unemployment. (C)

Alternatively, it could lead to the argument that schools should help pupils to understand the economic and political nature of the problem and to play their role in society in attempting to overcome it at that level. The staff meeting at Madeley Court identified some of the difficulties here: that it might adapt pupils to accepting the *status quo* ('give up and accept it'); that it might in practice take the form of political indoctrination, whether adaptive ('so behave yourself and do what you're told') or subversive ('thou shalt be a good left-wing rebel'). 'Balance' would be difficult, particularly if there was a concern to activate pupils:

I want to make them angry, but do I have the right to *require* the anger? (MC)

If the pupils were not activated with a sense of power to influence events, might not such discussions generate increased despair? And on top of all this, however delicately the teacher manoeuvred his or her way through the minefield, might not his or her efforts be misunderstood and/or exploited by people outside the school? Despite these difficulties, many of the teachers felt that the task still had to be attempted, partly to counteract the sense of self-blame and guilt that pupils might otherwise feel if and when they became unemployed. Moreover, concern was expressed by a teacher in one of my interviews that *all* pupils should be encouraged to think about such matters, even those who seemed certain to find employment:

Their attitude will help make the situation for those who don't get jobs. (MC)

In practice, systematic consideration of the economic and political causes of unemployment tended to be limited. At City School, for instance, it was restricted to the minority of pupils taking economics in the upper part of the school (though the recent introduction of economics into the third-year humanities course had created the opportunity to introduce key concepts earlier to all students); otherwise it arose only incidentally if at all. One teacher said that he would prefer the political responses to come from the pupils rather than being fed to them: if they came from the teacher, there was a danger of unquestioning acceptance or rejection of the interpretation being offered.

This latter was in general the stance taken at Springfield, where political issues came up to some extent in discussions within the social-education course, not least in the sessions with the YOP trainees:

The question then came up: "OK, but in the end it's never going to get any better than it is now. Mrs Thatcher's made a mess of things, and with the new technology and all the rest of it there's never going to be a position where people have lots of jobs. So that means that we've got to find other work at home. But is that right? Is it right that some people have work and some don't: that some people earn a good wage and live well, while other people don't? What can be done about it?"

A couple of my kids said: "Well, it's no good sticking your neck in the soil ... It's no good just talking about what it feels like, and how we will feel – people have got to stand up and do things." One of the things suggested was stopping YOP schemes altogether, and putting the money spent on YOP schemes into building more factories and creating more work. Then another of mine said: "Ah, but we've just said that microtechnology is going to take over, so if you build more factories, you still won't make more jobs, so that won't help."

Then a couple of them got round to saying, "The government needs to do something. They said somewhere that just because you haven't got a job, it doesn't mean you're no good, and maybe there's other things that could be done. People could go and do voluntary work and do voluntary things if they got a decent amount on the dole money. What we're on now is £16, and I pay my mum £10, so how am I going to manage on £6 a week?" So that's the sort of thing they got into. (S)

Because, however, these issues arose spontaneously rather than being structured, and because they arose within the 'personal' frame used in social education rather than in the 'academic' frame that might be used in a political-education or an economics course, they tended to be taken at face value rather than being subjected to any very rigorous critical examination by the teacher. One teacher confessed his lack of confidence in providing anything more structured:

If we try to provide something very detailed about the reasons for unemployment, I'm not sure we know what we'd say or how we'd get it over. (S)

Another teacher felt there were also other factors here:

I don't know whether we ignore the political area consciously or deliberately. Perhaps we find it too threatening: I don't know, but our main concern is for individuals, and we want to respond to individuals in a real way. The experience of employment/unemployment is a reality to them: the politics of it are not real to them in the same way. Too much of that might just make them feel powerless: perhaps the most practical way is to accept the situation and find out how we can best work within it. (S)

This was echoed in a more general comment made by the school's Acting Head:

To me, the nub of what we have to do is to make everything we do as relevant as possible, even if it's painful. Unless it's relevant there's no point. We're not interested in academe, in pie-in-the-sky, in futurology: we're interested in relevance. (S)

But might not this worthy concern with immediate relevance lead to problems like unemployment being defined as the *individual's* problems, without in any way challenging the structures which gave rise to those problems?

Considering the future of work. The issue of 'futurology' was picked up at Madeley Court, where there was a concern that while schools claimed to be preparing pupils for their future, they rarely did much to help pupils to consider the kinds of future social changes that might affect their lives – including, not least, their working lives. Accordingly, the last of the five themes that formed the social studies course in the fourth and fifth years was termed 'Towards the 21st Century'. It included attention to the impact of automation, genetic engineering, etc. on traditional patterns of employment and on life-styles. In line with the approach used in the rest of the course, efforts were made to use community resources. A difficulty here was that few people in the local community were concerned with thinking about the future: most were preoccupied with surviving in the present. Nonetheless, some use was made of a could of local firms which manufactured robots, and also of an Alternative Technology Museum which provided concrete material through which to explore alternative fuel sources etc. Video material was also used: schools programmes, current affairs programmes, the film of *Brave New World,* etc. In many ways the theme provided a fitting end to the course, projecting what had been learned earlier forward into the future. The perspective was a 10/20-year one, with an emphasis on what *could* happen rather than what *would* happen. The pupils' views were regarded as being as valid as the teachers', so long as evidence was given:

> What we're really doing is mentally gearing them up for change. (MC)

The same futurology focus was used in 1981 for a 'Year 2000' conference for fifth-year pupils held during the suspended-timetable week towards the end of the summer term. The school had previously run school-to-work conferences, but in the current climate it was felt – in the Head's words – that it was 'jeering' to run such a conference. On the other hand, it was generally agreed that one of the merits of these conferences had been the intensive contact over a concentrated period of time with 'adults other than teachers'. The 'Year 2000' conference was designed to provide an alternative, and more appropriate, framework for such contact.

A lot of people – parents, employers, and other community contacts – were accordingly invited in to work with small groups of pupils about the future in their particular 'patch'. For example, a local reporter took a group to visit his newspaper office and on an assignment, went back to school for lunch, and then explored with them some options for the future, using the media as a focus. The film *Fahrenheit 451* was then shown; and there was a disco in the evening to which the 'adults other than teachers' as well as pupils were invited – 'for the kids to see the woman army officer come back not in her uniform but in her jeans was very important'. On the following day, a brief input session was followed by small-group discussions about predictions for the future in various fields of interest (social services, police, manufacturing, education, etc.), and this led to the working-up of the pupils' conclusions regarding the year 2000 for a 'drama symposium' in the form of displays, videotapes, playlets, etc. The whole event was a 'happening', and was not very closely structured, though there was some preparation within the social studies curriculum. It was at times chaotic, and since it took place at the end of term, it was not properly followed up or evaluated. The Head felt it had strengthened the school's community links; another teacher felt it had shown that the pupils were more 'knowledgeable' about the future than were many of the adults. Nonetheless, it was not run again in 1982, but was replaced by a one-day conference on industrial relations which seemed to represent some reversion to the concept of a school-to-work conference.

Restructuring of the school day. The discussion so far has concentrated mainly on reactions to unemployment which involved additions or modifications to the existing curriculum. In all three schools, however, there was an awareness that unemployment also posed challenges to the existing structure of the curriculum as a whole. This was related to the growing concern expressed earlier about the diminishing power of the examination system as a source of motivation and validation for the school's activities. It was allied to an awareness that the current dominance of examinations in schools, and the extent to which schools were judged by their performance in such examinations, made it difficult for the curriculum to respond to unemployment or indeed to other realities:

> The exam system doesn't face up to any reality at all, except the demands of universities. (MC)

Furthermore, the examination system was considered by some teachers to place excessive emphasis on *knowledge* and on *written work*, which alienated many pupils, rather than on *skills* and on *capability*.

To some extent this could be modified by reforms within the examination system: 'mode three' exams which permitted more flexibility in curriculum content and method, graded tests, etc. All three schools had moved, and/or were thinking of moving, some way in this direction. The system could also be modified by adopting profiling procedures like the Personal Record of School Experience being introduced at Madeley Court, which provided a basis for valuing a broader range of interests, personal qualities, and capabilities, and for involving pupils actively in the assessment process. Alongside this, there was the possibility of entering pupils for fewer examinations, or entering fewer pupils for examinations of any kind:

> To a large extent the examination system was only ever there really to safeguard the needs of the 20 per cent or so, and then we applied it to all of them ... It's the schools' fault: they've allowed the thin ivory tower of universities to dominate them, not only for the 20 per cent for whom it is perhaps a legitimate affair, but to a greater extent for the rest. Now the

consensus that all kids should be examinees in one way or another has broken – it's certainly broken in this school. (C)

Beyond this was the idea of restructing the school day to permit greater flexibility. At Madeley Court there had been some discussion of the possibility of providing a traditional, formal curriculum on a compulsory basis from 8.30 a.m. to 1 p.m., followed by 'open activities' for any pupils who wanted to stay (and others in the community who wanted to come). This would widen the age-range, might produce a 'better atmosphere', and 'trains voluntary involvement'. It would however require LEA approval, and the school feared it would be resisted if it were applied to all pupils. At the time of my visit, therefore, it seemed likely that moves in this direction would be limited to a team-teaching block-timetabled course with a more open brief than any of the school's existing courses – possibly rather like Springfield's social-education course though, initially at least, for non-examination pupils only.

At City School, however, the idea of reforming the school day was being considered very seriously indeed. The notion was 'to do what we presently do in the whole day in the morning only, and to spend the afternoon enriching what we do in the morning with relevant experience unconstrained by the 80-minute slot'. The Head pointed out that 'the statutory minimum is four hours' secular instruction a day, spread over two sessions: the afternoon session by law need only be 10 minutes'. The aim was to use the remainder of the afternoon 'to give children more experience which will be more relevant to the lives they're going to lead after they leave school: I don't believe you can do this in 70-minute chunks, four times a day, three terms a year'. For example, 'at the moment we're terribly constrained in terms of community visits to old-age pensioners: doing it in 70-minute periods is drip-feed and thoroughly unsuitable'. More generally, it was hoped that the new structure would make it possible to do a much more varied range of visits etc. outside the school, and to be involved with a much wider range of 'adults other than teachers' within it. It was indeed hoped that this might be developed into a community-education role: not only using 'adults other than teachers' to benefit the pupils, but also offering activities of interest and value to the adults – a role which the present school regulations prohibited.

This proposal was not merely a response to unemployment. As one of the Assistant Heads said:

I like to hope that we would still be doing the same things even if all applicants were getting jobs. I don't want unemployment to have so much prominence here that it looks as though we're just adjusting and reacting. It's a proactive movement. (C)

The Head agreed that he and many of his colleagues had had doubts about the educational validity of a heavily examination-focused curriculum even in times of full employment. Nonetheless, he felt that unemployment had provided the essential spur without which change would not have been seriously considered. More direct links between the proposals and unemployment seemed to include enabling pupils to make constructive use of longer blocks of time, and extending the range of leisure interests which they might be able to draw upon after leaving school. Also important were the elements of involvement in the community, and the acquisition of skills, self-confidence and 'personal independence' which might give the pupils a better chance of getting a job if there was one available, and of coping with unemployment if there was not. Reference was made, for example, to the way in which projects like school plays (e.g. a recent production of *Yeomen of the Guard*) could bring out hitherto unsuspected abilities, and involve lots of people in a corporate task from which they could derive self-esteem and pride, as well as a sense of how to work with other people. At present, such activities had to be fitted into the curriculum in a reduced form, or in blocks of time specifically cleared for them. The aim was now to find a clear and regular basis for them within the structure of the curriculum itself.

The notion of the shortened day seemed to owe something to experiments in Chard, Somerset, which some staff had read about in the *Times Educational Supplement,* and also something to proposals made by Hargreaves (1982). Significantly, it was seen not just as a City School initiative but as an initiative being taken up by City School and two other schools in the area that had formed a consortium for sixth-form courses and as a result had established close working links which had now extended into other areas. Although the lead of the 'shortened day' had been taken by City School, it had been taken up enthusiastically by the other two consortium schools. It was recognized that setting it up on a consortium basis might complicate the negotiations that would be needed to institute it, but might also make it less vulnerable to opposition from the local community. Being thought of as the 'trendy' school could be a very destructive label in a solidly working-class area.

At City School, the specific proposal currently being discussed was that the length of periods in the morning should be shortened from 70 minutes to 45-50 minutes, and that 'enrichment' should be offered on the basis of voluntary options in years two and three for the final period (i.e. after 2.25 p.m.) and for years four and five for the final two periods (i.e. after 1.35 p.m.). For years two and three 'enrichment' would take the form of intensive short courses lasting a few weeks or a term: these might include music, physical education, religious education, art, computer club, technology club, further maths, a second (or third!) language, a writers' workshop, etc. For years four and five it would include trips and visits related to traditional subjects (e.g. geography field trips, theatre visits), up to two extra CSE/O-level/16+ options for the more academic pupils, and non-examination interests and pursuits (e.g. film, theatre arts, reading, physical education, computer education, music-making, crafts, construction, photography, business studies, etc.). The latter could be on the intensive-short-course basis proposed for years two and three, and might well be offered across years. It was recognized that the new timetable might mean different dismissal times for pupils during the afternoon, and flexible timetables for staff (e.g. 10.25 a.m.-4.00 p.m. instead of 8.50 a.m.-2.25 p.m.).

These proposals had been broadly approved by a meeting of heads of department and year tutors, and at the time of my visit were about to be discussed at a full staff meeting. The main stumbling-block so far was that the teacher unions had raised difficulties about the 'flexitime' for teachers that would be involved, and were insisting on an agreement for this to cover the whole of Sheffield. But within the school itself, as the Head put it, 'the lights are almost all green'.

Provision for local unemployed youngsters. A final response that had been considered by all three schools was not only to prepare pupils for the possibility that they might become unemployed, but also to offer something useful to young people who had already left school and failed to find a job. Both at Madeley Court and at City School, there had been concern about former pupils who had come back to the school, or who had hung around the school gates. The concern had stemmed partly from the sense that the school was not offering them anything concrete and positive, and partly from the disruption to the rest of the school caused by some of these youngsters. The latter had caused particular anxieties at Madeley Court because the school was built on an open-access basis and saw itself as an open and welcoming institution: the disruptive youngsters – small minority as they were – therefore challenged the school's view of itself. Accordingly, a working party had been set up by the school governors which included teachers, youth workers, probation officers, and representatives of the Social Development Department of Telford Development Corporation, looking into the issue of what the school should be doing in relation to the current economic and social realities within Telford. Efforts had also been made – so far unsuccessfully – to secure funds for youth workers to be attached to the school to 'pick up' such youngsters and to work with them in a constructive way.

At Springfield, the possibility had been explored of setting up a co-operative to provide employment for some of the school's unemployed leavers. The original idea was to produce goods and services that were not already being offered in the area: making mahogany toilet seats, for example, or providing loft insulation for old people. It did not get off the ground:

We had lots of ideas and lots of energy, but we couldn't raise the money, nor could we get to the point where we could find anyone to take the risk of floating it and carrying the can if anything went wrong. Finally, it looked as though all our problems would be solved by the MSC, but in the end they cooled off: we were told they were not going to back any more of these sorts of ventures because they had a far bigger scheme coming up. At that stage we didn't know what it was, but it was NTI (the New Training Initiative). (S)

There were still hopes that the idea might be revived when Springfield amalgamated with another school in 1983/4 and when, in view of falling rolls, more physical space might become available. The aim however would be less entrepreneurial than it had previously been:

What we feel we'd like to do now is to set up more of a – not a rehabilitation centre but a "habilitation" centre, if you see what I mean: somewhere where young people who are falling through the mesh of YTS can come in and find some sort of support. "Training" is too big a word to use here, but resources where they can gainfully use their time, have some learning experiences, do a little bit of life-skills work, and hopefully have some sort of workshop facility. (S)

Dilemmas and opportunities

The range of responses produced by these three schools was considerable, and a tribute to their concern and creativity. At the same time, the difficulties they had experienced in attempting to respond honestly and yet constructively to such an essentially negative phenomenon as unemployment should not be underestimated. At Springfield, for example, the session on co-operatives mentioned earlier caused some difficulties because the introduction to it was blunt about prospects regarding employment:

The person from the agency said, "I understand that you've been looking at alternatives for when you leave school. As you know, this area is an area of high unemployment, and the likelihood of your getting a job is poor. Therefore you're perhaps looking at alternatives: other things that you could become involved in. So we're coming in today with something that has taken off in this area in the last few years."
Some of the youngsters came back after this, and said they didn't like it. One girl said, "I've been more or less promised a job in engineering drawing, and I resent this person coming in and telling me to get into co-operatives and that sort of thing. I don't want to do this: it's useless to me. And anyway, I'm fed up with hearing about unemployment: I'm all right with what I want to do, and I don't want to hear about it." That picked up a lot of support – which I interpreted as being panic in facing up to the situation. It quite shook me: I

hadn't realized that they'd been so protected. I was ill-prepared for such a violent reaction. (S)

The reaction described in this passage showed how teachers' well-meant efforts to introduce pupils to less-desirable *options* and *possibilities* could be personalized by pupils and felt to be a judgement upon them. The fact that such a strong reaction was experienced even in relation to such a constructive and 'positive' alternative to traditional employment as co-operatives indicated how sensitive young people could be to such messages.

The passage also indicated pupils' resistance to 'bad news'. This resistance was reiterated elsewhere:

> What came out from the group was: "We have unemployment rammed down our throats at home, on the television: why should we have it in school? We shouldn't have to think about it at school: school should be a nice place." (S)

It could however mean that pupils were hiding themselves from the realities that faced them. This was illustrated in a brief conversation I had with four fifth-year boys at City School, who started by asserting firmly that 'most people from this school get jobs'. Although they subsequently modified this, it seemed that their awareness of the extent of unemployment was masked partly by the existence of MSC 'schemes' which were not always readily distinguished from 'jobs', and partly by the fact that their experience depended on the extent to which unemployment had affected people in their family, street, etc. – and the extent to which this was *known*. Thus they considered that 'the papers make it out to be worse than it is'.

The question then for teachers was how far they should confront this resistance. Was it better for pupils to be happy but blind, or aware but depressed, during their final two years at school? Too much realism could damage the intrinsic quality of their experiences within school; too little might make it more difficult for them to sustain this experience, and the confidence it induced, after leaving. Perhaps the aim should be to try to strike a balance, helping pupils to be realistic and yet remaining 'positive':

> Making them aware of the realities of life as it's going to be, but not destroying their hopes. (S)

At Springfield, the title 'change and alternatives' had been chosen for this reason; it sounded much more positive than 'unemployment'. The balance was however a very delicate one, and some Springfield teachers felt that it had now tilted too far in the realistic/negative direction:

> We've got to find a balance between being honest with them and not disillusioning them too much. In the past, perhaps we've over-encouraged the positive side; now perhaps we've gone the other way. (S)

I'm becoming worried about whether we're putting more pressure on them
than we mean to: whether we're being too dramatic about it. (S)

The problem of securing the right balance was particularly difficult because of
the mixed-ability nature of the social-education groups:

I don't think we cater enough for the bright kids. A couple of fifth-form girls
said to me, "Why are you always going on about unemployment? Why can't
you be telling us about the good things? I want to go to sixth-form college; I
want to go to university. You're not spending enough time talking about that
area." . . . How do you do it with 150 mixed-ability kids? Yet if we split them
up, and talk about unemployment only with some of them, that would be quite
wrong. (S)

It was wrong, presumably, partly because of its labelling effect, partly because
there was graduate unemployment too, and partly because – if the stigma and
destructiveness of unemployment was to be reduced – all must be helped to
understand what it involved. Another possibility was to avoid talking *directly*
about unemployment, but to keep it in mind:

I don't necessarily think it should be something that should be tackled as a topic.
I'm much more interested in presenting the kids with a selection of situations
and intellectual experiences from which they might be able to pull out a lot of
personal resources and skills that will enable them to cope with whatever comes
along. (S)

But might not the reluctance to provide an unemployment 'frame' have made
it more difficult for pupils to transfer the resources and skills they acquired to
the situation they would be in if they became unemployed? Was it enough for
only the teachers to 'keep it constantly in mind'?

These were difficult questions. They were not made any easier by the
attitudes of parents, who often knew about local unemployment all too well,
but had difficulty in relating it to their children's school, which they
frequently wanted to symbolize stability and traditional virtues. The
privileged position of teachers might not help:

If we try to prepare youngsters for unemployment, will we be seen to be
hypocritical, when we are more secure in employment than any of the parents?
(C)

Such difficulties focused around the status of unemployment in the
surrounding society. While it continued to be widely regarded as a negative
identity – making those affected, in social terms, 'non-persons' (see chapter
six) – attempts to 'prepare' for it would remain deeply ambivalent. This was
illustrated by the reaction of one teacher to two pupils who said they would
accept living off the dole and would not bother to look for jobs: he felt it was

important to counter this, since 'everything we do must be positive'.

In the end, the best hope was that it might be possible for schools to define a set of skills and competencies that would enable pupils both to secure employment and to survive unemployment. Perhaps the most optimistic point that emerged from my visits was the sense in all three schools that the search for such skills and competencies had impelled a fair number of teachers to return to basic educational questions. While employment prospects were good, schools had been increasingly pulled on to a production line to which their contribution was measured largely by examination results. The result was that schools had concentrated more and more not on education but on *schooling* based on the link between examinations and employment. Now, however, unemployment had fractured that link, and was giving schools a more ready opportunity to return to fundamental educational principles:

> We shouldn't be talking about "education for employment" or about "education for unemployment": we should be talking about education. If we develop independent learners, whether they go to work or not won't matter. (MC)

Or, as another teacher put it:

> Unemployment gives an added urgency to what we should be doing anyway, especially in encouraging the development of self-determination in pupils. (MC)

This basic educational task had never been an easy one. It was no easier at a time of high unemployment, particularly if it was accepted – as it widely was in these three schools – that self-determination, to be real, had to be grounded in the realities of youngsters' lives. But many teachers in these schools clearly felt that honestly addressing the harsh realities of unemployment had helped to make it possible for them to regenerate the educational principles that had attracted them to teaching in the first place. The sense of release, and of energy, was at times unmistakable.

Summary

Chapter three has described the responses to unemployment made in three schools situated in areas of high unemployment. The schools were selected because their responses were known to go beyond that of attempting to increase pupils' employability (though all attached importance to this too). In particular, steps had been taken to pay attention to 'official' alternatives to unemployment, to the notion of creating one's own work, to developing 'leisure' activities, to developing survival skills for use if one became unemployed, to raising awareness of the economic and political causes of unemployment, and to coinsidering the future of work. Some moves had also been made to review the structure of the curriculum as a whole, including the structure of the school day, and to make provision for local unemployed youngsters. Some of the difficulties and challenges experienced by the schools have been outlined.

CHAPTER FOUR

Practices, Options and Implications

Schools in general

How widespread are the practices outlined in chapter three? There is no firm evidence on this, but the way in which the three schools were selected implies that they are likely to have made stronger and more varied responses to unemployment than most other schools. In an unpublished MORI poll of 585 15/24-year-olds in Newcastle and Croydon carried out in autumn 1981, the majority said their school had spent enough time teaching reading, writing, arithmetic, and careers, but that among the items they had spent too little time on were how to use spare time and how to claim benefit; the figure saying 'too little' for the latter (78 per cent) was the highest for any item. Again, a survey by Sawdon *et al.* (1979) of 250 youngsters from five schools found that only 30 per cent reported having been told how to register as unemployed, though 50 per cent experienced unemployment within six months of leaving school. (p. 64)

Pupil reports do not always, however, accord with teacher reports on such matters. This was demonstrated in a survey by Fleming and Lavercombe. (1979) They found that when interviewed in their penultimate term at school, only 10 per cent of a sample of 209 young people reported having talked with their teachers about what it might be like if they could not get a job for a time after leaving school (p. 23); when re-interviewed nine months after leaving, 82 per cent said they could not remember doing anything at school about unemployment, 45 per cent said that when they left school they did not know where to claim social security, and 81 per cent said they had not got any ideas from school as to how they might use their spare time if they were unemployed. (p. 27) Yet all had attended schools where the heads of careers said that fifth-form leavers were prepared for the possibility of unemployment in terms of the practicalities (e.g. claiming benefits), possible psychological effects, and knowledge of alternatives to permanent work and unemployment. (p. 27)

This indicates the difficulties of getting messages about unemployment across, and suggests that pupils may erect defences against 'bad news' which enable them to avoid hearing such messages. It also poses the question of whether it is feasible to 'prepare' for the possibility of unemployment. Perhaps one has to experience the realities of unemployment before one can be taught how to deal with it? Yet this argument is applicable to most learning in school designed to 'prepare for adult life', whether it is concerned with careers education, with political education, with health education, etc. Certainly it is important to recognize the limitations of learning designed to prepare for experience as opposed to learning which is experience-based. But much of schooling is based on the premise that 'preparatory' learning is sufficiently useful to be valid.

Unquestionably, however, many schools prefer not to spend time preparing pupils for the possibility that they might become unemployed. As one careers teacher put it:

> In schools, unemployment is like cancer – it's something you don't talk about. (quoted in Wilby, 1983)

When a careers teacher in another school was asked about the extent to which preparation for unemployment was included in his careers-education course, he replied:

> This is the one area I spend least time on, I honestly have to admit it. Because I'm assuming when I start off that every one of the school-leavers at . . . are going to have a job, and there's no way they are going to leave this school and be out of work. (quoted in Ward, 1981, p. 226)

In part, this kind of attitude can be attributed to concern for the individual pupils involved. In part, however, it may reflect a fear of the political heat which the notion of 'preparation for unemployment' engenders. This was referred to briefly in both chapters one and three. Wrath can be evoked from both the political right and the political left: for the right, 'preparation for unemployment' dangerously exposes the idea that unemployment is likely to be persistent and is due to structural economic and political factors rather than the inadequacies of the unemployed; for the left, it suggests that particular groups of young people are to be conditioned to accept – at both a societal and personal level – an intolerable situation. The ensuing pressures encourage many teachers to evade the issue altogether.

If they do this, they may move in one of two general directions. One is to follow the broad policy pressures outlined in chapter two, and to increase efforts to enhance pupils' employability. The limitations of this have already been discussed in chapters two and three, and will be further discussed later in this chapter. The other is to use unemployment as an excuse to eschew all vocational concerns and to revert to an essentially 'academic' or 'personal' rationale for the curriculum, based on the notion of learning either for its own sake or for personal development abstracted from the realities of future destinations. The problem with the latter is that it can produce 'a cocooning and enclosing of young people in a comprehensive and self-preoccupying socialization that is more substitution than preparation.' (Stronach and Weir, 1983, p. 14) The problem with the former is that the notion of learning for its own sake tends to be transmuted into the maintenance of examination syllabi for *their* own sake. It is important in this connection to note many teachers' ambivalence about examinations: as Peterson (1975, p. 97) points out, 'on the one hand they will inveigh against the "tyranny" of external examinations and apparently long to be free of the shackles that prohibit teaching and learning for its own sake'; but 'on the other, they appear to love their chains, (and) vehemently oppose any proposals to reduce the amount of time given to examinations', perhaps because 'they see little or no hope of interesting the majority in the contents of what is taught'. For such teachers, 'an external examination system imposed from outside, which can be treated by pupils and teachers alike as a common enemy, is the ideal solution'.

Strategies of this kind may be strategies for a limited form of educational survival, but they invite a gradual erosion of confidence and commitment on the part both of teachers and of pupils. Since the motivation of pupils in schools derives to a significant degree from their perception of the utility of schooling for their subsequent lives, to evade the issue of future destinations is likely steadily to undermine such motivation. The pupils will be aware of unemployment and the uncertainty of their prospects beyond school: if the school does nothing to help them to articulate their fears and to confront them, the effect of these fears may be, in a subterranean way, to sap their sense of direction and the vitality of the curriculum. Mark Carlisle, when Secretary of State for Education, said in relation to technological change and unemployment that 'more than ever before the fundamental task of teachers must be to see that young people leave school with a sense of purpose' (DES Press Notice, 30 July 1981). How can a sustainable sense of purpose be developed without addressing the realities to which it will have to be related?

It is these kinds of situations which have led some schools to develop in the kinds of direction illustrated in chapter three. Whether these developments will continue to grow once the Youth Training Scheme is established is as yet uncertain. In chapter two it was pointed out that because YTS is 'end-on' to schools and is seen as a permanent programme, it could release some of the pressures on schools from the demands of employment: the same could be true of the pressures from the demands of unemployment. Taken to an extreme, this could mean that schools will become more insulated from the realities of the outside world, and will abdicate the unemployment problem as being the responsibility of YTS. It need not be so: the removal of some of the pressures of *selection* for employment could, for example, make it easier for schools to become *less* insulated from such realities. Certainly, however, the pressures of unemployment will bear strongly on YTS, and it is to this that we turn next.

YOP/YTS

As we saw in chapter two, both YOP and YTS have been essentially employment-focused programmes, and yet on completing them many of their participants have become unemployed. To what extent have the structure and content of the programmes reflected this reality?

At a structural level, there have certainly been elements of YOP/YTS that have reflected broader concepts of work than those of traditional employment. Within YOP, Training Workshops and Community Projects enabled young people's energies to be harnessed towards the production of goods or services of value to the community which were not being provided within the existing economy. Some creative and imaginative projects were established, including theatre projects, museum projects, and community work of various kinds. More generally, Stern (1980) argued that although in formal terms YOP could be seen as a 'reproductive' measure, attempting to reassert the continuities of the established employee work-culture, in practice a good deal of covert subversion was taking place which enabled it to perform more of a 'transformational' function, including preparation for post-YOP options outside formal employment. The decentralized method by which YOP was delivered meant that 'everyone is bending, re-interpreting or simply flouting the rules'. (p. 15)

In the early 1980s, however, the imposition of strong bureaucratic control began to make such covert subversion more difficult. The government became increasingly mistrustful of, and restrictive towards, what Ministers termed 'Yoppery', as opposed to work experience on employers' premises. The 'Yoppery' elements remained, simply because not enough places on the latter schemes could be found. But they were clearly in a subordinate role, and subjected to increasing restrictions. In particular, the hopes that YOP might become a framework through which young people could develop their own projects, as was done with the Local Initiatives Programme in Canada (Mukherjee, 1974, chapter 8) – for example, funding young artists and sportsmen, or providing phasing-out grants and advisory and training support for self-enterprise co-operatives, or supporting job-creation projects based on community needs but devised by groups of young people themselves (Watts, 1978, pp. 247-8) – receded further into the distance.

One of the criticisms made of the 'Yoppery' projects was that the placement rates following them were much lower than in the WEEP programme. Among those entering schemes in 1980/1, for example, 36 per cent of those on WEEP entered employment on leaving their scheme, but the parallel figures in the case of the other forms of work experience were only between 18 per cent and 26 per cent. (Bedeman and Courtenay, 1983, p. 22) The main reason for this was not any shortcomings in the projects themselves, but the fact that WEEP tended to 'cream off' more able youngsters (*ibid,* p. 9), and to offer direct contact with employers which could lead to offers of employment. Nonetheless, it reinforced the 'second-class' nature of the other projects, and meant that they were vulnerable to criticism as being cosmetic 'make-work' projects which, far from offering opportunities to their trainees, reduced their access to employment – a further reminder of the difficulty of developing 'positive' alternatives in a society in which paid employment continues to be accorded such importance.

In reality, of course, unemployment has been an issue for projects on employers' premises as well as in other YOP/YTS projects. But within such schemes, even more than in the case of schools, there are strong pressures to ignore it. The MSC's task is to train for employment, not to offer a liberal education or a social service. Those working in schemes often feel that if they address the issue in a way which goes beyond using it as a threat or a sanction, they are likely to be accused either of politicizing young people or of adapting them to unemployment – with the deprivation this involves. They frequently also feel that confronting the issue of unemployment may depress trainees, reduce their motivation, and make them less willing to conform. The trainees, too, can prefer to hide themselves from the realities: Knasel *et al.* (1982, p. 10), for example, pointed out how in some WEEP schemes, trainees were anxious to 'pass' as normal employees, in the hope that this would increase their chances of being kept on. The result, often, is a conspiracy of silence.

This silence, however, has its own corrosive effects, as was suggested at the end of chapter two. Beneath it, the unexamined sense that 'This is a waste of time, because there's no job at the end of it anyway' gradually wears away the trainees' and their mentors' confidence in the worth of what they are doing. Two fallacies are constantly embedded in this kind of statement: that there are *no* jobs; and that if the trainee fails for a time to get a job, the scheme has *necessarily* been useless. But because the statement is not open to exploration, these fallacies are not able to be challenged and worked through.

Within YOP, tensions relating to the issue of unemployment tended particularly to be focused around the 'social and life skills' element of the programme. Often mounted in colleges of further education, these courses — with their strong emphasis on how to present oneself in looking for jobs, etc. — were criticized by educationalists and youth workers as being exercises in social control and social manipulation both in design and in execution. (see e.g. Davies, 1979; Atkinson *et al.*, 1982) Certainly the early manual published by the MSC (n.d.) was very open to criticism in these terms, though subsequent publications (e.g. FEU, 1980; Lee, 1980) indicated the possibility of alternative approaches which were less mechanistic, based on broader educational values. On the whole, however, the emphasis tended to be exclusively on 'how' questions rather than 'why' questions: little MSC encouragement, for example, was given to helping trainees to acquire the conceptual and critical skills which would enable them to understand their situation and the structural forces that had given rise to it. Indeed, an MSC circular letter sent to colleges and other organizations which was 'leaked' to the press in 1982 explicitly stated that 'political and related activities could be regarded as a breach of your agreement with the MSC and could result in the immediate closure of your course'. (quoted in Waugh, 1983, p. 2) MSC officials were quoted as commenting that while they would not object to trainees discussing unemployment, they would want the teacher to be 'unbiased'. (*Times Educational Supplement*, 3 December 1982) Subsequently, though, a letter appeared in the *Guardian* (7 December 1982) from a scheme which claimed that it had been closed by MSC officials because it had involved a two-day residential course in which trainees had produced a report on unemployment: the report had quoted the views of various professional people and members of the public indicating that almost nobody expected the unemployment situation to improve in the next five to 10 years, and had concluded that many on the course did not expect proper, regular employment over that period — copies had been sent to MPs etc. This was hardly, it would seem, fomenting revolution.

The social and life skills element of YOP was not always popular with the young people themselves. Of the one-third of YOP trainees who were offered off-the-job training of any kind, nearly a quarter rejected it, and those who accepted it tended to attach greater value to vocational and practical courses and to aspects of social and life skills courses concerned with job-search and job-finding than with other aspects — including coping with unemployment, claiming benefit, etc. (Greaves *et al.*, 1982) This point should not be overstressed: a lot of trainees *did* enjoy the social and life skills work, and found it helpful. Nonetheless, it is worth enquiring why there were more reports of dissatisfaction here than in other aspects of YOP – including, in a few cases, 'mini-rebellions'. (*ibid*, pp. 21-2) Some of the reasons were clearly to do with poor organization, and resistance to learning in the classrooms which for some were associated with the 'failure' experience of school (though some colleges etc. tried hard to avoid such associations). Some also, however, seemed to concern the fact that in an employment-focused programme, moving outside the formal boundaries of the work-place – both physically and in terms of content – could pose difficulties. The trainees were beginning to see themselves, however inaccurately, as 'workers': to question this was threatening, and to extend into the non-work areas of their lives could seem like an intrusion redolent of the paternalism and dependency of school. The difficulty was exacerbated by the 'professional' and often middle-class background of the tutors, which meant that they could be rejected as talking from theory rather than from experience which could be related to the realities of the trainees' lives. On the other hand, the attempts made in some schemes to locate social and life skills teaching on the job, and to leave it in the hands of supervisors most of whom came from working-class backgrounds, could have more credibility but ran the danger of reinforcing working-class bigotry and prejudice on such issues as race and contraception – and, indeed, unemployment. (Williamson, 1982, pp. 112-3)

These difficulties are not insuperable, but emphasize the importance of sensitivity in moving outside employment and into issues like unemployment. Yet the need to do so is clear in YOP/YTS, because the future destinations of the trainees are so uncertain. The issue is in a sense more acute with YTS than it was in YOP, in view of the more formal specification of the areas in which learning opportunities should be offered.

It was indeed only in 1982 – as the mutation of YOP into YTS began to get under way – that documents published under MSC auspices started to pay significant attention to preparation for the possibility of unemployment. A manual on 'learning at work' (Hilgendorf and Welchman, 1982a) argued that:

> Schemes can help young people with planning for the future even when there are no immediate job prospects, especially in helping them to cope with being unemployed. Young people can be encouraged to be aware of their unemployment rights and entitlements: how to complete forms for unemployment and supplementary benefits, concessionary fares. Suggestions can be made about where they could look for help: drop-in and unemployed centres, helping agencies, unemployed and claimants' unions; how they can use informal networks; what courses are provided by further education colleges; what voluntary activities they might take part in. (p. 22)

More broadly, it pointed out that:

Encouraging self-reliance and mobilizing the resources that the young people themselves possess is particularly important if prospects for employment are limited. For example, outlining what steps need to be taken in setting up a delivery business or window cleaning firm; doing contract typing from home; painting and decorating or gardening for old people. Giving information about self-employment and tax, bookkeeping and invoicing may all be valuable. In fact, work experience schemes may benefit young people most by helping them learn how to survive in a world without full employment. (p. 23)

Again, Hayes *et al.* (1982), in a document which provided the basis for the curricular design of YTS, argued that the concern expressed in their report with vesting ownership of skills in individuals, rather than focusing them towards the needs of particular employers, meant that 'skills used in employment are merging with those used out of employment'. For example:

Skills in maintenance and repair, clerical work, construction (e.g. laying a garden path), woodwork and many others can be bartered or sold and can make it possible to retain links with society other than the receipt of benefit. (para 2.2.36)

Again:

Participation in community action groups, political or non-political, for one's own or for other people's benefit can become attractive and satisfying if one can be a contributor and not only a follower and a learner. (para 2.2.38)

After naming as a third area 'the skills needed for holding one's own in dealing with central and local government agencies' (para 2.2.39), they added:

It is worth noting that the utility of these three areas of skills is not confined to unemployment but applies to adult life in general, just as the skills discussed in relation to employment can often be transferred to unemployment. Building, therefore, on the world of work skills often found in YOP schemes, integrated learning objectives could be established which would help young people in the transition to adulthood, whether in employment or not. (para 2.2.40)

In addition to the advantages to the individual and to society in adopting such an approach, a more subtle argument began to be developed for legitimating a concern for 'the world outside employment' in relation to the MSC's own remit. (see Hilgendorf and Welchman, 1982b; Watts, 1983b; Hayes *et al.*, 1983, chapter 4) The Youth Task Group Report, on which YTS was based, stated clearly and explicitly that a primary concern of YTS was with making a 'central contribution to economic survival, recovery and growth' by producing a 'better equipped, better qualified, better educated and more motivated workforce'. (MSC, 1982f, para 1.3) Since training did not create jobs, the notion was presumably one of 'training for stock', so that appropriately skilled workers would be available if and when the economy picked up sufficiently to need them. As Annett *et al.* (1981) pointed out, however, skills once learned were not necessarily retained: they were easily lost. Skill loss could take place if there was no opportunity to practise and maintain them. Moreover, if the skills acquired through YTS were seen to be focused exclusively towards employment, and if further use of them was denied by lack of employment opportunities, they were likely to be so discredited in the eyes of the young people that they would not just wither but would be actively shed in disillusionment. If, on the other hand, their continued usefulness in other settings could be demonstrated and understood, there was more chance both that they would be valued and that they would continue to be practised.

Transfer of skills, however, did not happen automatically. If it was a desired outcome, it had to be addressed in the learning process itself. To some extent it could be addressed in a general way by involving the learner actively in the process, through practices like 'trainee-centred reviewing'. (Pearce *et al.*, 1981) But it also arguably required explicit attention to be paid to alternative settings in which the skills learned in a particular setting could be utilized – whether through *reflection* on alternative settings in trainees' existing experience to which transfer might be possible, and/or through repeated *practice* in different settings (preferably including settings as close as possible to those to which the desired transfer was to take place). Both suggested that, if the transfer of skills outside employment was to be facilitated, schemes must at least be prepared to encourage discussion of non-employment settings, and possibly to adapt the scheme design to incorporate such settings.

Two broad approaches – not mutually exclusive – were suggested by Hilgendorf and Welchman (1982b) for incorporating attention to unemployment into YOP/YTS schemes. One was the 'addition' approach of including a 'transfer programme' about three-quarters of the way through the scheme which should include, where young people were likely to be unemployed when they left the scheme, attention to coping with unemployment. The other was the 'infusion' approach of incorporating attention to unemployment into the general structure of the scheme. Hilgendorf and Welchman pointed out that in any case 'attitudes to the future use of skills are . . . expressed throughout the scheme particularly in the way the objectives of the scheme are conveyed to young people and also through assessment and review procedures'. (p. 23) Discrepancies could easily arise:

> For example, the scheme may quite seriously try to prepare young people to cope with unemployment by choosing work which might be useful in the community and running thoughtful sessions on unemployment. But their work group supervisors believe that having a steady job in a factory is the only conceivable way of living. Not only from their everyday conversations but

through the way they organize and run the work these supervisors in practice communicate a quite different message to young people than that which the scheme managers intend. (p. 28)

The difficulties in attending to options outside employment should not be underestimated. Hilgendorf and Welchman (*ibid*) pointed out that the boundaries dividing work-places from other aspects of people's lives tend to be rigid. For example, schemes can directly communicate attitudes to transferring skills over the work/non-work boundary by their practices and rules about the use of equipment, tools and time for non-work purposes:

> Not all schemes lend themselves to such activities but some do, for example, using typographic equipment to print leaflets for a trainee disco, typing trainee's job applications, using tools to mend a bicycle, taking home cuttings from a market gardening scheme. Many firms forbid or frown on practices of this kind. (p. 32)

Also, some employers may fear that by encouraging the application of skills related to their own operation to work outside employment, they may be reducing the market for their own products or services (it was presumably this kind of fear that lay behind the report, recorded by Handy (n.d., p. 8), that in Belgium it had been made illegal for unemployed people to paint their own houses). Further resistance could come from the trainees themselves. In view of the continued importance of employment in our society, anything which is seen to distract attention from the goal of finding a job may be opposed. Time is needed to work through and past this: to demonstrate that finding wider uses for the skills being learned within the scheme, far from reducing employability, should increase it.

The issue of the compatibility of the attributes required for employment and for surviving unemployment is a key one, and one we shall return to later in this chapter. From the point of view of skills, clearly some are common to both but some are not: some skills, for example, can only be practised if expensive machinery and equipment is available of kinds which are only likely to be found within formal employment. In broader attitudinal terms, too, there are similarities but also differences. Hayes (1983), for example, pointed out that training someone to perform well in work outside employment requires them to have a much higher degree of self-reliance and independence than does training them to perform well within the controlled and supportive environment of a place of employment. He subsequently argued that the additional competences required here could have a pay-off even in conventional employment terms:

> There is ample evidence that private and public employers increasingly want people who are adaptable, flexible and re-deployable, that is people who can learn and perform well in new and different environments.

Obviously, however, there is some tension between the capacity for taking responsibility for oneself and the willingness to adapt at the behest of others.

In general, then, there have been some attempts to respond to the issue of unemployment within YOP/YTS in ways which have gone beyond attempting to increase employability. But the fact that YOP/YTS has been an employment-based programme has meant that that they have taken a rather more limited form, and been based on somewhat different arguments, than those developed in schools.

Other sectors

Other sectors of the education service, too, have had to confront the issue of how to respond to the issue of unemployment. *Youth workers,* for example, have developed a number of schemes and projects which can be viewed as being complementary, alternative or even supplementary to MSC special measures. In addition to efforts to improve job-seeking skills, these include work projects concerned with self-employment, co-operatives, and job-sharing; voluntary-work projects; education and training projects; and other projects concerned with sport, hobbies, and campaigning for change within local communities. (National Youth Bureau, 1982) Youth workers also use group-work to enable young people to explore their own feelings about being unemployed, to increase awareness about the causes, and to support each other in finding positive alternatives. On some occasions this may result from chance remarks or questions in the course of general youth-work activities; on others it may be part of a more structured programme. (Swain, 1982) Some careers officers have also taken part in these kinds of activities.

In *further education,* the influential Mansell Report (FEU, 1979) – designed mainly to provide a basis for one-year full-time pre-vocational courses — included as one of its objectives that students should:

> Recognize the risk of future unemployment, understand its causes, and know the steps they can take to mitigate its effects on them personally (including knowledge of government schemes, voluntary opportunities, entitlement to benefit, the possible advantages of mobility and the possibilities of self employment). (p. 49)

This report has been widely read and applied not only in colleges but also in schools, and has provided the basis for much of the curriculum-development work leading towards the Certificate for Pre-Vocational Education. (DES, 1982a)

In *higher education,* careers services have run courses for unemployed graduates, and have also sometimes attempted to incorporate attention to unemployment in careers education courses for undergraduates. It is salutary to underline the extent of graduate unemployment: thus, for example, of those home first-degree students who left universities in 1980/1, 11.3 per cent were still unemployed at the end of December 1981 (UGC, 1982, p. 6); if this figure is represented as a proportion of those becoming available for employment (i.e. excluding those going on to further education and training etc., as is done with school-leaver unemployment statistics), it rises to 18.6 per cent. Most of the careers-service activities focus on job-hunting; some, however, include attention to group support and other forms of self-help. In addition, several careers services in higher education have begun to run courses and other events designed to encourage students to consider self-employment as a possibility, and at least one university (Sussex) has broadened this to include attention to co-operatives and various other forms of voluntary and community action which could provide alternatives to employment.

In *adult education* (broadly defined), increasing attention has also been given to unemployment, particularly in view of the fact that the longer-term unemployed can continue claiming supplementary benefit while attending courses lasting under 21 hours a week (though the inability or unwillingness of many providers to remit fees for the unemployed has meant that a lot of people who would have liked to take advantage of this dispensation are unable to do so). Many of the efforts have again been focused on helping unemployed people to regain employment, both by acquiring new skills and by learning how to 'market' themselves more effectively. There have also been courses in self-employment etc. In addition, the life-skills component of adult basic education has often paid attention to ways of helping people to cope on the dole, including skills of budgeting and planning, and awareness of welfare rights and sources of help.

Growing attention has also been given to ways of helping unemployed people to adopt various forms of mutual help, often focused around the centres for the unemployed which have been set up by various community groups all over the country (a number of them under the auspices of the Trades Union Congress). Thus, for example, one centre with a regular programme of educational activities organized discussion and activity sessions on such topics as keeping fit, growing one's own food, cooking, and changing family relationships. (ACACE, 1982, pp. 13-4) Others have set up 'skill-swapping' mechanisms whereby unemployed people exchange skills and services (see e.g. Senior, 1983a), and have more generally sought to provide a source of emotional support.

Some centres, too, have engaged in limited forms of political campaigning. Indeed, Gallacher *et al.* (1983) have argued that:

If these centres are to do more than merely help unemployed workers cope with unemployment, their potential as campaigning bases, as settings within which organized opposition to the economic and social policies responsible for the hardships of unemployment can take shape, must be developed. (p. 6)

They accordingly urge that community workers should do what they can to foster a political-campaigning role. There are however difficulties here, because the MSC, whose schemes are often used to provide funding for the centres' staff, tend to prohibit such activities. The TUC's acceptance of such funds has accordingly been widely criticized, though defences have been offered. As one commentator put it:

It has been pointed out that with the TUC's declared overall policy of urging on the Government an alternative economic strategy for full employment, an agreement not to politicize the unemployed is disturbingly similar to an act of hara-kiri. But such criticism, plausible as it may sound ... makes the extremely shaky assumption that the unemployed in general are, or would cheerfully become, partisans of one single political doctrine. Suppose a group of unemployed decided to run a cell of the National Front from one of the centres – would that be acceptable? (Martin, 1982, p. 13)

The same commentator also quoted one centre co-ordinator as saying:

I'm a member of the Labour Party and CND. I'm always thinking about politics. But in this job you're dealing with ordinary people, and you have to be where they are – not where you want them to be. (*ibid*, p. 13)

Even Gallacher *et al.* (1983) argued that, 'while the politicizing of the unemployed may be the appropriate next step from initial contact, care needs to be taken in ensuring that individuals are not overwhelmed by the political strength of some groups within centres'. (p. 7)

People in adult education more generally are also divided on the issue of whether its aim in relation to unemployment should be to help unemployed people to make the best of their lot, or should be more radical. A strongly radical stance was taken by the Association for Adult and Continuing Education (1982) in its evidence to the enquiry by the Advisory Council for Adult and Continuing Education into education for unemployed adults:

Adult education should not be about patching up shattered personalities, persuading unemployed people that life without work can be rewarding, useful and worthwhile, *unless* it is also convincing the population as a whole that the current levels of unemployment are not acceptable or inevitable but are the results of a definite economic strategy, and ensuring that the population as a whole faces up to the impact of new technology, to fewer jobs, to shorter hours and to work-sharing. It is pointless and deceptive to persuade unemployed people to change their deeply held views about the importance of work in society if the rest of the population remains soundly wedded to the work ethic, and unemployment continues to place severe limitations both financial and otherwise on a person's freedom and ability to participate effectively in that society. (p. 24)

The ACACE (1982) in its subsequent report was less forthright. It did however acknowledge that the stigma often attached to the unemployed was undeserved, and that:

> If the truth were generally understood, about the structural changes taking place in the economy and about the personal experience of unemployment, the kind of local co-operative action which we are advocating would be much easier to set going ... Here is a further task for adult education, to raise the level of public information and awareness about the whole matter of unemployment. (pp. 10-11)

Some adult-education initiatives with an explicit political base have sought to go beyond awareness-raising to more active development of economic alternatives. Fisher (1983) describes some of the Greater London Council's initiatives in 'education for popular planning', designed to develop and implement alternative plans for local economic development within a socialist framework. The main focus of the initiatives is people who are motivated to seek to change their economic circumstances through some kind of collective action, based on meeting people's needs both as workers and as consumers. Such efforts require access to practical skills, and this tends to be a difficulty:

> Socialist accountants, lawyers, architects and so on tend to be few, whilst those like sociologists who can explain the crisis of capitalist society tend to be thick on the ground.

On the other hand, Fisher argues that it is important for those involved in such ventures to keep sight of their political context, and not to permit the pressures of day-to-day routine, targets and deadlines to subject them to 'the tyranny of the immediate'. Apart from anything else, maintaining a political context could help to avoid disillusionment if the ventures break down due to wider forces hostile to the ideology underpinning them:

> Much "alternative activity" will be, in the last analysis, a political and educational experience.

Even without this degree of political commitment, there would seem to be a strong case for some form of political education with the unemployed themselves. The AACE (1982) stated firmly that, in offering guidance and counselling to unemployed people, adult education:

> ... should quite clearly begin such counselling by rejecting the frequently held view that unemployment is the personal problem or fault of the individual without a job. The social, political and economic causes of unemployment must

be clearly stated. (p. 24)

The paranoia about this issue in official circles was revealed yet again when the adult-education elements of the MSC's Voluntary Projects Programme were drawn up in 1982. According to a report in *New Society* (29 July 1982):

> The Workers Educational Association drew up an ambitious plan with special courses ranging from welfare rights to "The political economy of unemployment". This smacked too much of "liberal education" for ministers. The scheme was postponed on the pretext that the guidelines took the MSC outside its statutory remit; and then, when the guidelines had been redrafted, it was postponed again out of fear that it would be infiltrated by politically-motivated courses. New guidelines will limit the educational element to courses directly relevant to getting work, such as basic literacy and numeracy.

Options and implications

It will have been evident from this chapter and from chapter three that there are a number of recurrent themes and dilemmas which people in education and training face in attempting to respond to unemployment. In this final section, an attempt will be made to outline the main options and to analyse their underlying aims and implications.

Figure 4.1 Some possible curricular objectives relating to the issue of unemployment

1 *Employability skills.* To equip people with skills which will increase their chance of finding and keeping a job:
   (a) Social and technical skills required for employability
   (b) Job-search skills
   (c) Job-acquisition skills (interview techniques, application forms, etc.)
   (d) Job-retention skills
   (e) Skills of foreseeing forces which may affect prospects in particular kinds of employment
2 *Adaptability awareness.* To extend the range of employment opportunities which people feel are possible for them.
   (a) Awareness of jobs other than those which are immediately attractive
   (b) Awareness of possibilities for travelling further to work or living away from home, and relevant skills training (how to ride cheap mechanized transport, etc.)
3. *Survival skills.* To equip people with the knowledge and skills they will

need to survive if they are unemployed:
- (a) Knowledge of unemployment benefits and supplementary allowances
- (b) Knowledge of redundancy rights
- (c) Knowledge of welfare rights in general
- (d) Skills of claiming rights
- (e) Skills of handling a limited budget
- (f) Awareness of local possibilities for 'fiddling' (e.g. 'illegal' part-time jobs), and of its possible consequences
- (g) Awareness of psychological effect of being unemployed, and skills for coping with it
- (h) Awareness of social pressures on the unemployed, and skills for coping with them
- (i) Knowledge of after-care and support services in the community

4 *Contextual awareness.* To help people to determine the extent to which the responsibility for being unemployed lies with society rather than with the individual:
- (a) Awareness of possible alienating effects of work
- (b) Awareness of effects of technological change
- (c) Awareness of possible economic and political solutions to unemployment
- (d) Awareness of possible alternative patterns of work and leisure

5 *Leisure skills.* To equip people with knowledge and skills which will help them to make good use of their increased 'leisure' time while they are unemployed:
- (a) Knowledge of courses in educational insitutions, skillcentres, etc.
- (b) Knowledge of local possibilities for voluntary community work, skill exchanges, etc.
- (c) Skills of managing use of own time

6 *Alternative-opportunity awareness.* To make people aware of official alternatives to employment and unemployment:
- (a) Knowledge of courses in educational institutions, skillcentres, etc
- (b) Knowledge of government work schemes for the unemployed

7 *Opportunity-creation skills.* To equip students with the knowledge and skills they need to be able to create their own employment:
- (a) Knowledge of job-sharing possibilities and procedures
- (b) Knowledge of self-employment possibilities, and of legal and social security problems involved
- (c) Awareness of alternative, self-sustaining life-styles (communes, etc.)
- (d) Skills of thinking about work in a proactive rather than a reactive way

In figure 4.1, a number of possible curricular objectives related to the issue of unemployment are listed. Many are not exclusively related to this issue: all, however, represent direct responses to the possibility that the students involved are, or may become, unemployed. Most have emerged at various points in the preceding discussion: a few additional possibilities have been added, including the notion of helping people to develop skills for foreseeing forces which may affect prospects in particular areas of unemployment (1e), awareness of the possibility of travelling further to work or living away from home (2b), and awareness of alternative, self-sustaining life-styles (7c).

Within these objectives, a basic distinction can be drawn between those which are concerned with helping the unemployed to secure employment (1-2), and those concerned with helping them to cope with being unemployed and to respond to it in other ways (3-7). Some of the issues related to the balance to be struck between these two broad approaches have already been discussed, but they are sufficiently crucial to merit review and elaboration.

The difficulty stems from the fact that there is some conflict between the two approaches. Within a society in which paid employment is the most important source of identity, status and income, the case for maximizing people's chances of securing employment is a powerful one. Even a Marxist writer pointed out the dishonesty on the part of teachers which any approach that negated this would involve:

> Don't refuse to be an agent in the reproduction of bearers of labour power by going to the extent of disqualifying your pupils from getting jobs. They need jobs as much as you need yours. (Harris, 1982, p. 151)

There is certainly evidence that there are ways of increasing employability, even among the hard-core unemployed (for a useful review of the relevant research, see Hayes and Nutman, 1981, chapter 8). At the same time, however, the fact has to be confronted that such efforts do not increase the number of jobs. Moreover, there are good reasons to suppose that if they do *not* lead to a job, they may aggravate rather than alleviate the individual's problems.

The main reason for this is that the attributes required to increase employability are not simply technical skills but also include attitudes and values. And some attitudes and values that are functional for employment are dysfunctional for unemployment. Bakke (1933), for example, found that among the unemployed, it was the most ambitious that lost heart most quickly:

> The quality that *on the job* leads to rapid achievement of greater and greater satisfaction, *off the job* leads to rapid retreat into hopelessness and discontent, despair and even sullenness. The incentive to work hard, the desire to push ahead, and ambition to perfect one's technique, these are basic qualities for

satisfaction at work. They are just the qualities that make it hardest for a man to be out of work. (p. 71)

Again, Stafford *et al.* (1980) found that 'work involvement' – the degree to which a person wants to be engaged in work – was positively related to mental health among employed young people, but negatively related to it among unemployed young people.

Moreover, some of the attitudes and behaviours of the unemployed (or those fearing unemployment) which reduce their chances of securing employment represent defences that protect them against negative experiences. Thus, for example, they may decide, whether consciously or unconsciously, that the chances of job applications leading to a job offer are so slim that they prefer to avoid the stress and the likely sense of rejection by ceasing to apply for jobs at all. This reduces their chances of securing a job to nil, but it may nonetheless represent a rational decision which may make it easier for them to maintain their mental health and self-esteem.

A further difficulty relates to Rotter's (1966) concept of 'locus of control' – the extent to which people believe that what happens to them is determined by their own actions or by forces and events beyond their control. There is general evidence that people with an 'internal' locus of control are more effective at controlling their world that those with an 'external' locus of control (Phares, 1976), and this seems to be applicable to unemployment. Poole (1981), for example, found that 'internals' were more successful at obtaining work than were 'externals', who experienced longer periods of unemployment. But those who found employment tended to develop a still more 'internal' locus of control, whereas those who were unemployed did not. (see also Gurney, 1981) It does indeed seem plausible to suppose that for those who are unemployed, to believe that their condition is due not to their individual inadequacy but to external forces is a powerful means of enabling them to maintain their sense of self-respect. Thus to encourage people to believe that they command their own fate – that they can find jobs if only they try hard enough – may increase their chances of finding a job; but it also means that if they still fail to secure one, which with current levels of unemployment they well may, the psychological impact of this failure may be more acute.

The difficulties become more complex when they are removed from a purely psychological context and placed within a political framework. For it has to be recognized that the notion that unemployment is due not to economic and political forces but to the personal deficiencies of the unemployed – including their lack of willingness to look hard enough for work – itself serves a powerful political function. It maintains the economic and political *status quo* by shifting attention away from it: it suggests that what is needed is not economic and political reform but ways of making good the inadequacies of unemployed individuals. It also incidentally means that to the poverty and sense of purposelessness experienced by the unemployed are added the sense of being social pariahs and the need to cope with the insults of the media, of politicians, and, not infrequently, of their family and associates. (for a fuller treatment of this point, see chapter six)

The confused nature of the social messages received by the unemployed can be illustrated by referring to the concept of 'realism'. In some parts of the country, the chances of employment for certain groups are so low that 'realism' would seem to dictate that they should cut their losses and cease looking for jobs. Yet public criticisms of the laziness of the unemployed suggest that they should resist such realism and *maintain* the optimism and pride needed to continue their job search. On the other hand, the same public critics often suggest that the unemployed should be 'realistic' in accepting the jobs and wages offered by the economy. The implication is that they should *avoid* the traps of optimism and pride which – as Roberts *et al.* (1982) showed in the case of unemployed young people – lead them to reject 'trash jobs' and 'shit-work'. Which forms of 'realism' should educational provision encourage?

The political issues here suggest that at least some attention should be given to addressing the economic and political causes of unemployment. Here too, however, there are dilemmas. Increased awareness of the size and complexity of the forces which cause unemployment can lead people to feel a sense of impotence in the face of these forces. It accordingly can easily lead to a fatalism which not only reduces their chances of finding a job but also produces a more general passivity and disenchantment. It need not of course do this: it could lead to a sense of empowerment which results in political action. If so, however, it is more likely to attract criticism and opposition from the public authorities, on whose financial support most educational provision depends. Moreover, it could have the effect of encouraging the individuals involved to sacrifice their immediate interest to the supposed long-term health of society. If this is truly their own free individual choice, this is of course perfectly acceptable, but as a curricular aim it is a grave responsibility for teachers etc. to take on. The dilemma was well expressed by some of the teachers, careers officers and youth workers interviewed by Fleming and Lavercombe. (1982, p. 30) One said:

> What I'd like to do ... is to say "Get angrier about it; get on the streets and demonstrate." I've never said that to anyone ... but I think if any of them were to come in and say they were going to do that, to have a raid on the Benefits Office or something, I would encourage them.

But others voiced concern as to what it might mean for young people to become politicized:

> I've never felt I had any right to put youngsters at this stage in the front line politically, as it were.

> They can't articulate it and they can't write it down. If they get angry then they just get into trouble. They can't get organized – as soon as anything happened they'd get scared and they'd be exploited like mad. They'd just be labelled "bad" and left at the bottom of the heap again.

It is not of course necessary to polarize the issues too sharply. Compromises are possible. An *exclusive* focus on a political level of analysis poses acute difficulties. But as a secondary aim, linked with others, political and economic education would seem to have a useful role to play in helping individuals to understand their situation in broader terms. Not only may this help them maintain their self-respect and sense of identity if they become unemployed, but it may also help them to show more understanding for the position of other unemployed people, and to play their role as citizens in confronting the issue at the economic and political level from which, the evidence clearly shows (see chapter six), it stems. The growing pressure for attention to be paid within education to 'learning about work' – to develop greater understanding of the place of industry in our society – is, as we saw in chapters one and two, an argument for economic and political education. There seems little defensible reason why such education should not also embrace the structural causes of unemployment.

Similarly, it may be possible to aim to help people to understand that at a 'macro' level the causes of unemployment are structural, but that at an individual level people can still increase their chances of securing employment through their own efforts. Moreover, it may be possible to help them to recognize that although if they become or remain unemployed this may be due to forces outside their control, what they make of that situation even in an immediate sense is something which they themselves can influence. For example, there is a tendency for unemployed people to reduce their 'leisure' activities (see chapter seven). Yet Hepworth (1980) found that people's capacity to occupy their time was the best single predictor of mental health among the unemployed, and similarly Donovan and Oddy (1982) found among unemployed young people that those with more social and leisure activities tended to have fewer psychological problems. Furthermore, activities such as voluntary work or undertaking an educational course may help to reduce the stigma attached to being unemployed, and arguably also are likely to increase one's chances of impressing a potential employer. Accordingly, encouraging leisure activities does not necessarily have to be seen as encouraging unemployed people to accept the inevitability of unemployment.

Here too, though, there are some limits to what can be done within an employment-oriented society in which there appears to be a strong need to ensure that life on the dole is characterized by poverty and guilt (see chapter six). Attempts to present the possibility that unemployed people can construct positive social identities for themselves are likely to be constrained by the feeling that social pressures make it difficult for such possibilities to be developed, or at least to be publicly acknowledged. The basic issues here are whether educational institutions should reflect society's attitudes to the unemployed or should question these attitudes, and how far – even if the latter course is desirable – it is feasible in view of the pressures against which they will be working.

The various objectives outlined in figure 4.1 are therefore not mutually exclusive, but there are some tensions between them. The balance that is adopted between them is likely to vary between different teachers and different educational institutions. Broadly, there would seem to be four possible underlying aims. The first is the *social-control* aim of seeking to reinforce people's motivation to seek work and to make them feel that unemployment is a result of personal inadequacy. The second is the *individual-change* aim of seeking to maximize people's chances of finding employment. The third is the *social-change* aim of seeking to help people to see unemployment as a social phenomenon which can only be resolved by political and economic change. And the fourth is the *individual-coping* aim of seeking to make people aware of the nature of unemployment, and help them to determine how they might cope with it. These aims can be distinguished along two dimensions: one concerned with whether the primary focus is on society or individuals; the other with whether the aims accepts the *status quo* or is concerned with changing it in prescribed directions. Although in figure 4.2 each is represented as being divided into two discrete categories, for practical purposes they are better regarded as continua: any curriculum programme responding to unemployment will inevitably find a place somewhere within the two-dimensional space represented by the continua. In figure 4.2, the seven objectives outlined in figure 4.1 have simply been assigned to aims with which they seem to be most directly linked . Some of the assignments are disputable: it has already been suggested, for example, that objective 1 (employability skills) has a clear social-control function, even though in figure 4.2 this is considered subsidiary to the individual-change function of maximizing people's chances of finding meaningful 'employment'; the converse could be true in relation to objective 2 (adaptability awareness). The implication· of the analysis, however, is that as objectives more directly linked to other aims are added, the overall stance being taken moves closer to the central part of the figure. It is important that

Figure 4.2 Four alternative curricular aims relating to the issue of unemployment

	Focusing on society	Focusing on individuals
Change	*Social change* 4 Contextual awareness	*Individual change* 1 Employability skills 6 Alternative-opportunity awareness 7 Opportunity-creation skills
Status quo	*Social control* 2 Adaptability awareness	*Individual coping* 3 Survival skills 5 Leisure skills

Note: The seven objectives listed are those elaborated in figure 4.1

the assumptions and values implied by such decisions be explicitly recognized and accepted.

The issue of who should define the objectives of the curricular response to unemployment is an important one. It is of course related to more general issues regarding the control of the curriculum, but unemployment is a sufficiently controversial topic to focus these issues in a particularly sharp way. Should the decision be made by teachers? by the Local Education Authority? by the Government? What part should be played by members of the local community? – and which members? What part should be played by students themselves? Senior (1983b), for instance, has suggested at the adult-education level that unemployed people should be encouraged to set their own goals and remain in control of their own learning experiences. She also, however, points out that 'any provision must have as a starting point the opportunity for unemployed individuals to understand what is happening to them and why', so that this can provide a base on which a process of self-assessment and then of goal-setting can be built. In other words, some level of consciousness-raising covering all of the possible objectives would seem to be needed before students can be expected to choose between them. Who is to control the balance of the consciousness-raising?

Whoever makes the choice, the stance adopted will depend in part on values. For example, someone who basically believes that the unemployed are layabouts is unlikely to devote much attention to the economic and political causes of unemployment or to ways of coping with it. One 'litmus-paper' indicator of values in this respect might be whether the belief is held that unemployed people should always accept a job offered to them, whatever that job may be, rather than 'live off the state'. Another might be the attitude that is taken to 'fiddling' (i.e. black-economy activities).

In addition to values, though, the balance that is adopted will depend on whether unemployment is viewed as a passing or an enduring phenomenon, and what the future of work is seen to be. Such matters are often alluded to in educational debate, but rarely examined in any depth. Yet arguably any response to unemployment, if it is to be adequate, should be subjected to rigorous scrutiny in relation to such questions: otherwise it can easily become part of the problem, rather than part of the solution. It is these questions, then, that will provide the basis for part II of this book.

Summary

Chapter four has explored the responses to unemployment that have been made in schools in general, in YOP/YTS, in youth work, in further education, in higher education, and in adult education. In each case, particular attention has been paid to responses that have gone beyond a concern to increase employability. Seven possible curricular objectives relating to the issue of unemployment have been distinguished: employability skills, adaptability awareness, survival skills, contextual awareness, leisure skills, alternative-opportunity awareness, and opportunity-creation skills. These have been related to four broad alternative aims: social control, individual change, social change, and individual coping. It has been suggested that the balance that is adopted between these aims and objectives will depend partly on values, and partly on what the future of work is seen to be.

Part II

EDUCATION AND THE FUTURE OF WORK

CHAPTER FIVE

Futures for Work?

The concept of unemployment

Ultimately, the implications of unemployment for education depend on what are seen to be its causes, how durable these are likely to be, and how society responds to them. It is important to recognize at the outset that unemployment in the form in which we know it implicitly refers to a particular type of economic and social organization, based upon liberal capitalist principles. (Mouly, 1979) 'Unemployment' has meaning only where work relationships are based largely on the concept of 'employment', and 'work' has come to mean paid 'employment' as a result of the development of capitalist productive relations. (Williams, 1976, p. 282) In a subsistence economy, people work for their own survival; in an economy based on slave labour, slaves are obliged to labour for life and cannot 'lose their jobs', much as they might wish to do so; in a feudal society, serfs are bound to their lords by a range of obligations, rights and protections which are inviolable and extend far beyond work. Again, within advanced centrally-planned socialist economies, unemployment is officially unthinkable, since the whole of the available labour force is in principle assigned to production units.

It is only when workers are free to offer or withdraw their labour, but, in Marxist terms, are separated from the means of production, that unemployment becomes meaningful. Small businessmen who control the means of production are not employed, but clearly are not unemployed either. As Garraty (1978) puts it: unemployment 'presumes a curious mixture of freedom and dependence ... only those who work for wages or salary, who are at liberty to quit their jobs yet who may also be deprived of them by someone else, can become unemployed.' (p. 5)

Even within a liberal capitalist society, therefore, the concepts of employment and unemployment have peculiar limits. Their special focus is on work which has exchange value rather than use value. This is reflected in the way the Gross National Product (GNP) is calculated. A man who marries his housekeeper reduces national income and employment at a stroke, because her work, hitherto regarded by society as productive, now becomes mere 'housework'. Conversely, as Stretton (1974) points out, if it was decided that the work in the domestic economy should be paid for by exchanging it – with households agreeing to do each other's cooking, gardening, household repairs, child-minding, etc. at exchange rates – employment and GNP would be massively increased at a stroke (especially if we all went to bed next door at regular massage-parlour rates!). (pp. 28-9) The effect is to attach social value to productive activities which take place within the market-place of the formal economy, and to discount those outside it. Those whose work is not based in the formal economy are officially regarded either as economically inactive or as unemployed.

The causes of unemployment

Unemployment was barely written about by economists until the nineteenth century. In general, it was assumed that if people were not working, this was voluntary: it was because they were malingerers (Garraty, 1978). The Statute of Artificers of 1563 began by enunciating the principle that everyone had an obligation to work, the assumption being that work was available for all who were willing to take it. Marx, however, argued that the capitalist system caused, and indeed required, what he called 'a disposable industrial reserve army' to adjust to the cyclical booms and contractions that were characteristic of capitalist economies: this army could be employed during the booms, and laid off during the contractions, and its existence would reduce the pressure for wage increases and thereby keep workers' 'pretensions' in check. (1976 ed., Volume 1, pp. 781-94) Moreover, Marx believed that one of the internal contradictions of capitalism was that, while the capitalists' profits were initially extracted largely from labour, the process of automation drove them inexorably to reduce the proportion of their capital invested in labour, so that labour played an ever-decreasing role in the production of social wealth. (see McLellan, 1971, pp. 73-4) The inevitability of growing structural unemployment within a capitalist system was seen as one of the elements which would bring about the system's inevitable demise.

The issue of the extent to which unemployment is voluntary, cyclical or structural continues to be hotly disputed. The usual form of the *voluntary* thesis – that unemployment is caused by the erosion of the will to work due to increases in state benefits – is not supported by the available evidence: such increases as there have been in benefit levels have had little or no direct effect on unemployment rates (Showler, 1981, pp. 42-5; also Atkinson, 1981); few of the unemployed are financially better off than they would be in employment (Marsden, 1982, p. 222; also Davies *et al.*, 1982); and not only would the vast majority prefer to be in a job, but a fair number are willing to accept cuts in their previous real earnings. (e.g. Daniel, 1981, chapter IV; Moylan and Davies, 1981) The thesis can of course be pushed further, suggesting that if the principles of a true free-market economy were more fully established, state benefits reduced, and wage rates permitted to fall to their proper market level, unemployment would be demolished. (see e.g. Minford, 1983) In this version, it should be noted, the 'voluntary' behaviour which causes high levels of unemployment is not only that of the unemployed (in refusing to work below certain rates) but also that of organized labour (in sustaining excessive wage levels) and of society as a whole (in offering benefits and maintaining other institutional interventions that distort market forces). Apart from the political and social issues involved here, it is questionable whether moves towards such a reduction in wages and benefits would necessarily help to 'solve' unemployment in the short and medium term, since they would affect not only the cost and competitiveness of goods, but also the level of demand for those goods. To give a simple illustration, poorly-paid workers in, say, the glass industry would not be able to afford to buy new television sets, and by failing to buy them would not only depress the electronics industry but also, eventually, the demand from television manufacturers for glass. (Merritt, 1982, p. 201)

The *cyclical* thesis asserts that unemployment is due to the recession, and that it will decline when the economic system recovers. But the pattern of unemployment in the 1960s and 1970s showed, beneath the cyclical pattern, an underlying upward trend; since then, the upward trend has been unbroken (see chapter two, and especially figure 2.1).

It would seem, then, that the cyclical theory is inadequate, and that unemployment is being caused to a significant degree by *structural* changes in the economy. There appear now to be serious doubts about the feasibility of continued economic growth. (see e.g. Meadows *et al.*, 1972; Mishan, 1977) But even if sustained growth were resumed, it seems unlikely that this would in itself solve the unemployment problem. The recession has been used by many manufacturing companies to 'shake-out' surplus labour: if there is resumed economic growth, they are unlikely to re-employ them. Instead they are likely to invest not in labour-intensive methods but in capital-intensive methods, using the potential of robotics etc. to achieve the productivity increases that will enable them to compete in world markets. This trend is exacerbated by the fact that such labour-intensive industries as there are now tend to migrate to 'less developed countries', where labour costs are cheaper.

As Gershuny (1978) points out, 'the potential for the increase of manpower productivity must by far outrun the potential for sustained economic growth in the developed world'. (p. 136)

It is important to emphasize here that there is no evidence that the impact of microelectronics in particular has so far been a significant cause of unemployment. (see e.g. Northcott and Rogers, 1982) It seems likely, however, that it will have a more substantial effect if and when Britain emerges from recession, and as telecommunications, microelectronics and computing converge into a single information technology. The extent of this effect is a matter for dispute. Some argue that the advent of microelectronics will not produce any more dramatic net displacement of labour than other previous technological changes: by increasing productivity, and making available new products and new services at lower prices, it will create as many jobs as it destroys. (Sleigh et al., 1979) Others argue that its effect is likely to be far more pervasive than previous changes, and that it will destroy so many jobs as to cause a 'collapse of work', with five million or more officially registered as unemployed in Britain by the end of the century. (Jenkins and Sherman, 1979; see also Barron and Curnow, 1979) A careful analysis by the University of Warwick Institute of Employment Research (1982) estimated that an acceleration in the pace of technological change could have an initial displacement effect of some 340,000 jobs, but that this might in due course be turned into a very small net increase if it led to a significant improvement in domestic demand and in Britain's trade performance. Certainly most commentators agree that if Britain does not invest heavily and effectively in new technology, this will lead in the end to higher unemployment than if it does so. But this investment seems likely at best to ensure that the existing high levels of unemployment will not be durably reduced, and possibly to increase them still further, at least in the short and medium term.

A post-industrial society?

It thus appears that structural changes are taking place in the economy which mean that high levels of unemployment are likely for the foreseeable future. Beneath the changes identified so far lie deeper forces. Of particular note is the gradual transformation that has taken place in the balance between the primary sector of the economy (primarily agriculture), the secondary sector (primarily manufacturing), and the tertiary sector (primarily services). In feudal times, the vast majority of the population worked in the primary sector; during the Industrial Revolution, the majority came to work in the secondary sector; more recently, there has been a gradual shift towards the tertiary sector – into trade, finance, transport, health, recreation, research, education and government. This shift seems to be characteristic of all industrialized countries. (Clark, 1940) Indeed, Gershuny (1978) has demonstrated empirically that beyond a certain level of national product per head – which Britain passed in the 1970s – the proportion of employment in manufacturing starts to fall, largely due to the greater potential for productivity increases in this sector. Thereafter, the secondary sector becomes characterized by the phenomenon of 'jobless growth'. (Rothwell, 1981) An unpublished MSC study of the investment plans of Britain's 90 largest manufacturing firms revealed that any new investment in capital equipment would result not in the recruitment of labour but in a reduction of up to 30 per cent in their labour forces. (quoted in Thornton and Wheelock, 1979, p. 3)

The recognition of these trends led a number of writers in the late 1960s and 1970s to announce the advent of a 'post-industrial society'. (see e.g. Bell, 1974; Drucker, 1969; Kahn and Wiener, 1967; Touraine, 1971) While some of their more extreme and more naive assumptions have been convincingly demolished by Kumar (1978, chapter 6), it does seem that major changes are taking place in the economic system that has evolved since the Industrial Revolution. These changes are particularly problematic because it can no longer be assumed that they will be allied to sustained economic growth. The changes have particular significance for the nature and distribution of employment.

A key issue is whether the service sector can be expanded sufficiently to absorb those now surplus to the needs of agriculture and manufacturing. The proponents of the notion of the 'post-industrial society' tended to assume that it could, and that the expansion of the tertiary sector would take place reasonably smoothly on the base of the productivity increases within the primary and secondary sectors. Now, however, this assumption seems increasingly questionable. Parts of the service sector – notably insurance, banking and finance – are already among the prime targets of firms manufacturing the new microelectronics-based labour-saving office equipment. Moreover, as Gershuny (1978) and Pahl (1980) have argued, many personal services are beginning to price themselves out of the market. Although productivity rises faster in the manufacturing than in the services sector, various institutional forces – notably trade unions and government incomes policies – tend to maintain or even to narrow wage differentials between sectors: therefore the costs of service outputs tend to rise faster than those of manufacturing industry. At the same time, the declining costs of tools and appliances, and the development of new materials whose use requires lower levels of skill, tend to make informal production of certain services cheaper and more viable. The result is the substitution of self-service for the production of services from the formal economy: examples include the increasing popularity of 'do-it-yourself' and of household construction work paid for in cash; and the purchase of cars and TV sets as a substitute for the purchase of transport and entertainment services. As Gershuny (1978) graphically puts it, people whose cultural requirements 'may approximate to those of an eighteenth-century Prince Esterhazy . . . are more likely than he to possess a stereophonic record player, and less likely to employ Haydn and a full orchestra.' (p. 89)

Many services, of course, are offered not in the market economy but in the public sector. This is true particularly of the kinds of services which Bell (1974) saw as the key ones in his vision of the 'post-industrial society', notably health and education. Bell considered that the inadequacy of the market for meeting needs in these areas, or for meeting other needs such as a decent social and physical environment, would lead to a growth in the public sector. Indeed, the decline of employment in the manufacturing sector in Britain in the 1970s was for a while masked by the increase in public-sector employment. Now, however, the so-called 'tax revolt' (evident in a particularly populist form in the USA, but prominent too in Britain and other European countries) has led to pressure for reductions rather than further increases in public expenditure. This pressure has been fuelled by rising wage costs, which have led to accusations that such expenditure increases are simply adding to wage bills rather than improving the quantity and quality of the services to the consumer. It has also been fuelled by those who maintain that only jobs in manufacturing are 'real jobs'. Bacon and Eltis (1976), for example, influentially argued that Britain's economic problems were significantly due to the rate at which workers had been leaving 'productive' jobs and moving into 'non-productive' jobs – this despite the lack of any evidence that the growth in manufacturing had been curtailed by labour shortages, or that growth in the services sector had inhibited manufacturing growth. (see Gershuny, 1978, p. 111)

Part of the difficulty with these arguments within a mixed economy is that three separate distinctions tend to be conflated and confused with one another: the distinction between manufacturing and services; the distinction between the private and the public sectors; and the distinction between the market economy and what Handy (n.d.) terms 'the redistribution economy' (which redistributes some of the 'added value' created by the market economy to the general public). Although manufacturing is wealth-generating and is largely located in the private sector, some of it takes place in the public sector (nationalized industries). Moreover, services are offered in both the private and the public sector, and can either be marketed (e.g. financial services, tourism) or 'distributed'. Again, although the market economy provides the wealth for the redistribution economy, it also depends heavily on non-market services provided by that economy (e.g. for the education of its future labour force) and on the demand for goods and services from people employed within it. Though careful balances need to be struck between the various sectors, simple prescriptions often tend to confuse categories and to underestimate their interdependence.

Thus, for example, attempts to cut back public expenditure have the effect of reducing demand, which adversely affects the market for goods and services, and in return reduces the tax yield and thereby causes still further public-expenditure reductions. Each stage in the vicious spiral feeds the dole queue. Yet governments have become unwilling to adopt the converse approach of stimulating the economy during recessions through increased public expenditure, along the lines advocated by Keynes. (1936) For a while in the post-Second-World-War era these and other demand-management methods seemed to work well. But although they produced unprecedentedly low levels of unemployment, they also increasingly produced inflation, and evidence of the relationship between these two phenomena (Phillips, 1958) attracted growing concern. Moreover, changes in the international economy meant that the methods of stimulating growth that were used increasingly had the effects not of boosting industrial investment and output, but of leading to consumer booms of spending on imported goods, which led to balance of payments crises and to the rapid return of deflationary policies – the notorious 'stop-go' cycle; at the same time, attempts to control inflation through government incomes policies seemed to have at best only short-lived successes. Governments' confidence in the effectiveness of Keynesian demand-management methods started to erode, and priorities shifted from maintenance of full employment to control of inflation. (for an excellent description of the course of this shift, see Deacon, 1981) Increasingly it seemed that governments, far from wishing to intervene to reduce politically unacceptable levels of unemployment, were prepared to use them as a tool of policy to reduce wage demands and so to limit inflation. They were aided in this politically by the fact that although inflation directly affects everyone, unemployment directly affects only those who are unemployed. In this sense, Showler and Sinfield (1981) argue, 'the unemployed are the government's conscript army in the war against inflation'. (p. 238)

As a result, recent government policies have oscillated between increasingly tepid forms of Keynesian intervention and ever more determined attempts to promote the free-market policies of classical economics. (Marsden, 1982, p. 244) Yet in view of what has been said, there must be strong doubts about the capacity of the market to solve the problems of a society moving uneasily into a post-industrial phase of development. The market with its inevitable imperfections does not seem likely to be an effective mechanism for distributing the kinds of services that tend to be valued in such a society.

Moreover, by limiting many such services to a restricted section of the population, and by denying employment to large numbers of those who want to work, it tends both to produce a deflationary spiral and to result in increasing social divisions that threaten political and economic stability.

The implications were spelt out by Bell (1974), who contended that whereas industrial society was characterized by 'the co-ordination of machines and men for the production of goods', post-industrial society was 'organized around knowledge, for the purpose of social control and the directing of innovation and change'. (p. 20) Hence:

> The problem of a post-industrial society is the growth of a non-market welfare economics and the lack of adequate mechanisms to decide the allocation of public goods . . . Because such goods are distributed to all, there is a disincentive on the part of a citizenry to support such expenditures. Most important, the nature of non-market political decisions invites direct conflict: as against a market which disperses responsibility, in politics the decision points are open and visible, and the consequences of political decisions, as to who would lose and who would gain, are clear. (p. 118)

Nonetheless:

> The decisive social change taking place in our time – because of the inter-dependence of men and the aggregative nature of economic actions, the rise of externalities and social costs, and the need to curtail the effects of technical change – is the subordination of the economic function to the political order. The forms this will take will vary . . . But the central fact is clear. The autonomy of the economic order . . . is coming to an end, and new and varied, but different, control systems are emerging. In sum, the control of society is no longer economic but political. (p. 373)

Such a process is likely to result in considerable political tensions. These tensions could certainly be *contained* more easily if significant rates of economic growth were resumed, but such growth of itself now seems unlikely to *resolve* them. Moreover, the tensions are themselves beginning to threaten the chances of achieving resumption of growth. The issue can be posed in terms of two questions. Should Britain, and other advanced industrialized countries, continue to place all their faith and resources in measures to achieve growth, in the knowledge that this seems likely at best to ameliorate rather than to solve basic underlying problems about the distribution of work (and of wealth)? Or do these wider issues need to be addressed immediately in their own right, recognizing that their resolution will be easier if there is economic growth, but asserting that it is also a prerequisite for removing the social and political obstacles to such growth?

The future of work is thus a deeply political as well as economic matter. If the political decision is to let narrow economic forces prevail, this means that unemployment is unlikely to be significantly reduced and may well grow. This is certainly one possible scenario for the future. But there are others, which depend upon acts of deliberate political will. It is possible, for example, that those outside employment, instead of being stigmatized, could form the basis of a new leisure class. Alternatively, it is possible that ways could be found of distributing employment, and the income and status associated with it, more evenly. A further alternative is that the concept of work could be broadened beyond that of employment, and that greater value could be attached to self-employment and to forms of work outside the formal economy. The implications of these four scenarios are that groups similar to those who are at present unemployed (a) remain unemployed, (b) are regarded as being 'at leisure', (c) are offered employment, and (d) are seen as 'working', if outside formal employment structures. We will term them (a) the unemployment scenario, (b) the leisure scenario, (c) the employment scenario, and (d) the work scenario. The next four chapters will be devoted to an exploration of these different scenarios.

Summary

Chapter five has attempted to place unemployment in a historical perspective, by pointing out that it is characteristic of a particular type of economic and social organization. Three possible explanations for current levels of unemployment have been explored: the 'voluntary' thesis, the 'cyclical' thesis, and the 'structural' thesis. It has been concluded that the first two are invalid or inadequate, and that unemployment is being caused to a significant degree by structural changes in the economy. Although new technology has not so far been a significant cause of unemployment, it is likely to ensure that, within current policy assumptions, levels of unemployment will remain high for the foreseeable future. The proportion of the working population employed in manufacturing is falling, and it now appears unlikely that the service sector will absorb the surplus. Economic growth is important for the creation of jobs, but it is not likely of itself to solve the unemployment problem.

CHAPTER SIX

The Unemployment Scenario

The identity of the unemployed

If unemployment continues at its currently high level, or at higher levels still, what are its implications likely to be? Because 'unemployment' is an essentially negative concept, the identity it bestows is a negative one. The notion underlying many official regulations and social attitudes is that those who are unemployed should be spending their time looking for jobs, or engaging in passive pursuits which require no commitment so that when a job is offered to them they are immediately available to take it. There are strong restrictions on the extent to which unemployed people can engage in money-making activities, in formal education, or even in voluntary work, without imperilling their benefits. (see e.g. Jordan, 1980) The opportunities for constructing a positive identity are severely limited, and have not been helped by the effects of public-expenditure cuts on leisure and adult-education facilities.

A few do manage it. One person, for example, wrote to me in 1980 about the variety of activities he had engaged in during his period on the dole:

> Unemployment has never bored me, which is more than I can say about many of the clerical jobs I have done in the past ... I have really enjoyed being unemployed, and I have developed many talents, and met many people, as a result of this.

But he also spoke of the difficulties he had experienced:

> The drawbacks are obvious – lack of money, and the sense of vulnerability one

experiences as a claimant, especially as your time on Supplementary Benefit lengthens. Strictly speaking you are not supposed to write books or do voluntary work while claiming, as this is supposed to prove that you are not interested in finding "real" work. It was this feeling of vulnerability, and lack of freedom, plus the worry that I might become "unemployable" at a time when chances for the self-employed were thin, which made me change my tack completely, and try to get into computer programming.

He felt some resentment about this and about the general social pressures on the unemployed:

Those people who are perfectly *happy* being unemployed are being hassled at a time when there is no work available – they are also forced to compete for work they do not want with people who *do* want a job, which seems very hard on the latter. If this country is lucky enough to have people who are prepared to accept a "low" standard of living . . . and will remain happily and productively unemployed, it ought to make the most of it.

Because of these pressures, there is little sign of significant groups of unemployed people being able to construct positive alternative life-styles. The interest in communes and other radical life-styles was more characteristic of the 1960s and early 1970s (e.g. Rigby, 1974), when unemployment was relatively low; as unemployment has risen, it seems to have waned rather than waxed. Some groups certainly seem to cope with unemployment better than others. They include those who are unemployed for reasonably short periods, those who did not like their previous jobs, those who have sufficient savings or redundancy payments to manage financially for a time, and/or those who feel they have legitimate reasons for not being in employment (e.g. the disabled, parents of one-parent families, those looking after disabled or sick relatives). (Hayes and Nutman, 1981, pp. 50-60) Again, some school-leavers, who have not experienced much occupational socialization, and who are not impressed by the employment opportunities open to them, will not be as adversely affected by unemployment as most older adults. A number of such young people are able to retreat into sub-cultures – for example, in the case of young blacks, sub-cultures built around Rastafarian doctrines and the status attached to successful 'hustling'. But even these groups rarely celebrate their confinement to the fringes of the formal economy. (Roberts *et al.*, 1982) In general, as Marsden (1982) concluded from those interviewed in his study, 'talk about the "opportunity" or "leisure" afforded by unemployment seems decidedly premature'. (p. 210)

The negative status associated with being unemployed is demonstrated by unemployed people's strategies for avoiding being labelled with it. Unemployed people sometimes try to hide the fact that they are unemployed – even occasionally from their families. Marsden (1982, p. 113) records how one man when he went out wore an old BRS coat as a work uniform, and how a young woman sometimes pretended to be a student. Others seek to distance themselves from what they perceive to be associated with the label of being unemployed, in an attempt to avoid being tarnished with it themselves. Hayes and Nutman (1981), for instance, note how some unemployed people seem concerned to explain that they are not like 'those lazy scroungers who haven't done a day's work in their lives', and often show considerable venom in the way they castigate others in a similar predicament to themselves. (pp. 89-90) This reluctance to accept the identity of being unemployed may explain the difficulties experienced in organizing sustained collective protest among unemployed people (Galland and Louis, 1981), a point to which we shall return shortly.

Social attitudes to the unemployed

The problems of the unemployed are certainly greatly exacerbated by the general social attitudes manifested to them. Williams (1976), for instance, points out how the term 'idle' is used in news reports to describe workers laid off, as well as those on strike:

> With its strong moral implications *idle* in this context must have ideological intentions or effects. "Many thousands idle" sticks in the mind. (p. 275)

Yet, as we have seen, the effect of social security regulations is to tend to *make* unemployed people 'idle' even if they do not want to be.

The same social hypocrisy is evident in a more blatant form in the way in which the unemployed are presented by some politicians and by parts of the popular press for public obloquy as being 'work-shy' and as 'scroungers'. (Deacon, 1978; Golding and Middleton, 1982) There are persistent newspaper stories of individuals – usually men with large families, pictured with a cigarette in one hand and a drink in the other, in front of large television sets – who apparently are able to construct affluent life-styles on the basis of their social security payments. An example of the *genre* was a story in the *Daily Mail* (13 July 1977) which indignantly assured its readers that:

> The seaside social security offices are thick with subsidized cigarette smoke, the smell of alcohol paid for by the state, and the smugly tanned faces of the leeches feeding off the hard-working, ordinary, silent majority.

Often, these stories are not subsequently substantiated. (Golding and Middleton, 1982) Moreover, the evidence shows clearly that most of the unemployed live in considerable poverty. A 1978 survey of men unemployed for over three months showed that they tended to have been low-paid workers in the first place. Yet for 75 per cent their total family income was now over one-fifth less than what it had been when they were in employment, and for 35 per cent it had been more than halved; only 9 per cent were better off, and these were largely men with dependent children who had received particularly low wages when in a job. Only 10 per cent had received a redundancy payment of more than £300. The situation represented by these figures is likely if anything to have worsened since 1978. (Davies *et al.*, 1982)

Some newspapers and politicians also delight in parading examples of social security frauds. The excited and distorted media treatment of the mass arrest of homeless claimants in Oxford in 1982 was a good example. (Franey, 1983) That such frauds exist is undeniable, and the 'Rayner Scrutiny' (DE/DHSS, 1981) estimated that at least 8 per cent of claims were fraudulent. Some, however, are likely to be due to ignorance or misunderstandings rather than anything more deliberate. They also tend to be for small amounts: in 1976/7 the total money involved in detected fraud was only 0.12 per cent (or 1p in £8) of all social security payments. (Public Accounts Committee, 1977, para 56) This may be due in part to the substantial staff involved in investigating social security abuse. It is, however, notable that the number of such staff far exceeds the number involved in investigating tax evasion, even though a lot more money is lost to the government through the latter, and though the yield on investment in employing specialist investigatory staff is likely to be far higher there. (Field, 1980)

Thus, 'of all the myths of the Welfare State, stories of the "work-shy" and "scroungers" have been the least well-founded on evidence, yet they have proved the most persistent'. (Marsden, 1982, p. 2) Moreover, they often tend to increase at times of high or rising unemployment: in other words, people on benefit frequently become more likely to be condemned as work-shy and as scroungers as it becomes more difficult for them to get a job. (Deacon, 1978) Much the same phenomena have been noted in other countries, as for example in the Australian government's 'dole bludger' campaign. (Windschuttle, 1979, chapter 9; Pemberton, 1980) What, then, is their meaning? It seems that they perform a number of psychological and social functions. Those in the employed population find it easier to avoid confronting the reality of the threat of unemployment if they can believe that it only affects people who are different in character from their view of themselves. Moreover, if they feel any sense of guilt at their relative privilege, this can quickly be allayed by 'blaming the victim' – believing that those out of work are less deserving than they themselves are. Such beliefs are examples of a kind of 'moral panic' which tends to arise when a tension-ridden society experiences a perplexing threat to social order. (Cohen, 1972) Governments themselves are not exempt from such panics, and in addition have a more calculated vested interest in fostering them so as to distract attention from policies that might be seen as being responsible for high unemployment levels. (see also chapter two)

The effects of all this on the unemployed are considerable. The suspicions about social security abuse mean that the very process of applying for the benefits essential for economic survival becomes surrounded by suspicion and anxiety. Apart from receiving little or no help in identifying the benefits to which they are entitled, they are made to feel guilty about applying for such benefits. The anxiety this produces is exacerbated by uncertainties about social security officials' discretionary powers, and about the room these powers offer for the exercise of moral judgement: Marsden (1982) found in his study that 'applicants could not decide whether it was best in applying for grants to let standards slip and appear needy or to keep up standards and risk being ignored or refused'. (p. 191) Moreover, derogatory social attitudes towards the unemployed develop a political climate in which it is possible to reduce benefit levels, whereas rationality suggests that – as Galbraith (1970) argues – *higher* levels of benefits should be paid when unemployment grows and the fear of weakening incentives to work becomes less valid. Beyond this, they also mean that on top of all the poverty, dislocation and stress associated with their condition, those who are unemployed have to contend with being regarded as social pariahs. It is difficult for them to avoid internalizing such attitudes. As Orwell (1937) commented when he first saw unemployment at close quarters: 'The thing that horrified and amazed me was to find that many of them were *ashamed* of being unemployed.' (p. 85)

Some have argued that these social attitudes have changed. Garraty (1978), for instance, asserts unequivocally that 'the irrational tendency of so many of the unemployed of the 1930s to blame themselves for their unfortunate position ... is fast disappearing among the unemployed of the 1980s'. (pp. 251-2) Little evidence, however, is offered for this statement, and it seems clear from what has been said above that many unemployed people do still feel a sense of shame and of social stigma. According to a 70-year-old man in the North-East, the change within his own community had been in the reverse direction:

"I pity those who haven't got work now. When we were unemployed, people were generally more sympathetic to us than they are now. When we marched, there were always a few who stood on the pavement calling us Commies and Reds, but on the whole, people's goodwill was with you. Nobody ever called us scroungers; I'd never heard the word layabout. But now, they make you feel it's your own fault." (Seabrook, 1981b, p. 4)

Although in the 1980s the attention of the media has shifted somewhat to lay greater stress on examining the economic causes of unemployment and its personal consequences, the punitive attitudes to which the unemployed are subjected have by no means disappeared.

In part these attitudes stem from the nature of welfare benefits. Discussion of the levels of such benefits are readily couched in terms of what the taxpayer can afford, and where the taxpayer will draw the line, thereby implicitly defining claimants as non-citizens. Tawney's argument that 'since unemployment is the result of a social breakdown, society must pay for it', and that 'since the maintenance of the willing worker is a matter of right, not of grace, the sum paid must be sufficient, not merely to keep him in physical existence, but for a self-respecting life' (Tawney, 1964 ed., p. 148), is easily lost to view. So is the fact that the welfare system is based on an insurance principle, so that many of those involved are simply drawing on what they themselves have 'invested' through their insurance contributions.

Effects on the unemployed

The notion that the unemployed are, in important senses, 'non-citizens' is indeed implicit in a society in which status is determined, both in official statistics and (to a large extent) in social attitudes, in terms of one's occupation. 'What do you do?' is the most illuminating question to ask when one meets someone for the first time, because it is indicative of so much else in terms of attitudes, life-style, etc. It is a question which expects an occupational answer. The result of withdrawing people's occupational status altogether is thus to threaten both their status in the eyes of others and their own sense of identity. As Hayes and Nutman (1981) put it:

> When this status is removed it is not simply a question of the individual who loses the status of a working person, but more importantly he or she loses the means by which the integrity of the self-image is maintained. (p. 86)

It has been argued by some that these effects are tempered by the fact that the material situation of the unemployed is less devastating that it was, say, in the 1930s. While this is true in terms of *absolute* deprivation, it is not true in terms of *relative* deprivation. In a society which values the hedonistic attitudes associated with consumer commodities, to be deprived of these commodities is experienced as an assault upon status and identity:

> For many people consumer activities (planning, searching for and buying goods and services) occupy a great deal of their non-work time; acquiring a new item is experienced as pleasurable, often being used as a compensation for boredom and frustration in other spheres of life; possession of a standard range of goods which are replaced regularly gives reassurance of psychological security and social status. (Hilgendorf and Welchman, 1982b, p. 8)

At the same time, the sense of solidarity in many working-class communities has been eroded. As Seabrook (1981b) eloquently puts it:

> In the 1930s, hope remained public and collective; whereas in the 1980s there is room only for individual fantasy – the big pools win, a lucky night at Bingo, the sudden access to money of individuals . . . The anger and frustration tend to turn inward, people turn on each other, or even on themselves. Violence, family breakdown, mental illness are part of the price people pay. (p. 13)

Certainly it seems that, on the whole, unemployment results in a sense of normlessness and of alienation from the mainstream of society rather than in any cohesive political stirrings. Most unemployed young people, for instance, have no interest in politics (Roberts *et al.*, 1981, p. 5): their public demonstrations tend rather to involve roaming the streets in pursuit of their own totems – associated with football teams, for example – and engaging in random acts of violence. The riots which took place in many British cities in 1981 did not centre around any clear set of political goals, but appeared to be an incoherent release of deep ,pent-up frustration which both nationally and locally was widely attributed as stemming, in significant part, from unemployment. (e.g. Southgate, 1982) The growth of such delinquent and anarchic behaviour is not hard to understand: it is difficult to see how a society can expect loyalty from able-bodied people to whom it has denied the opportunity to be productive and responsible members. Its main result, however, is a demand for an increase in public spending on law and order: for more public money to be spent on the police force, and less on social services. Repressive police methods then cause further resentment and accentuate the sense of oppression. So the repressive forces in society grow, and feed on each other. And although the unemployed do not form any coherent political force, it does not mean that they may not eventually be susceptible to extreme right-wing or left-wing politicians offering instant remedies to their problems, as happened in Austria in the 1930s. (Jahoda, 1982, p. 28)

The effects of unemployment on crime and delinquency are not easy to prove irrefutably. Nonetheless, the indicative evidence is strong. Fleisher (1963), for example, demonstrated that in the USA there was a significant relationship over time between delinquency rates and unemployment rates, and suggested that a 100 per cent increase in unemployment over a given period might be expected to lead to an increase in delinquency of between 10 per cent and 25 per cent (depending on which age-group was in question). Again, Phillips *et al.* (1972), in another American study, found that young people who were not working had significantly higher crime rates than those who were, and concluded that changing labour-market opportunities were sufficient to explain the increase in crime rates for youth. Although similar studies have not been conducted in Britain, Gladstone (1979) suggested, on the basis of a preliminary analysis of Home Office statistics, that the North American conclusions might be relevant to contemporary British experience as well: for example, the fluctuations in the number of youths aged 17-20 admitted to prison and borstals in recent years seemed to reflect the unemployment figures for late adolescence. Furthermore, Box and Hale (1982) have showed that the frequency and severity of *imprisonment* varies positively with the rate of unemployment even when the level of *crime* is controlled: this may be because unemployed people are less likely to be given bail, are more likely to be given custodial sentences, and are less likely to be granted parole. Finally, there seems to be a clear association between unemployment and recidivism: Martin and Webster (1971), for instance, found that those with good employment records were relatively unlikely to be reconvicted, whereas the reconviction rate among those who committed their original crimes while unemployed or in casual work was as high as 73 per cent. (pp. 194-5) Of course, in all these studies the possibility exists that both unemployment and crime/imprisonment/reconviction are not causally related but are each caused by other factors ; moreover, in some studies, the possibility that unemployment is the *effect* rather than the *cause* of any relationship between the two must be given due consideration. Nonetheless, the weight of evidence makes it extremely likely that there are *some* direct effects stemming from unemployment itself.

Much the same is true of other 'social indicators'. Thus in the case of suicide – which Durkheim (1952 ed.) classically regarded as an index of anomie (i.e. normlessness) – there is evidence from longitudinal studies of a relationship between fluctuations in unemployment and in suicide rates in the USA (Hammermesh and Soss, 1974; Brenner, 1977a; Vigderhous and Fishman, 1978), in Australia (Windschuttle, 1979, pp. 106ff), and in other countries (Boor, 1980), even if evidence in Britain has been more mixed. (Swinscow, 1951; cf. Boor, 1980) Again, cross-sectional studies in Britain have consistently found that the proportion of suicides who are unemployed at the time of their death is significantly greater than the proportion unemployed in control samples or in the population at large. (Sainsbury, 1955; Robin *et al.*, 1968; Shepherd and Barraclough, 1980) Although neither set of studies proves causality, and each is subject to methodological limitations, the fact that they confirm each other is strongly suggestive.

On the broader phenomenon of mental health, there is evidence from the USA that the unemployed are overrepresented among psychiatric patients (Jaco, 1960, p. 193); moreover, it is significant that employment is widely used as a form of rehabilitation, and this becomes progressively more difficult to provide when general unemployment is high. (Morgan and Cheadle, 1975) In other words, not only does unemployment seem to be associated with an increase in the numbers of people suffering some form of mental ill-health, but it also reduces the provision of a key form of 'treatment' available to them.

The relationship between mental health and unemployment is complicated by the fact that there is evidence from a number of studies conducted both in the 1930s (e.g. Bakke, 1933; Jahoda *et al.*, 1972 ed.) and in the 1970s (e.g. Hill, 1978; Marsden, 1982) that the subjective experience of unemployment tends to pass through a number of stages. From a review of some of these studies, Harrison (1976) suggests that there is an immediate drop in morale due to *shock;* that this is followed by a period of *optimism* in which efforts are made to find a job and confidence is still reasonably high; that when these efforts fail, there is a much greater drop in morale in which money worries, boredom, declining self-respect, and the recognition of the diminishing chances of obtaining another job, all take their toll, inducing acute *pessimism;* and that this is finally succeeded by *fatalism,* in which people adapt themselves to their unemployed state by adopting, as Eisenberg and Lazarsfeld (1938, p. 378) put it, 'a broken attitude'. (for a more extended discussion of this and other versions of the cycle, see Hayes and Nutman, 1981, chapters 2-3) Though clearly not *all* unemployed people pass through this cycle, many seem to do so. The level of stress and mental health is accordingly likely to depend on the length of unemployment and on the stage individuals have reached in the process.

It seems that the stresses associated with unemployment have a considerable effect not only on mental but also on physical health. Kasl and his colleagues, for example, identified a variety of physical changes – high blood-pressure, etc. – which seemed likely to increase chances of illness, and even, eventually, of death. (see e.g. Kasl and Cobb, 1970; Kasl *et al.*, 1975). More recently, Fagin (1981, p. 116) has catalogued the symptoms that are associated with job loss: these include asthmatic attacks, skin lesions, backaches, and headaches. Although a DHSS longitudinal study (Ramsden and Smee, 1981) found no evidence that men's health deteriorated significantly during their first year of being unemployed, Brenner (1976) argued that many of the deeper symptoms would need time to develop, and related mortality rates to unemployment by introducing time-lags varying – according to the symptom – from one to five years. On the basis of these analyses, he estimated that in the USA a 1 per cent increase in unemployment, sustained over six years, was associated with an increase of nearly 37,000 deaths. He also applied the same kind of analysis to data from England and Wales, with similar results. (Brenner, 1979b) These data have come under some attack. Eyer (1977a; 1977b), for example, has claimed that the time-lags allowed for by Brenner were excessive, and that the death-rate variations associated with the business cycle were due not to the unemployment during the downswings but to the overwork, lack of workers' solidarity and increased worker mobility during the upswings. This ingenious claim has however been refuted by Brenner (1979a), as has a claim that the British results were an artefact of the particular time-period chosen. (Gravelle *et al.*, 1981; cf. Brenner 1981) Again, there is evidence that effects on health may vary according to previous employment: when people have been working in unhealthy occupations, unemployment may actually result in an increase of health. (Jahoda *et al.*, 1972 ed., p. 34; Fagin, 1981, pp. 44-47; see also, in relation to mental health, Kasl, 1979) This underlines the importance of not assuming that generalizations apply to all groups; it does not, however, challenge their overall validity *as* generalizations.

Wider effects

The effects of unemployment do not only apply to the unemployed themselves. Fagin (1981), for example, showed that in families where the main wage-earner was unemployed, signs of distress were often displayed by all the family – husbands, wives and children. Bakke (1960) elaborated this by describing how unemployment had a dislocating effect on all the relationships within traditionally-structured families in which the husband had previously been the main wage-earner: after becoming unemployed, his status began to decline in the eyes of both his wife and his children, and increasing challenges to his authority – allied to financial pressures and over-proximity – caused growing conflicts and tensions. Where the wife has a job and becomes the main earner, this may relieve the financial pressures to some extent, but may exacerbate the psycho-social pressures. In practice, though, various factors – including the structure of means-tested benefits – mean that wives of unemployed men are less likely to be in employment than are wives of employed men (Moylan and Davies, 1980, p. 832), and this adds to the financial pressures within such families.

Within communities, too, unemployment can have a corrosive effect. Although it has affected all parts of the country, it is still much higher in some regions than in others: in March 1983, for example, regional unemployment rates (excluding school-leavers) ranged from 9.3 per cent in the South-East to 16.6 per cent in the North and 19.7 per cent in Northern Ireland. (Department of Employment, 1983c, table 2.3) These figures can conceal even greater variations: within the East Midlands, for example, rates ranged from 5.4 per cent in Market Harborough to 25.3 per cent in Mablethorpe (*ibid*, table 2.4); and even within a city like Liverpool, the male unemployment rate for different wards in the 1981 Census varied between 8.2 per cent in County and 39.2 per cent in Everton. (OPCS, 1981, table 2) Unemployment rates tend to be particularly high within inner-city areas, and in communities dependent on a single industry that is in decline. In such areas, high unemployment can damage the community's infrastructure, and can lower the morale not only of those without work but also of the community as a whole. This can produce a downward spiral which is hard to reverse, deterring possible external investors, and developing a sense of resignation which makes it difficult for local people's energies to be sustained and harnessed. (for a classic account of such a community, see Jahoda *et al.*, 1972 ed.)

Unemployment has wider effects still. There are, for example, the stresses caused by those in jobs who fear they may become unemployed. There are also the effects of 'under-employment': factory workers on short time; 'trading down' (i.e. people being pressurized to accept jobs that do not make full use of their skills and abilities – e.g. at the entry level, graduates being forced to accept jobs traditionally filled by A-level leavers, A-level leavers those traditionally filled by O-level leavers, etc.); and 'job stagnation' (i.e. people dissatisfied with their jobs who at other times would have been prepared to risk a period out of work in order to find something better but who are now unwilling to do so). Unemployment has ripple effects which run through the whole labour market and the whole society, reducing people's sense of confidence and fulfilment.

Costs of unemployment

All of these factors have costs for the individuals concerned. They also, however, have costs for the society as a whole, not only in social but in economic terms. These costs can be divided into four categories. First, there are the transfer payments made to the unemployed in the form of unemployment and supplementary benefits (including rent and rates rebates, cheap school meals, and the like): Dilnot and Morris (1981) estimated these as totalling £4.6 billion. Second, there are the revenues foregone, in terms of income tax and national-insurance contributions: these were estimated by Dilnot and Morris as totalling a further £5.7 billion. Third, there are the so-called 'second-round' effects such as the loss of indirect taxes like Value Added Tax (VAT) which the unemployed would have paid if they had been in work and spending money: this covered an additional £2.6 billion. On these three sets of costs alone, the cost to the Exchequer of each unemployed person even in 1981 was £4,500 per year. Beyond this, there is also the more controversial issue of the public-expenditure costs associated with the pathological effects of unemployment – the lost income due to illness and mortality, and the added expenditure on prisons, hospitals, etc. In the USA,

Brenner (1977b) estimated that the 1.4 per cent rise in unemployment in 1970 cost nearly $7 billion in these terms over the years 1970-5, to set alongside $14 billion spent in welfare payments.

The burden of these costs can easily produce a 'downward spiral' effect, in which unemployment adds to the pressure of demand for benefits and public services, and yet reduces the state's capacity to pay for them. This results in pressure to cut the level of benefits and services. Such cuts in turn cause increased social dislocation and also mean that unemployed people's level of consumption falls. This affects the economy as a whole, because it reduces domestic demand for goods produced within the market economy. So although the market sector may be achieving greater productivity in relation to its direct costs – partly because of its slimmer labour force, and partly because of limited wage-demands due to fears of unemployment – this may simply conceal a continuing deterioration in total output. The only way out of this is for reduced production costs to lead to a boost of export demand and so to export-led growth. But this is made more difficult by the sustained tax burden of supporting those driven out of work. This burden, along with the declining market demand from these groups, can accordingly mean that the market economy winds itself into an ever tighter and more exclusive spiral, serving the needs of fewer and fewer people and thereby making likely its own continued decline. (Newland, 1982)

How long a society can endure such costs and their associated social effects without causing intolerable economic, social and political frictions is uncertain. Certainly if people in the mid-1970s had been told of the sustained high levels of unemployment that Britain was to experience in the early 1980s, many would not have believed that the country could contain the strains which such levels would produce – particularly since communication systems are now so powerful that the relatively deprived are reminded constantly of their relative deprivation. Yet by 1982 it seemed that a mood of fatalistic acquiescence had developed: an *Observer*/NOP poll (Taylor, 1982) showed that although one in four of Britain's workers – about six million people – had been unemployed at some point during the preceding 12 months, over two-thirds thought that none of the political parties had the right answer to cure unemployment, and 64 per cent said they did not believe politicians who said they could solve it.

Groups at risk

One possible policy response frequently canvassed is to reduce unemployment not by creating jobs for the unemployed but by finding means of excluding some of them from the labour force altogether – in other words, preventing or dissuading them from making themselves available for employment. It is important in this connection to emphasize that, although unemployment has affected all groups in all areas of the country, it has tended to be disproportionately concentrated among the weaker groups within the labour market. It has been suggested that there is in reality a dual labour market: in the primary sector there is relatively low turnover, high earnings, and relatively good advancement and on-the-job training opportunities; in the secondary sector, by contrast, turnover is high, earnings are low, and promotion and training opportunities are limited or non-existent. (Doeringer and Piore, 1971; Bosanquet and Doeringer, 1973; Barron and Norris, 1976) Certain groups tend to be concentrated in the secondary sector: they include the young, the old, the women, the disabled, the unskilled, and ethnic minorities. When labour demand is low, it is their labour that is shed.

Certainly it is true that these groups have suffered particularly acutely from unemployment. So far as the *young* and the *old* are concerned, the unemployment rate in October 1982 for those aged under 20 was 28 per cent; it then declined until for the 45-54 age-group it reached 8.5 per cent; thereafter it rose to 15.5 per cent for those aged 60 and over. (MSC, 1982b) The figures in the higher age-groups in particular would have been even greater had not some older people who in better times would have been glad to have remained in the labour force decided to seek early retirement. (Department of Employment, 1980)

The position regarding *women* is a little more complicated. The official unemployment rate for women in October 1982 was actually much lower than that for men – 10 per cent as opposed to 16 per cent. (MSC, 1982b) This has traditionally been the case, partly because of women's lower labour-force participation rate, and partly because married women in particular often gain no financial benefit from registering as unemployed. Between 1971 and 1981, however, the number of women registering as unemployed increased nearly seven-fold, compared with a tripling among men. (Department of Employment, 1983a, table 2.1) Although this was partly attributable to changes in regulations governing national insurance contributions and benefits which increased the incentive to register, it was still the case in 1981 that 41 per cent of married women who declared themselves as unemployed in the Labour Force Survey had not registered, as opposed to 25 per cent of non-married women and 10 per cent of men. (OPCS, 1982b, table 4.14) Also, the increase in married women's economic activity rates, which had grown rapidly from 50 per cent in 1971 to 59 per cent in 1975, slowed to reach only 62 per cent in 1980. (OPCS, 1982a, table 5.2) It seems likely – as was argued in chapter two – that to the registered unemployed and the non-registered unemployed who are looking for work should be added a fair number of married women who have been 'discouraged' from seeking work but would do so if jobs were available. The particular threat posed by microelectronics to, for example, the clerical and retailing jobs in which many women are concentrated suggests that the position represented by these figures may well worsen much further. (Arnold *et al.*, 1982) There has, incidentally, been an extraordinary lack of studies of female unemployment: most of the existing studies concentrate exclusively or mainly on men.

The *disabled* also face particular problems in the labour market, and their employment prospects have worsened rather more quickly than those of able-bodied job-seekers during the recession. (MSC, 1982c, p. 10) Protective measures designed to force employers to offer a proportion of jobs to handicapped people are less likely to be effective at such times, because of the easy availability of alternative labour. Disabled workers accordingly find it particularly difficult to get back to work once they have lost a job, and form a disproportionately large number of the long-term unemployed. In October 1981, 50 per cent of disabled unemployed men had been out of work for more than one year and 27 per cent for more than two years, compared with 29 per cent and 10 per cent respectively for *all* unemployed men. (MSC, 1982a, p. 8)

Much the same is true of the *unskilled*. Although just over one-fifth of the male working population are semi-skilled and unskilled workers, these groups provide over half of the long-term unemployed. (*ibid*, p. 37)

Finally, *ethnic minorities*, too, tend both to be more likely than indigenous groups to become unemployed and, when they are unemployed, to take longer to find a job. This is partly because they tend to be less skilled, and employed in more insecure work (Smith, 1981); and partly because of discrimination by employers in hiring. (Smith, 1974; McIntosh and Smith, 1974; Smith, 1976, chapter X) After reviewing the various sources of evidence, Showler (1980) concluded that unemployment rates among ethnic minorities exceeded the general rates in the late 1970s by at least 40 per cent, and that the difference was even greater for young and female workers from these groups.

In principle, some of these groups could be encouraged or even forced to leave the labour market. This applies particularly to the young, to the old, and to women. For example, there have been strong hints from government ministers that the proper place for mothers is in the home – a point that will be returned to in chapter nine. There have also been measures like the Job Release Scheme (see Makeham and Morgan, 1980), designed to encourage older workers to take voluntary early retirement so as to make way for young people, as well as pressure from various groups to reduce the official retirement age (as was done in 1925, when the pensionable age for men was reduced from 70 to 65 to release jobs for the younger unemployed). (see Hawkins, 1979, p. 123) So far as young people are concerned, though no serious lobby has emerged for a further raising of the school-leaving age, there have been proposals for various forms of compulsory military or community service. (e.g. Colombatto, 1980; cf. Jeffs, 1982) In the event, the advent of the Youth Training Scheme means that few school-leavers will henceforth enter the labour market at the age of 16: instead they will be 'trainees', paid by the government to engage in various forms of education and training and of 'work experience'. (see chapter two)

Significantly, these three groups (women, the young, the old) are among the groups for whom the stresses of unemployment – though still marked – seem to be relatively tolerable. For example, recent American evidence (Radloff and Cox, 1981) showed that unemployed wives were less depressed than unemployed husbands, though it interestingly also showed that the reverse was true in unmarried groups – unemployed single women were significantly more depressed than unemployed single men. It seems plausible to suppose that this is because the role of being unemployed as a married woman is sufficiently close to the socially acceptable role of 'housewife'. Similarly, for young people, as was mentioned earlier in this chapter, it has been suggested that lack of occupational socialization, relatively limited financial responsibilities, and access to sub-cultures in which to be unemployed is the norm, may all help to ameliorate the experience of being unemployed (Hayes and Nutman, 1981, pp. 52-4): the evidence collected by Roberts *et al.* (1982), while not including comparative data for older age-groups, would seem to bear this out. Being unemployed as a teenager is perhaps sufficiently close to the socially acceptable roles of 'child', 'student', and 'trainee', to carry less of a stigma than for other people. Finally, older unemployed workers seem to be able to reconcile themselves to the fact that they will not be able to secure another job, and gradually to take on the role of being retired.

Since the roles of housewife, child/student/trainee and 'senior citizen' respectively are accessible to these groups, the argument seems to run, why not press them to take up such roles, and lose the stigma of unemployment altogether? The idea is superficially attractive, but it fails to take account of the extent to which substantial numbers of people who *have* assumed one of these three roles have expressed dissatisfaction with their dependent status and have pressed for access to the labour market. Oakley (1974), for example, has shown how many housewives experience their role as possessing low status, and as being socially isolating; as a result of these and other pressures, more and more women through the 1960s and 1970s sought to enter the labour force, and to secure the same pay and opportunities as men. Again, it was argued in the 1960s and early 1970s that the student's lack of a fully accepted social role was a significant cause of student unrest (e.g. Hatch, 1972; see also Silver, 1965); and the raising of the school-leaving age to 16 in 1972 was widely perceived as 'an act of hostility, a use of power by those who wish to prevent or at least inhibit the process of taking up adult roles'. (Bazalgette, 1978b, p. 182) Similarly, in a recent survey of retired people, 37 per cent of women and 46 per cent of men said they would have liked to have gone on working (Hunt, 1978, p. 63); and the lack of an active and fully accepted social role has been adduced as an explanation for the distress and anomie experienced by many people once they retire. (e.g. Burgess, 1960, p. 20) In the USA, the 'grey power' movement in the 1970s accordingly pushed through Congress a statutory *increase* in the minimum compulsory retirement age, which is now 70.

Discussing these three groups together conceals some important differences between them. For example, housewives tend to be dependent on their husbands, whereas retired people tend to be dependent on the state (though drawing, in most cases, on their previous insurance contributions); students/trainees tend to be in an intermediate position here, partly dependent on state grants or allowances, and partly on continued support from their parental families. In this respect, adding to the stock of housewives and students/trainees would seem in purely fiscal terms to be a more attractive policy option than lowering the age of retirement (though in the end it simply means that the 'burden' of the increased dependency ratio has to be borne by wage/salary earners privately rather than through the tax system).

It is however important to discuss the groups together because otherwise the problem of access to employment tends simply to be transferred from one group to another. Those promoting the interest of old people argue that encouraging earlier retirement at a time when increasing numbers of people feel at the peak of their vitality and competence between the ages of 55 and 75 could lead to social strains; they also argue that it could extend poverty in old age, which is associated with the length of time that has elapsed since leaving the labour force. (on this latter point, see e.g. Walker, 1982a) The usually unstated implication is that young people and married women are better able to bear the burden of dependency. On the other hand, those promoting the interests of young people argue that to raise the age of dependency at a time when physiological adulthood is occurring earlier is to cause a dangerous gap to grow between the age of sexual maturity and the age of economic responsibility. They point to evidence that entering work is important for promoting psycho-social development, and that lack of employment can impede such development. (Gurney, 1980; Poole, 1981) Further, they point to the greater threat to public order caused by rearing a generation denied access to jobs. Implicitly, they suggest that young people should be given preference over older people – an idea given official legitimacy in the Job Release Scheme. They also imply that young people should be given preference to married women, who after all have a husband to depend upon and a proper role to attend to in child-rearing. The fact that many working women live in families that depend crucially on their earnings is ignored, as is the possibility that men might have an equal responsibility for child-rearing.

The danger with all these arguments is that by focusing on the needs of one group, they tend to seek to meet them at the expense of the needs of others, and to fail to address the underlying problem. The fact is that in a society in which employment is the main source of identity, status and income, and in which consciousness of this is high, groups that do not have access to employment will feel themselves to be deprived, and will resist such deprivation. Voluntary methods are accordingly unlikely to be effective, as was shown by the limited response of older workers to the Job Release Scheme, largely because they accurately perceived it as increasing their prospects of poverty in retirement. (Makeham and Morgan, 1980) Compulsion, too, will be firecely resisted. Such resistance may take sufficiently private forms to be publicly containable, but it will have a cost in terms of social energy, social cohesion and individual fulfilment.

The cost will be greater in the case of the other groups that suffer particularly acutely from unemployment and for whom no socially acceptable alternative roles currently exist. These include, in particular, the unskilled and ethnic minorities (the disabled would seem to occupy, in this respect, an intermediate position between these and the other groups). It seems that there is beginning to emerge what could become a permanent underclass of people – including many middle-aged males – who are unable to secure more than an occasional tenuous toe-hold in employment, if that. As a group, they are not sufficiently strong or broadly-based to exert any effective political leverage, particularly in the short term. As Shanks (1981) argues, 'as the pattern of income distribution starts to move from a pyramidical to a diamond-shaped structure – as is now happening generally in the West – the political pressure for equalization is starting to diminish, and income and wealth differentials are widening', to the point where 'the natural inequalities within society could widen dangerously'. (p. 31)

In some areas, the exclusion extends beyond minorities and unskilled groups. Here and elsewhere, the sense of permanence about unemployment distinguishes the experience from that of the 1930s:

> In the 1930s, those who wanted work had a sense that they had only to wait before their labour would be required again. When they talk of those years, they evoke the idle machinery, the eerie silence over shipyard and pithead. Unemployment impaired their sense of worth, assailed their dignity, denied them and those they loved adequate food and comfort. But it didn't rob them of the skills themselves. Now, on the other hand, there is a terminal sense of the extinction of work itself. Something elusive and despairing pervades those towns and cities which were built only for the sake of their purpose in the old industrial processes. It is as though the working class were being wounded in its

very reason for existence, work itself.' (Seabrook, 1981b, p. 14)

Is it possible for socially acceptable roles to be created for such groups and communities outside employment? Is it possible for their depression and deprivation to be transformed into something more positive, building the base of a new 'leisure class'? It is to this scenario that we turn our attention in the next chapter.

Summary

Chapter six has explored what the implications are likely to be if unemployment remains at high levels, and continues to be defined in such an essentially negative way as it is at present. The difficulties which the unemployed have in constructing a positive identity for themselves have been discussed. These difficulties are exacerbated by social attitudes to the unemployed, which tend to transfer guilt for their situation to the unemployed themselves. The effect of unemployment on crime, delinquency, suicide, mental health, physical health, etc. has been analysed, along with its wider social effects and economic costs. The groups particularly at risk of unemployment have been identified: they include the young, the old, the women, the disabled, the unskilled, and ethnic minorities. Some of these, notably the young, the old, and married women, have access to socially acceptable roles which offer alternatives to unemployment. But many people in these groups resist such roles, because of their dependent character. There is a danger that unemployment gets passed from one relatively weak group to another, without ever addressing the underlying problem: the importance attached to the status of being employed, access to which is denied to many who want it.

CHAPTER SEVEN

The Leisure Scenario

Prophets of an age of leisure

The notion that Britain and other 'developed' societies are moving into a new leisure age has been promoted by a number of writers in the twentieth century. As long ago as the early 1920s, Bertrand and Dora Russell (1923) estimated that if waste and extravagances were cut out, an average of four hours' work per day would be sufficient to produce the goods that were needed for a good life. (p. 40) Keynes (1931), too, concluded that 'in the long run ... mankind is solving its economic problem'. (p. 364) Thus:

> For the first time since his creation man will be faced with his real, his permanent problem – how to use his freedom from pressing economic cares, how to occupy the leisure, which science and compound interest will have won for him, to live wisely and agreeably and well. (p. 367)

If people could learn to use this freedom and leisure, they would be able to lead a fuller and more virtuous life:

> I see us free, therefore, to return to some of the most sure and certain principles of religion and traditional virtue – that avarice is a vice, that the exaction of usury is a misdemeanour, and the love of money is detestable, that those walk most truly in the paths of virtue and sane wisdom who take least thought for the morrow. We shall once more value ends above means and prefer the good to the useful. We shall honour those who can teach how to pluck the hour and the day virtuously and well, the delightful people who are capable of taking direct enjoyment in things, the lilies of the field who toil not, neither do they spin. (pp. 371-2)

Keynes offered, however, a parting cautionary note:

But beware! The time for all this is not yet. For at least another hundred years we must pretend to ourselves and to every one that fair is foul and foul is fair; for foul is useful and fair is not. Avarice and usury and precaution must be our gods for a little longer still. For only they can lead us out of the tunnel of economic necessity into daylight. (p. 372)

The same kinds of ideas seized the imaginations of various writers in the 1960s and early 1970s. Kahn and Wiener (1967) argued that the wholehearted adoption of new technology would lead to unimagined levels of economic abundance while massively reducing the need for human labour. Gabor (1964) saw the 'age of leisure', to be created by 'the technological paradise in which the work of a small minority is sufficient to keep the majority in idle luxury' (p. 10), as the most formidable of the 'trilemma' facing our civilization. Again, Dumazedier (1967) claimed that we were on the verge of a 'society of leisure' in which our self-identities and values would be derived from leisure interests.

In the late 1970s and 1980s, such optimistic visions have seemed difficult to recognize in the prevailing gloom. The credibility of the notion of a society of plenty in which all needs can be met have been undermined, partly by the increasing recognition of the limits of the world's natural resources (Meadows *et al.*, 1972; Mishan, 1977), partly by increasing recognition of the immense gulf between the developed world and the Third World and the threat this poses to world stability (Brandt *et al.*, 1980; 1983), and partly by the recognition that many human needs are not absolute but are 'positional goods' which because they are essentially relative can never be fully satisfied. (Hirsch, 1977) Nonetheless, Jenkins and Sherman (1979) have argued that 'if governments, unions and employers take the right decisions in short and long terms the "collapse of work" may be referred to in historical terms as the "ascent to leisure".' (p. 13) Again, two ex-Labour Members of Parliament, Clemitson and Rodgers (1981), have urged the Labour Party to forego its traditional preoccupation with labour and with the 'work ethic' and to replace it with a 'life ethic'.

The basic assumptions that lie beneath these various statements are two-fold. The first is that, because of technology, work in the dimensions we have known it is no longer *necessary*. Echoing the earlier statements of the Russells and of Keynes, Stonier (1983, p. 24) has estimated that by early in the 21st century it will require no more than 10 per cent of the labour force to provide us with all our material needs – food, clothing, textiles, furniture, appliances, automobiles, housing, etc (for a report of the basis for this estimate, see *The Times*, 13 November 1978) The second is that since much work is no longer necessary, it is also no longer *desirable*. As Russell (1935) put it: 'only a foolish asceticism, usually vicarious, makes us continue to insist on work in excessive quantities now that the need no longer exists'. (p. 19) The point was put graphically in a story told by Lord Ritchie-Calder (1979) about a sun-tanned Italian youth, lying on the beach at Naples:

> An American tycoon berates him: "You lazy layabout, why don't you do some work? Why don't you get yourself a piece of string and a bent pin and go out on that rock and fish? You could sell your catch and buy yourself a proper line and hook and you'd catch more fish and earn enough to hire a boat and go out and catch more fish and get your own boat. And you would catch enough to buy a trawler and hire yourself a crew. Then more trawlers and more ships. And you'd end up a millionaire like Onassis." "Si, signor, then what?" "Then you could lie on the beach at Naples". (p. 73)

Even modern economics attributes no intrinsic value to work as such: as Schumacher (1973) points out, it is seen as 'little more than a necessary evil', so that 'the ideal from the point of view of the employer is to have output without employees, and the ideal from the point of view of the employee is to have income without employment'. (p. 49)

The leisure ethic

The ultimate preferability of a 'leisure ethic' has deep roots in Western culture. Indeed, it is expressed clearly in the Book of Genesis, which tells us that work is punishment for sin, and that idleness is the natural condition of the blameless soul. The yearning for the return to the Garden of Eden is a basic thrust in Christian tradition.

Aristotle, too, clearly saw leisure as superior to work undertaken for gain, which 'absorbs and impoverishes the mind' (1959 ed., p. 222). Accordingly:

> . . . in a state which has an ideal constitution . . . the citizens must not lead the life of mechanics or tradesmen, which is ignoble and far from conducive to virtue. Nor . . . must they be drawn from among the farming class, because leisure is necessary for the growth of virtue and for the fulfilment of political duties . . . No one can rule satisfactorily without the leisure derived from easy circumstances. (*ibid*, pp. 203, 60)

But in Aristotle's vision, leisure was not equated with idleness: it was a disciplined quest for higher values. Moreover, these values were not just moral and spiritual: they were to form the basis for political action, which was the responsibility of all citizens. Their attainment was dependent upon the existence of foreign traders and, particularly, of slaves. Citizens could aspire to virtue only if slaves were condemned to endless toil:

> 'As the proverb says, "There is no leisure for slaves".' (*ibid*, p. 214)

Aristotle's views represented a broad strain within Greek civilization: as

Clayre (1974) points out, 'apart from some sayings of Hesiod, and a few remarks of Socrates, there is little praise of work itself, or even respect for it, accorded in any ancient Greek texts, at least in the Classical period'. (p. 158) Indeed, the Greek language defined work in negative terms as lack of leisure – ἀσχολια (a fascinating contrast with the precisely opposite way in which word 'unemployment' is now used in our own society). It was only in Roman times, as slavery began to decline, that work began to be taken seriously. (Anthony, 1977, p. 22)

These two rather different traditions have continued to exert their influence down to our own day, and to cross-cut pagan and Christian cultures respectively. Thus the notion of leisure as idleness, freedom and gratification – expressed in the Christian tradition of the Garden of Eden – has been reflected in Marcuse's invocations from California for people to liberate themselves from a cycle of ever-increasing production and obedient consumption to rediscover the primacy of sensuality and the enjoyment of nature. (Marcuse, 1955; 1964) Conversely, the Aristotelian notion of leisure as a quest for virtue, dependent on a servile class, continues to be reflected within Christianity in the Benedictine and Cistercian monastic tradition, in which lay brothers perform the menial work, leaving the monks to devote their attention wholly to the higher-order concerns of spiritual contemplation and prayer. (Moorhouse, 1969, pp. 27, 29)

A new leisure class?

The distinctions between the two traditions are, however, important for our purposes here, because they both influence people's concepts of the leisure society, and yet portend very different visions. They can be distinguished not only in the *moral* terms of the values they espouse, but also in the *political* terms of whether satisfaction of these values is to be made available to all or only to select groups.

These different views have influenced the prophets of the leisure society quoted earlier in this chapter. When writers like Keynes and Gabor talked about the imminence of such a society, they recognized that some work would still be necessary, and referred somewhat vaguely to the need, for the present, to permit all workers to have access to it. As Keynes put it (significantly calling upon Genesis imagery):

> For many ages to come the old Adam will be so strong in us that everybody will need to do *some* work if he is to be contented. (1931, pp. 368–9)

Similarly, Gabor refers to the need to enable everyone to do some work as 'occupational therapy'. (1964, p. 109) Nonetheless, Gabor is also clear that some people – 'recruited from the most gifted part of the population' (*ibid,* p. 104) – will be required to make a much stronger commitment to work. They will produce the wealth that will create the leisure for others.

It would seem then that what is being described here is a distinction between a new working class and a new leisure class. Whether the latter is larger or smaller than the former, it will be dependent on their labour. To refer to a 'leisure class' is to conjure up images, if not of Athenian citizens, then of an eighteenth and nineteenth-century pseudo-aristocracy engaged in the effete self-display of 'conspicuous consumption' (Veblen, 1899); what is promised is 'a kind of mass aristocratic society'. (Seabrook, 1981a, p. 135) It is important, however, to point out that the eighteenth and nineteenth-century 'leisure class' were not idle: they were landowners engaged in managing their own estates and in political activity. Above all, they were the ruling class: it was they who held political power. At the same time, their level of protection from the forces of their environment contained within it in many cases the seeds of their corruption, their incapacity to adapt to change, and hence their eventual demise. (Veblen, 1899)

The position of a 'new leisure class' would almost certainly be very different. Though they too would be protected from the forces of their environment and thereby in danger of effeteness, they would not possess political power. The conditions of their existence would be dependent on those who generated the wealth, and it would be this 'new working class' which would ultimately control the levers of power: the 'leisure class', after all, would not have any significant control of capital, nor would they have the power to withdraw their labour. Moreover, there would have to continue to be incentives to encourage the working class to create the wealth on which the livelihood of the leisure class would depend. Yet it would be essential for the conditions of this livelihood to be sufficiently attractive to the members of the leisure class to prevent them from seeing themselves as dependent and inferior, and thereby being tempted to challenge the power of the working class. Again, it would be important that joining the leisure class should be a matter of choice rather than an imposition due to, for example, one's age or sex. Finally, it would be important for income to be distributed to the leisure class without any connotation of personal inadequacy or any implication that an undeserved income was being received from an over-generous state.

A guaranteed minimum income

One device for achieving this is the notion that instead of social security provision being offered as means-tested *relief* for those unable to support themselves, there should be a minimum income allocated as a *right* to all families or to all individuals in society. Although some people refer to the present complex range of benefits and allowances, and free and subsidized services, as a 'social wage', they are so diffuse and complicated that many are not claimed; and the fact that they are widely seen not as a right but as a gift from a munificent state means both that there is a stigma attached to them and that at times of recession they can be readily reduced. (see e.g. Walker *et al.*, 1979, chapter 3)

More radical visions have however been proposed. An early minimum-income proposal was the Social Credit scheme put forward by Douglas (1920), who argued that the way to avoid 'stop-go' policies was to increase incomes without increasing costs, by introducing universal dividends to all citizens in line with increases in output: as technology conferred the benefits of non-manual production, these dividends would gradually replace wages and salaries as the main source of income for all citizens. (for a recent account of Douglas's ideas, emphasizing their contemporary relevance, see Jordan and Drakeford, 1980) A number of proposals have also been put forward from very diverse ideological positions for a Negative Income Tax system, under which there would be a minimum guaranteed income for all families, and a sliding scale for families having other sources of income, with a break-even point below which net income would be gradually increased but the negative-income-tax income gradually reduced, and above which families would pay 'positive income tax' as at present. (see e.g. Tobin, 1965; Friedman and Friedman, 1980, pp. 120-6) More recently, Roberts (1982) has proposed a National Dividend system, under which a basic subsistence income would be paid to all citizens irrespective of any other income, being funded by a massive increase in VAT, and replacing most existing social security provision; citizens would then be free to receive additional earned and unearned income at a level determined by the market, subject to income tax which would be used to achieve an equitable distribution of total income and employment and to finance the 'collective sector' (schools, hospitals, etc.). A proposal similar in many respects to Roberts' has been put forward by the Ecology Party. (1980, pp. 30-2, 58-60)

It is important to note that these schemes do not necessarily imply a 'leisure class' scenario. Indeed, one of the aims of Roberts' scheme in particular is to remove the rigid distinction which now exists between the employed and the unemployed: there would be a continuous gradation between those who decided not to work at all and those who chose to work full-time; and since everyone would already have enough to live on, true market principles could operate in the labour market, so that employment at market rates could be available for all those who wanted it. Nonetheless, from the point of view of our present discussion, the important aspect of all these minimum income schemes is that people would be able freely to choose not to work, and yet still to have sufficient income for subsistence.

The notion of a guaranteed minimum income is, however, likely to meet with strong resistance from those who feel their interests are vested in the *status quo* – including those who currently possess the work and the wealth. It would require an act of altruism or at least of unusually enlightened self-interest to realize the importance of making what Theobald (1963) terms 'basic economic security' available to all. In particular, it would require an unambiguous acceptance of the principle that all the members of a society have a proper call on some part of the society's wealth, and that if economic structures prevent members from contributing to the generation of that wealth, this should not in any way inhibit the principle but rather should enhance it, on the grounds that the exclusion of their labour has permitted the productivity increases that have aided the creation of the wealth. The emotive refrain 'the world doesn't owe them a living' would have to be generally confuted. In short, the implication would be that employment would cease to be seen as the chief legitimate form of income distribution.

This attacks not only vested interests, but also more widely-held assumptions about the relationship between reward and effort: it basically means rewarding existence rather than usefulness. When an NOP opinion poll in 1978 asked a nationally representative random sample of adults in paid employment, 'Do you think it would be a good thing for society if people didn't have to work to get money, but could choose whether to work or not?', 77 per cent replied 'no', and only 16 per cent replied 'yes'; the rest said 'don't know'. (private communication from NOP Market Research Limited, 11 September 1979) It could be argued that if improvements are made in the quality of working life, so that jobs become inherently satisfying, many people will want to work and will not have any reason for reviling others for not doing so. Whether it is even *possible* to substitute such a benign view of work for the ambivalent view which most people hold about it at present is, however, open to question; whether it is wholly *desirable* to do so in a society which does not offer work for all is equally disputable. As Robertson (1978) points out, a leisure-class society would need to be able to hold together a deeply contradictory attitude to work:

> The *hoi polloi* would have to be persuaded that work was unimportant, un-satisfying, unfulfilling, unnecessary; while the élites and their potential recruits have to be continually impressed with the value of work and the high status which it conferred. It just doesn't add up. (p. 92)

Much would depend on the level of the minimum income, for this would measure the 'social worth' attached to the leisure class. Unless it were reasonably substantial, those in this class would be cast into relative, if not absolute, poverty, and would feel themselves to be an 'under-class'. If, however, it were too substantial, it might make it difficult for the labour market to fill all its posts – particularly the more unpleasant forms of unskilled work. Moreover, it might more generally provoke the resentment of those in employment, especially if the change to a minimum-income arrangement were made at a time of limited or nil growth, when it would have to be to some extent at their direct expense. At present most of those in employment already feel inadequately rewarded for their labours, and press for a reduction rather than an increase in taxation. Interestingly, even Roberts (1982), who shows a considerable concern for social compassion, implicitly suggests that the level of the minimum income should be low, for he argues that those unable to work for medical reasons should receive additional support (p. 37): in other words, there should be a distinction between the standard of life offered to those who *cannot* work and those who *choose* not to do so.

There are also implications here for political structures. Who would decide the level of the minimum income? Would democratic structures be sustainable? Handy (1980) suggests that to the pessimist ('which probably means most Britons') this kind of scenario evokes the image of 'an army of dependent layabouts living on their social wage, desperate for the modern variety of bread and circuses, growing obese in front of their television sets in human battery coops, with successive governments trying to extract more and ever more from the "productive" sector to buy off these indolent voters. When bribes fail, as they always do, governments will perforce turn to other forms of social control, including not only regulations but the mass media, education and, perhaps, religion.' (pp. 436-7)

There is a danger that these tensions and pressures will lead towards the kind of society envisaged by Vonnegut (1953) in his novel *Player Piano*, a dystopia predicting an increasing gulf between a technological élite and an unskilled, leisured majority subsisting on state benefits. Apart from make-work projects in the Reconstruction and Reclamation Corps (the 'Reeks and Wrecks'), Vonnegut's leisure class have no opportunities for rewarding occupations outside the household. Even though in this scenario they are materially well provided for, they are mere machines for consumption, confined to a particular geographical area where their existence can be closely controlled.

Can leisure replace work?

The image of leisure as pure consumption – of an orgiastic society of bread and circuses, providing a new opium for the masses – is not the only image that can be conjured. Others see the new leisure class as offering opportunities for a renaissance of artistic and spiritual values, liberated from the presures of materialism.(see e.g. Reich,1970) But, as Gershuny (1978) asks: 'though some middle-class individuals ... may certainly be happy to exist on bread and Sophocles, can we assume all members of a society can be satisfied in this way?' (pp. 48-9)

Some writers have seen signs that society is already moving towards more positive identities based on leisure. Kelvin (1980), for example, has asserted – despite the evidence to the contrary cited in chapter six – that the 'work ethic' is disappearing. He argues that to be unemployed is ceasing to be automatically deviant and stagmatized, and is increasingly becoming compatible with being a 'normal', respectable member of society, entitled to be treated as such: he sees the problem as being that of developing or inventing leisure activities capable of replacing the role of employment in people's lives. Precisely the converse argument, however, is put by Frith (1981). He proclaims that young people are already constructing their own leisure identities, but are being inhibited by 'DHSS officials, the police, teachers, every adult concerned to stop the young carving out their own space':

> The state's fear (evident in every Manpower Services Commission report) is that the more successfully the young do survive nonwork, the less they'll ever be willing to do "real" work. Hence the ideological and physical crackdown (which black youth have long experienced) on any suggestion that the young unemployed are enjoying themselves ... If the young learn to enjoy "unearned" leisure then the concept of earned leisure itself is thrown into question. Youth's most disruptive demand is not the right to work, but the right not to work. (p. 5)

The direct contradiction between these two views reflects continuing ambivalence and contradictions within society at large, which are unlikely to be easily resolved.

Any consideration of the feasibility of 'leisure' as an alternative to 'work' must recognize Frith's point that in our society it has conventionally been seen not as an alternative to work but as essentially complementary to it. Most definitions of leisure define it in relation to work: Parker (1976), for instance, defines leisure as 'time free from work and other obligations'. (p. 12) So close is the link between the two that it is questionable whether unemployed people – or indeed retired people – have 'leisure' at all: they have plenty of spare time, but to call it 'leisure' may, within the current usage of the term, be more misleading than illuminating. Significantly, studies of the unemployed suggest that the extension of their negotiable time results not in an increase but in a diminution both of the range of their leisure activities and of the enjoyment they derive from such activities. Thus the Marienthal study showed how the inability of unemployed people to fill their time meaningfully led to apathy, depression, and increasing passivity, with most social and political organizations declining in membership, and the number of library loans dropping substantially despite the abolition of borrowing charges. (Jahoda *et al.*, 1972 ed., chapter 5) A more recent study by the Economist Intelligence Unit (1982) found that few unemployed people had used their free time to develop new interest or hobbies; nearly half watched more television, with nearly a quarter watching four hours more a day. (p. 55)

Consideration of the extent to which leisure can adequately replace work also has to take account of the considerable range of functions which work as employment performs in our society. Jahoda (1979) proposes that in addition to its manifest fuctions – pay and conditions – it performs five psychologically important latent functions. First, it imposes a time structure on the working day. Second, it implies regularly shared experiences and contacts with people outside the nuclear family. Third, it links an individual to goals and purposes which transcend his or her own. Fourth, it defines aspects of personal status and identity. And fifth, it enforces activity.

Some of these functions will be explored further in the next chapter. For our present purposes, it is sufficient to point out that while some leisure activities can fulfil one or more of these functions, few can combine all of them. As Kelvin (1981) points out, many leisure activities are essentially individualistic, like reading; some may have certain social activities 'in parallel', in the form of clubs; but very few indeed demand the interdependence, on a continuing basis, which is the essence of most working relationships. (p. 8) Moreover, leisure activities, however taxing and productive, are not endowed with a sense of *necessity*: they remain, ultimately, 'play'. Although 'play' is a significant and essential part of civilization, enabling people to explore and express parts of their selves that would otherwise be suppressed (Huizinga, 1949), it is not psychologically sufficient:

> The sense that the world and life have a structure and are "real" comes from the sense of "having to" meet demands other than just one's own, demands which are, as it were, "external". To be "mature", "sound", "stable", "adequate", and so forth, is to be able to cope with this reality of external obligations and demands. (Kelvin, 1981, p. 10)

Of course, employment is not necessarily the only form of 'work' that can provide this sense of necessity: domestic roles, and community and political roles of a voluntary character, can also provide them to some extent. Once again, it is a question of whether we define 'leisure' in its Aristotelian sense or in its 'Garden of Eden' sense: such forms of non-employed work are more readily embraced within 'leisure' in the former case than in the latter. These forms of work will be discussed in more detail in chapter nine.

Linked to the sense of necessity is the sense of *reciprocity*: that in return for fulfilling one's obligations, one has access to true freedom. The dependence of the one on the other is embedded in Christian tradition: to regain the Garden of Eden, one must fulfil one's duties sufficiently to achieve absolution from sin. The capacity of Western societies in particular to escape such notions is open to question. Even in purely political terms, some such element of reciprocity would seem important as a way of relating the individual to the common weal.

More fruitful would seem to be the possibility that other forms than employment can be found through which the principle of reciprocity can be mediated. Jahoda (1982) points out that in many more primitive societies, where employment as an institution does not exist, psychological and social functions are met by religious rituals and community practices. The fact that such radically different institutions meet such similar needs 'lends support to the idea that enduring human needs are involved while at the same time demonstrating the variability of institutions that can satisfy such needs'. (pp. 59-60) Employment has been the dominant focus of reciprocity in industrialized societies: it could, in principle, be replaced by something else in post-industrial societies. This seems more likely, however, to be some form of non-employed work than of leisure in its purer sense.

But it is also possible that such societies will find ways of sharing or redefining employment so as to make it available to all. This is the possibility that we shall examine next.

Summary

Chapter seven has explored the notion that fewer people will need to work in future, and that the remainder might form a 'new leisure class'. The underlying assumptions are that, because of technology, there is less *need* for human labour; and that since much work is no longer necessary, it is also no longer *desirable*. The cultural tradition which affirms the ultimate superiority of leisure over work has been briefly traced, and the distinction between two rather different traditions has been identified: the notion of leisure as idleness, freedom and gratification; and the notion of leisure as a quest for virtue. The political difficulties inherent in the notion of the 'new leisure class', and its relationship with the 'new working class', have been noted. The concept of a guaranteed minimum income offers a way round some of these difficulties, though by no means all. The diverse functions performed by employment need to be recognized: few if any leisure activities can fulfil them as satisfactorily. In particular, leisure activities are not in general endowed with a sense of necessity or of reciprocity. New social institutions would be needed to meet the human and social needs which are currently met by employment.

CHAPTER EIGHT

The Employment Scenario

The work ethic

Just as there is a continuing tradition in Western culture espousing the superior virtues of leisure, so too there is a contrary continuing tradition espousing the superior virtues of work. Indeed, Anthony (1977) has suggested that political theories can be divided clearly into these two traditions in a way which 'has nothing in common with any traditional division between conservative and radical, left and right, progressive or reactionary'. (p. 7) Thus the division between capitalism and communism, for example, is narrower than is usually supposed, since both share a basic preoccupation with the importance of economic values built around an ideology of work. (The difference between them is that whereas capitalism is concerned to maintain the ideology by rehabilitating work so that society will continue to take it seriously, communism asserts the need to do so by rehabilitating society). *(ibid.* pp. 7–8)

Christian tradition contains strong references to the importance of work. As St Paul put it: 'If any would not work, neither should he eat.' (I Thessalonians, 3:10) In contrast with the notion of work as a product of the Fall, there is the view that it represents an opportunity to share in the divine activity of creation and recreation of the universe. It is thus through the routines of work that one discovers and grows in one's understanding of God, a notion epitomized in the lines of the Christian hymn:

> Raise the stone and thou shalt find me
> Cleave the wood and I am there.

As Entwistle (1970) points out, the emphasis here is on simple men discovering an ultimate purpose in life through the worshipful activity of work. (pp. 21-2)

In medieval times, elements of these ideas were incorporated into political theory by St Thomas Aquinas, who saw society as a closed system in stable equilibrium, in which each group contributed by doing its proper work – the farmer and artisan by supplying material goods, the priest by prayer and religious observance. He saw man as a being distinctively endowed with brain and hands, who achieved fulfilment by being engaged in using both to good and fruitful purpose. But work was to be done according to rhythms dictated by the natural cycle and by the performance of social obligations: 'there could be little point in working harder or more productively because, as the market economy was rudimentary, there would be nothing to do with a surplus.' (Anthony, 1977, p. 30)

These concepts were assimilated into the medieval church, which elevated work from the base position accorded to it by Aristotle, but saw it strictly as an instrument of spiritual purpose. The Benedictine rule, and its injunction *'laborare est orare'*, emphasized the spiritual danger of idleness, and saw work as contributing to Christian obedience and resignation. The distinction between labour as a spiritual discipline and labour as a means to economic ends was however drawn clearly by Groote in the fourteenth century: 'Labour is holy, but business is dangerous.' (*ibid*, p. 37)

It was the Reformation which developed the work ethic in a way which made it adaptable to capitalism. Luther saw *beruf* (vocation, or calling) as the work specifically assigned by God to the individual so that in performing it he might at one and the same time do his duty to God and his service to his fellow men. Calvin's notion that a minority 'are predestined unto everlasting life, and others are ordained to everlasting death', encouraged men to apply their talents with sobriety and thrift to the particular work to which they felt 'called', so that they could prove – not least to themselves – that they were among the 'elect'. It also helped to protect men from their propensity to sin. Weber (1930 ed.) argued that these ideas were partly responsible for the development of Western capitalism; Tawney (1926) modified this by emphasizing that any such effect was 'without design, and against the intention of most reformers'. (p. 84) Certainly both Luther and Calvin in their attitudes to usury differed little from the teaching of the contemporary Catholic church. (Green, 1952, p. 180) Nonetheless, the Calvinist emphasis on industry and austerity was readily adapted to the economic needs of the Industrial Revolution. As Anthony (1977) put it:

> The engagement of God as the supreme supervisor was a most convenient device; a great part of the efforts of modern management has been aimed at finding a secular but equally omnipotent equivalent in the workers' own psyche. (p. 43)

The Reformation thus transformed work, more firmly than before, from something which was necessary to something which was virtuous – and then made a necessity of virtue. (Kelvin, 1980, p. 296)

In more modern times, the work ethic has been secularized. At the same time, its invocation in support of capitalism has been challenged. For Marx, the capacity to invent tools and *produce* the means of subsistence was what distinguished man from other animals. (1963 ed., p. 69) The need to work was, accordingly, the essence of man's humanity, and the means whereby he created his world. In capitalist society, however, man was alienated from his work in two ways: first, because the product was the possession not of the worker but of the capitalist, so that 'in work he does not belong to himself but to another person' (*ibid*, p. 178); and second, because the concern of capitalists for maximization of profits led them to lengthen working hours and to reduce the content of work through division of labour, to the point where work ceased to be fulfilling and became meaningless drudgery. In a real sense, therefore, capitalism robbed man of his identity. It was accordingly necessary that, through revolution, restitution could take place, creating a communist society. In such a society,

> where nobody has one exclusive sphere of activity but each can become accomplished in any branch he wishes, production as a whole is regulated by society, thus making it possible for me to do one thing today and another tomorrow, to hunt in the morning, fish in the afternoon, rear cattle in the evening, criticize after dinner, in accordance with my inclination, without ever becoming hunter, fisherman, shepherd, or critic. (*ibid*, pp. 110-11)

The distinction between 'useful work' and 'useless toil' was also drawn by William Morris:

> It is of the nature of man, when he is not diseased, to take pleasure in his work under certain conditions. And, yet, we must say in the teeth of the hypocritical praise of all labour, whatsoever it may be . . . that there is some labour which is so far from being a blessing that it is a curse . . . What is the difference between them, then? This: one has hope in it, the other has not . . . hope of rest, hope of product, hope of pleasure in the work itself. (Morris, 1888, p. 142)

To Morris, the craftsman and the artist were the epitome of useful work:

> . . . to all living things there is a pleasure in the exercise of their energies, and . . . even beasts rejoice in being lithe and swift and strong. But a man at work, making something which he feels will exist because he is working at it and wills it, is exercising the energies of his mind and soul as well as of his body. Memory and imagination help him as he works. Not only his own thoughts, but the thoughts of the men of past ages guide his hand; and, as a part of the human race, he creates. (*ibid*, p. 144)

Indeed, Morris defined art itself as 'the expression of man's pleasure . . . in his work,' (see Briggs, 1962, p. 140)

More recently, Arendt (1958) has reaffirmed the craft ethic, pointing out that the making of things for use gives man a sense of objective permanence in his transitory experience of the world. But while maintaining that this kind of work is more satisfying than labour designed to produce the necessities of life, she also argues that such labour, too, is made pleasurable by its closeness to the natural elemental cycle of life:

> The "blessing or the joy" of labour is the human way to experience the sheer bliss of being alive which we share with all living creatures, and it is even the only way men, too, can remain and swing contentedly in nature's prescribed cycle, toiling and resting, labouring and consuming, with the same happy and purposeless regularity with which day and night and life and death follow each other. (p. 106)

Support for the importance of work also comes from very different religious and philosophical traditions. Schumacher (1973, chapter 4), for example, has drawn the attention of the Western world to what he terms 'Buddhist economics':

> The Buddhist point of view takes the function of work to be at least three-fold: to give a man a chance to utilize and develop his faculties; to enable him to overcome his egocentredness by joining with other people in a common task; and to bring forth the goods and services needed for a becoming existence. (p. 49)

He points out the consequences that flow from this view:

> To organize work in such a manner that it becomes meaningless, boring, stultifying, or nerve-wracking for the worker would be little short of criminal; it would indicate a greater concern with goods than with people, an evil lack of compassion and a soul-destroying degree of attachment to the most primitive side of this worldly existence. Equally, to strive for leisure as an alternative to work would be considered a complete misunderstanding of one of the basic truths of human existence, namely that work and leisure are complementary parts of the same living process and cannot be separated without separating the joy of work and the bliss of leisure. (p. 50)

Two points need to be made about these various statements about the importance of work. The first is that they are selective in what they define as 'work'. Certainly it is not equated with 'employment'. Morris's notion of exercising the mind, soul and body in unity, or even Arendt's notion of congruence with nature's prescribed cycle, are not recognizable in the monotony and fragmentation of the forms of employment that characterized the Industrial Revolution. Indeed, such forms of employment are explicitly condemned by writers like Marx and Schumacher as perversions of true work. More widely, Thompson (1967) points out how the imposed time-discipline characteristic of industrialization meant that natural work rhythms were disturbed: time became currency not to be passed but spent, and work became divorced from the other parts of life.

Linked to this is the second point, which is that most of these writers emphasize men's work as opposed to women's work. While their use of the word 'man' predated concern about sexist language, and could at times be interpreted as embracing both sexes, nonetheless there is an implicit preoccupation with the forms of work traditionally ascribed to men, and a neglect of the forms traditionally associated with women. Yet in a sense women who have held to their traditional role within the household are more closely linked to, for instance, the natural cycles than are men. As Thompson points out:

> . . . despite school times and television times, the rhythms of women's work in the home are not wholly attuned to the measurement of the clock. The mother of young children has an imperfect sense of time and attends to other human tides. She has not yet altogether moved out of the convention of "pre-industrial" society. *(ibid,* p. 79)

The implications of attending more closely to such roles, as well as the implications of the pressure for greater flexibility of sex-roles which has developed in the twentieth century, will be returned to later. (see chapter nine)

Meanwhile, it is nevertheless clear that writers from very different traditions have agreed that work represents a deep human need. In psychological terms, Freud (1930) argues that 'laying stress upon importance of work has a greater effect than any other technique of living in the direction of binding the individual more closely to reality', since 'in his work he is at least securely attached to a part of reality, the human community'. (p. 34) Freud recognized some ambivalence here:

> . . . as a path to happiness work is not valued very highly by men. They do not run after it as they do after other opportunities for gratification. The great majority work only when forced by necessity, and this natural human aversion to work gives rise to the most difficult social problems.' (p. 34)

Yet work was invaluable for the maintenance of mental health:

> Work is no less valuable for the opportunity it and the human relations connected with it provides for a very considerable discharge of libidinal component impulses, narcissistic, aggressive and even erotic, than because it is indispensable for subsistence and justifies existence in a society. (p. 34)

In a society in which work has become largely identified with employment, such needs are seen as being best met within the employment structure. Despite the ambivalence described by Freud, the critiques offered by Marx and others, and the contemporary evidence of alienation in employment (e.g. Braverman, 1974), it is clear that most people continue to want jobs. When Morse and Weiss (1955) in the USA asked a sample of employed men, 'If by some chance you inherited enough money to live comfortably without working, do you think you would work anyway or not?', 80 per cent said they would keep working. Work – i.e. employment – gave them a sense of being tied into a large society, of having something to do, of having a purpose in life. Similar if somewhat less marked tendencies have emerged in more recent American studies. (e.g. Vecchio, 1980) Again, in a recent British survey, some 69 per cent of employed men and 65 per cent of employed women said they would continue in employment even if it was no longer financially necessary; only 15 per cent and 18 per cent respectively said they would want to stop work and never start again. (Warr, 1982) In a parallel US study among the hard-core unemployed, the proportion saying they would want to work even if it were not an economic necessity was 84 per cent. (Kaplan and Tausky, 1972, p. 475)

The 'right to work'

Beyond the personal needs met in work, there is also an argument for asserting its social and political importance, as 'the major point of connection between the individual's creative energies and the purposes and policies of the whole society'. (Chanan, 1976/7, p. 43) Indeed, one can view employment in its modern sense as a key aspect of the contract between the individual and the wider society, whereby individuals agree to devote some of their time and energies to wider social purposes, in return for which they are given a social status and identity, as well as access to income which they are then free to use in whatever way they choose in their own time. If this is the case, then access to employment is a right which should be available to all its adult members.

A clear statement of this right occurs in the Universal Declaration of Human Rights issued by the United Nations in 1948:

> Everyone has the right to work, to free choice of employment ... and to protection against unemployment. (article 23)

The problem is how to deliver this right. In socialist countries, the right to work is written into the constitution, and is given primacy in policy decisions: because the state can make the production side of the economy as responsive to political decisions as the demand side, it is able deliberately to overman certain industries and to reduce productivity so as to employ more people. (Jenkins and Sherman, 1979, p. 81) In liberal-capitalist countries, the problem is more difficult to solve. Nonetheless, Beveridge (1944) in his classic report on *Full Employment in a Free Society* argued that its solution was as important as adequate social security provision:

> Idleness is not the same as Want, but a separate evil, which men do not escape by having an income. They must also have a chance of rendering useful service and of feeling that they are doing so. (p. 20)

He did not believe that there were simple panaceas, but he considered that if the aim of full employment was given sufficient importance, it could be achieved:

> Pursuit of full employment is not like the directed flight of an aircraft on a beam; it is a difficult navigation, in which a course must be steered among shifting, unpredictable, and to a large extent, uncontrollable currents and forces. All that can be done is to see that the pilot has the necessary controls, and an instrument board to tell him where and how to use the controls. It is necessary also that the pilot should always have the will to use the controls by which alone he can reach his destination. (p. 38)

For a period after the Second World War, this will was strongly represented in government policies. It has since been eroded, and given lower priority. (see Deacon, 1981) Nonetheless, in principle, the possibility of full employment remains, even without massive economic growth. Two different broad approaches can be distinguished: to share the existing employment more equally, or to generate additional forms of employment through government intervention in the labour market. Each of these will now be considered in turn.

Work-sharing

A number of approaches to work-sharing have been canvassed. One – to increase the age of entry to the labour market or to reduce the retirement age – has already been considered. (see chapter six) Although it can be seen as an approach to sharing work more equally between individuals if their full life-cycle is taken into account, it does so by excluding certain age-groups from the labour market and so reducing the size of the work-force. The concern here will rather be with ways of reducing the time worked by the existing work-force.

In these terms, there are five main possible approaches. One is *encouraging part-time jobs*. The number of people working part-time doubled between

1961 and 1980 – a period during which the number of people employed full-time dropped by 2.1 million. Most part-time workers are women or men aged over 60. (MSC, 1982c, pp. 23-4) It has however been suggested that there might be other groups which might welcome a reduction of working hours, particularly if the legal and financial arrangements for part-time working were made more attractive (at present, people who work less than certain specified hours a week lose a number of rights and benefits). These groups might include handicapped people who find it difficult to sustain a full day's work, fathers who wish to spend more time with their children, and people with outside interests and economic needs which can be met by working less than full-time. There are, though, clear limits to the extent of these groups.

The second approach, *job-splitting,* is a specific variant of the first. It involves the division of one job and its pay between two people. A number of experimental schemes have been launched (EOC, 1981), and in 1983 the government announced a pilot programme of grants to encourage it. Although job-splitting involves some additional costs to the employer – additional recruitment, training, administration, etc. – it may also offer some compensating advantages, including greater continuity and flexibility. (see CBI, 1982, p. 63) Again, such schemes seem unlikely within the foreseeable future to cover significant proportions of the working population, and are likely to be resisted if they are seen to be forcing people who want a full-time job to accept less – especially if the number of hours is restricted to exclude them from the cover of employment-protection legislation.

The third approach is to *reduce the length of the full-time working week.* The TUC (1978, p. 12), for example, argued that a move towards a normal working week of 35 hours could have a significant effect on unemployment. In France, the government in 1982 adopted a legal reduction of the basic working week from 40 to 39, with a target of 35 hours by 1985. (MSC, 1982c, p. 27) Jenkins and Sherman (1979) have argued that such modifications are too modest, and that the aim should be a 24-hour week (three eight-hour days) by the year 2000. (pp. 164-5) Such proposals need to be set in the context of the long-term trend for some of the gains from increased productivity to be translated into reduced hours of work rather than higher income levels. (Gershuny, 1980a) There are difficulties, though, in seeking to increase or accelerate this trend. Reductions in the basic working week do not necessarily mean reductions in hours actually worked: often they are bargaining devices which enable workers to work more of their hours as overtime at higher rates of pay. Even if this is not the case, the unions normally insist that where hours are shorter, earnings are not reduced: the risk is that, unless there are compensating productivity increases, the unit labour cost of production rises, pushing up the cost of the product and thus reducing competitiveness, thereby, in the end, threatening jobs. (Allen, 1980)

Moreover, unless the productivity increases are also sufficient to increase output, there is no leeway for the reduced working hours to create new jobs. Recent studies have demonstrated that such reductions as there have been to the working week in particular industries in recent years have had little or no effect in increasing employment opportunities. (White, 1980, pp. 79-80; Incomes Data Services, 1982, p. 2) In short, it seems that reduced working hours may have an important role to play in ensuring that productivity increases do not produce further job losses, and in making it possible for output increases to create new jobs, but they are unlikely within a voluntary system to have a significant effect on unemployment levels in the short and medium term.

Much the same is true of the fourth approach, which is *longer holidays and sabbaticals*. Again, there is a long-term trend towards longer holidays (Central Statistical Office, 1981, p. 71), and the French scheme for reducing working hours, quoted above, included provision for a fifth week of paid leave. The House of Commons Expenditure Committee (1978) argued that, although higher costs were still involved, longer holidays were more attractive than a shorter working week as a response to unemployment, because they were less likely to lead to increased hours being taken up in overtime, and so were more likely to lead to the provision of additional jobs. (para 352) This is also true of sabbatical leave (including paid educational leave), which has been available for some time to university teachers, Fleet Street journalists, some senior managers (and US blue-collar workers) (Jenkins and Sherman, 1979, p. 165), and could in principle be extended much more widely. A variant of the notion of sabbatical leave is paid educational leave. (see Killeen and Bird, 1981) A further variant is the practice of permitting paid leave of absence to care for infants: Sweden, for example, has an insurance scheme entitling parents to an income for seven months at the birth of the child, and fathers are encouraged to take advantage of this as well as mothers. (Scase, 1976, p. 614)

The final approach is *banning overtime*. In 1982 around 10 million hours of overtime were being worked in manufacturing industry (Department of Employment, 1983a, table 1.11): the equivalent of 250,000 jobs if no-one had worked more than a 40-hour week. The Department of Employment (1978) argued that reducing overtime was a more immediately promising way of attempting to alleviate unemployment than other forms of work-sharing. Nonetheless, it has to be recognized that many manual workers have become dependent upon the income which their overtime provides, while employers also often see it as an effective way of organizing their work.

The basic problem which all these approaches eventually confront is that work-sharing implies income-sharing, which in immediate terms means reducing the living standards of those whose incomes are cut. There are also likely to be limits to the interchangeability of skills and the mobility of labour, as well as resistance from overheads-conscious employers, though these are relatively surmountable difficulties. Certainly the various forms of work-sharing outlined above may on a voluntary basis have a contribution to make to the reduction of unemployment, particularly in the long term. But in the short and medium term only compulsory enforcement of measures implying reduced income for many workers would seem incapable of having any substantial impact on unemployment levels. And such measures would be likely to produce such fierce resistance from organized labour as to make them difficult if not impossible to enforce.

Employment creation

The alternative approach to achieving full employment without massive economic growth takes a more radical stance. Instead of seeking to share out the existing employment more equally, it seeks to create new forms of employment. After all, there is no shortage of *work:* only a shortage of *paid employment.* If the existing economic, social and political mechanisms are not making employment available to all, these mechanisms could in principle be changed. People could be paid for forms of work which are not paid for at present.

One way of seeking to implement this approach is by attempting to return to pure market forces. If the labour market were permitted to operate strictly according to market principles, then – in accordance with classical economic theory – the price of labour would fall to the point at which it would be purchasable. Arguably, however, the nature of advanced economies is so complex that even if this is regarded as an ideal, it is unattainable. In particular, social and political forces will prevent it being attained. In part these forces are motivated by the compassionate concern to avoid poverty for the weak. Roberts' (1982) proposals for a National Dividend system, already discussed in chapter seven, seek to take account of this by providing an assured basic subsistence income to all citizens, and then establishing market principles as fully as possible beyond this point. This would permit people not to work if they wished (hence its relevance to the leisure scenario): in principle, however, it would also make it possible for all who wanted employment to find it.

An alternative method is to accept that the structural constraints on market forces either cannot or should not be removed, and to seek instead to extend them in a way which creates jobs for all who want employment. After all, it is already the case that a great many jobs are based not in the market economy but in the 'redistribution economy', which consists of public-sector goods and services that are not traded but are made available to the general public – these include the armed forces, roads, police, and most schools and hospitals, as well as the direct subventions of 'welfare'. (Handy, n.d.) This redistribution economy depends on the added value created by the market economy, but it adds value on its own behalf, and – in the course of doing so – also creates a substantial number of jobs.

Moreover, even within the market economy there is evidence of a fair degree of 'over-manning'. (see e.g. Taylor, 1976) Some government policies encourage such practices. An unpublished report from the National Economic Development Council in 1982 (quoted in *New Society*, 23 September 1982, pp. 505-6) showed that government support for industry amounted to £20 billion a year, much of it being given to ailing industries like aerospace, cars, ship-building and steel, to avoid politically unacceptable job losses. Moreover, schemes like the Temporary Employment Subsidy introduced in 1975 – which, until it was outlawed by the European Community, offered government allowances to encourage employers to retain employees whom they might otherwise have made redundant – are designed positively to support 'over-manning'.

These practices are periodically condemned as encouraging inefficiency and waste. This is the view taken, for example, by Collins (1979) in the USA, who says that 'we have elaborated a largely superfluous structure of more or less easy jobs, full of administrative make-work and featherbedding because modern technology allows it and because of political pressures from the populace wanting work.' (p. 55) If this process goes too far, it can be self-defeating because it adds to costs and thereby reduces competitiveness in foreign markets, so ultimately causing further unemployment.

On the other hand, such over-manning can stimulate domestic demand. It is thus arguable that within reasonable limits over-manning is economically preferable to the wastage of unemployment, particularly if forms of social accounting are used which cover the public costs of unemployment, as outlined in chapter six. Mukherjee (1976), for example, calculated that even on the basis of savings in transfer payments and revenues foregone, the government could afford to pay a rate of up to 90 per cent of the average earnings of industrial workers to enable people to work rather than to be unemployed, without this leading to any increase in the budget deficit; and this took no account of the public-expenditure costs associated with the pathological effects of unemployment, or indeed the benefits of their output. (for an application of similar social accounting to a local works closure, see Newcastle City Council, 1979) Moreover, some writers have suggested that high levels of over-manning on more prosperous countries have helped to make their workers accept new technology and the productivity increases it brings. Sleigh and Boatwright (1979), for example, quote an estimate by the

Japanese equivalent of the CBI that up to 2.5 million workers in employment in Japan are really surplus to requirement, and suggest that the 'lifetime employment system' has combined with other factors to make the Japanese unions extremely acquiescent to technological change. Again, Jacobs *et al.* (1978) suggested that the higher priority attached to stability of employment by management in West Germany as opposed to Britain had helped to make German workers more confident about accepting changes in technology etc. (p. 118)

These arguments present a case for artificial job creation regardless of the uses to which it is put. Keynes (1936), for instance, argued with tongue in cheek that, rather than presiding over high unemployment, it would be better for the Treasury to 'fill old bottles with bank notes, bury them at suitable depths in disused coalmines, which are then filled up to the surface with town rubbish, and leave it to private enterprise on well-tried principles of *laissez-faire* to dig the notes up again'. (p. 129) Some commentators, indeed, identify all artificial job-creation with this kind of innately pointless activity. Thus Gabor (1964) argues that 'people artificially employed are socially useless; this could be altered only by changing the most fundamental conventions of our civilization'. (p. 99)

Often implicit in this kind of statement is the notion that the only 'real jobs' are those created by the market. It should be noted that unless modified this excludes, for instance, all jobs within the redistribution economy. It is often linked with the idea that a policy of increasing such jobs merely produces a swollen bureaucracy serving its own ends, rather than an improvement in services to the general public. That this *can* be so is indisputable. It does not however *need* to be so. Moreover, it should be pointed out that unemployment itself creates additional bureaucracy at the expense of, for example, productive personal and caring work: economic cutbacks have meant that in social security offices more and more staff are engaged in the routine completion of forms for the increasing number of claimants, including the many more unemployed, while there has been a reduction in the visiting of elderly and other recipients of benefits to ensure that they obtain all the benefits and services that can be provided for them. (Showler and Sinfield, 1981, p. 221)

Accordingly, Beveridge (1944) in urging the importance of full employment emphasized that the unemployed should have the chance of rendering *useful* service, and be given the feeling that their work is valued: 'employment is not wanted for the sake of employment, irrespective of what it produces'. (p. 20) The point is well illustrated by examining what government support for car companies like Chrysler UK (Young and Hood, 1977) has meant: it arguably has involved the investment of large sums of public money, to support classically alienating production-line jobs (Beynon,

1975), to produce environment-polluting cars, for which there is inadequate market demand.

Contrast this with what has happened in Lucas Aerospace, where a group of shop stewards – faced with a similar threat to their jobs stemming from the declining market demand for their products – were disturbed by the realization that their initial struggle to stay in work implied a struggle for society to continue making products which, in their own wider judgement, were anti-social. They recognized, however, that the company contained rich resources both of equipment and of skilled manpower. They accordingly formed a combine which developed an 'alternative corporate plan', designed to identify ways of harnessing these resources in the production of socially-useful products – kidney machines, domestic solar heaters, wind-powered generators, road-rail vehicles, etc. (see Wainwright and Elliott, 1982) The issue of who would buy the product and at what price was largely neglected, and it was never clear whether the plan was basically concerned with the more efficient operation of a capitalist company or with the exposure of capitalism to hasten its replacement by socialism. The plan was resisted by management, partly on the grounds that it represented a union challenge to managerial prerogatives, and partly because of the difficulties of responding within a single company to social criteria that were not subjected to the overall objective of profit maximization. Nonetheless, the plan confronted head-on the issue of the *purpose* of work. It challenged the notion that jobs should be maintained simply for their own sake, and at the very least suggested that where they were not justified by market forces, direct criteria of social usefulness needed to be applied.

The definition of what is socially useful depends, of course, on the nature of society's values. A theocratic society will honour the employment of a sizeable priesthood; an atheistic society will not. (Mouly, 1979, p. 113) Where there is strong agreement on values and needs, the criteria for jobs outside the market mechanism will be easier to apply. In times of war, when a society's existence is threatened, the general recognition of the primacy of its survival needs will enable it to organize itself so that as many as possible of its able-bodied population are engaged in the armed services or the essential services required to maintain and supply them, thereby virtually eliminating unemployment altogether.

An area of job-creation that has attracted a fair level of political support has been the notion of highly selective public investment in the infrastructure of roads, sewers, rail transport and power supply. The argument is that this will not only provide jobs in the short term, but will also sustain extended and more efficient market activity in the long term. It is therefore less likely to be inflationary than are other forms of demand management. A related approach is to make more use of government investment not to support ailing industries but to support the innovations and new industries which are needed to provide the base for renewed economic growth (Rothwell, 1981): this again is designed to provide 'subsidized' jobs in the short run but also to create 'real' jobs in the longer run.

A major modification of this approach, and one which underlay many of the ideas in the Lucas plan, is to steer short-term support for innovation towards alternative technologies that will themselves be labour-intensive and less likely to exhaust the world's natural resources. Ward (1979, pp. 128-9), for example, points to the French car industry, where energy consumption has increased massively and the labour force but little. She quotes a study by the Battelle Geneva Research Centre which showed how various factors of production might be altered if the industry aimed to produce a car with an operational life not of 10 but of 20 years. Its energy input for each year of life would be little more than half that of the 10-year vehicle; while the design for regular maintenance would mean that the labour input for each year of car use would be increased by half. Moreover, the work of maintenance, repairing and refurbishing is far more interesting and creative than the monotony of the assembly line.

Other job-creation activities are more firmly based within the redistribution economy. An area of employment where the potential for expansion is infinite is services based on human relationships: health care, education, and social welfare (including care of the elderly, the mentally ill, the physically infirm, the very young, etc.). While based largely on wider social values, such work can have benefits even in narrow economic terms. In particular, Stonier (1983) argues that education, coupled with research and development, constitutes the most effective form of investment a society can make, especially as it moves into a post-industrial phase: he regards it as investment in the intellectual infrastructure of the economy, complementing investment in its physical infrastructure. He accordingly contends that governments should enter into a massive expansion of the education system, extending it to include more computer-assisted, home-based and community-based learning.

There are also other areas where work can readily be generated. One is conservation and environmental improvement: improving housing, tidying up derelict sites, tree-planting, building trails and adventure playgrounds, converting warehouses into community centres, etc. Another is the arts and entertainment.

There are however constraints on the extent to which these kinds of work can be artificially created within a redistribution economy based on the public yield from a market economy. Some of them – teaching, for example – involve high levels of skill and professional preparation and are therefore likely, particularly where they are union-protected and resistant to any erosion of occupational power (e.g. through appointment of ancillaries), to be expensive in salary/wage terms, costing much more than the savings on unemployment benefits etc. Other areas of work — housing, for instance — require large additional costs in terms of materials. Again, there are likely to be considerable 'mismatch' problems — redundant assembly-line workers are not going to be transformed easily into social workers or even into bricklayers — and in so far as these problems are soluble, they are likely to involve substantial retraining costs.

All these additional costs are important, because although artificial job-creation can be justified to some degree by its output, the additional economic activity it generates, and the offset savings in benefits, nonetheless it is finally restricted within a mixed economy by the extent of the wealth generated within the market sector, and by the extent to which organizations and individuals within that sector can be persuaded or compelled to permit their wealth to be filtered into the redistribution economy. In the late 1970s and early 1980s, the 'tax revolt' created a political climate in which governments became concerned not to increase the size of this redistribution economy but to reduce it. Moreover, fears grew that artificial forms of job-creation would not only fuel inflation but would interfere with the normal workings of the market, providing unfair competition to products and services within the market sector, and fostering inefficiency. As Brown (1979) put it, in a diatribe against all forms of artificial government-supported job-creation: 'you cannot encourage drive, hard work and the challenge to compete through providing subsidies, soft options and feather-bedding'. (p. 150)

A compromise that has been sought in an attempt to avoid at least some of these obstacles and objections has been to confine direct government supported job-creation to a carefully insulated sub-sector within the redistribution economy, characterized by modest wages and short contracts which offer no job security, and restricted to deliberately circumscribed forms of work, of benefit to the community, which would not otherwise be done. Recent years have been a variety of programmes of this kind, including the Job Creation Programme (1975-8), the Special Temporary Employment Programme (1979-81), the Community Enterprise Programme (1981-2), and the Community Programme (launched in 1982). Within the Community Enterprise Programme, payment was at union rates; in the other programmes, however, it has been lower. Age limits have varied, but training has on the whole been limited or non-existent.

An evaluation of the Community Enterprise Programme by Sawdon and Tucker (1982) found that some schemes provided interesting, challenging and satisfying work which was unlikely to lead to comparably satisfying work in the mainstream economy; on the other hand, some work was unpleasant, repetitive and gave little satisfaction. In relation to the latter, the report concluded that 'given the opportunity to choose between creating such jobs and something more rewarding it seems perverse to plump for the former'. (p. 51) It accordingly recommended that 'the basic focus of the programme should shift to provision of what will be interesting and challenging work which is also of benefit to the community, rather than work which is of benefit to the community regardless of the quality of jobs which it provides'. (p. i)

This raises an important point. Employment-creation schemes of these kinds can be seen as a way of ensuring that people have something useful to do instead of being unemployed; alternatively, they can be seen as a cynical attempt on the part of government to reduce the official unemployment figures and keep the unemployed in contact with the disciplines of work at the lowest possible cost. (Loney, 1979, p. 229) Since wage levels tend to be low, they are particularly likely to be seen as exploitative if the kind of work they offer is unpleasant and demeaning, and offers no intrinsic satisfaction. In such situations, the unemployed may resent or even reject the work that is offered. As Garraty (1978) argues, 'the spectacle of WPA officials distributing snow shovels during blizzards to gaunt and ragged men was somehow heartening in the America of the 1930s because the men had no other source of income; in the 1970s the idle are less gaunt and ragged and are unlikely to accept such work unless threatened with the loss of available public assistance'. (p. 255)

A further major limitation of such programmes is the short period of time that any individual is permitted to stay in them – in the programmes outlined above, the maximum duration has normally been one year. At the end of the programme, many of the people involved have to return to the dole. Yet another limitation is the level of centralized bureaucratic control that is required. Although the Manpower Services Commission, which has been responsible for these various programmes, has attempted to operate through local agencies, it has been forced in the interests of financial and political accountability to maintain tight regulatory control over the ways in which the programmes have been used.

There have, however, been some experiments in establishing more locally-based initiatives of a kind aimed at creating more permanent jobs. These have gone under various names – community business, community enterprises, local enterprises, local initiatives – and have in general been formed by local community groups coming together with existing institutions (including companies, trade unions, and voluntary bodies). Their aim has been to create an organization owned and controlled by the local community which will generate ultimately self-supporting and viable jobs through which local people can meet locally perceived needs, and to use profits either for reinvestment in the business itself or for community benefit. Among the fields of product and service covered have been: joinery and wood products, knitwear and clothing, pottery and crafts, printing, toy manufacture, construction, landscaping and gardening, office cleaning, retailing, catering, and recyling and refurbishing of furniture and household appliances. (Community Business Ventures Unit, 1981; Calouste Gulbenkian Foundation, 1982a)

Such organizations cut across the market and the redistribution sectors. They are indeed part of a third sector, termed by Weisbrod (1977) 'the voluntary non-profit sector', which is a source of collective goods but is not directly subject to state control. (It was indeed the chief source of collective goods in, for example, Elizabethan England (*ibid,* pp. 63-4).) The organizations normally depend at least in part on funds from central and local government, private industry, or independent foundations and trusts; frequently they combine a number of such funding sources. Yet they also 'trade' and often seek to become increasingly self-sufficient over time. Their aim is not profit maximization (as in the market sector), yet neither is it the simple provision of free services: it is rather the provision of services within commercial constraints, but not subject wholly to market criteria. They attempt to recognize the extent to which some community needs can best be met not by market forces nor by large-scale government intervention but by communities taking initiatives on their own account. Their ambiguity causes problems: for example, there has been some resistance from existing businesses within the market sector fearing unfair competition. Efforts to use the government-sponsored job-creation programmes as a 'seed-bed' for organizations of this kind which might then establish their own broader viability – whether within the market economy or within the 'third sector' – have so far been largely resisted. They offer, however, an alternative approach which may help to generate forms of work that respond to community needs in ways which the market and redistribution economies in their pure forms are unable to do, and provide a closer point of identification for their workers.

Concluding comments

It would seem, then, that apart from the problems of *delivering* the right to employment – which, though not insuperable, are considerable – there are three possible caveats that need to be expressed in relation to the 'right' itself, even if the basis for the 'right' is granted. One, which has already been discussed at some length, is the possibility that the moral and social virtues of employment will only be substantiated if it is directed towards some evidently useful end. It is arguably an essential quality of work in its broader sense that it is 'an activity that produces something of value for other people'. (O'Toole *et al.*, 1973, p. 3) The market mechanism, whatever its limitations, does at least ensure that this criterion is met at some level (even though the 'value' may, for example, have been artificially induced by clever advertising). If, in order to provide employment for all, recourse is to be made to other mechanisms, care must be taken to ensure that the demanding criterion of utility continues to be addressed.

The second caveat is that attention should be paid not only to the product of the work but also to the needs of the worker: in other words, the extent to which the work permits and encourages workers to use and develop their individual interests, skills and values. In the USA, O'Toole *et al.* (1973) proposed that policy should be based on the principle not just of 'full employment' but of 'total employment', 'in which everyone who desires a job is able to find a reasonably satisfying one'. (p. 158) This is a demanding injunction. The reality at present is that much employment is unpleasant, monotonous and unfulfilling. (see e.g. Braverman, 1974) It is far removed from the high-minded claims of the proponents of the work ethic:

> 'If there is little Calvinist compulsion to work among propertyless factory workers and file clerks, there is also little Renaissance exuberance in the work of the insurance clerk, freight handler, or department-store saleslady . . . For the white collar masses, as for wage earners generally, work seems to serve neither God nor whatever they may experience as divine in themselves.' (Mills, 1951, p. 219)

Marx argued that alienation was intrinsic to productive relations within a capitalist system. Others contend that even within such a system, work can be organized in a way which avoids alienation and encourages individual fulfilment, if sufficient will and imagination are applied. Improved technology has been seen as the necessary if not sufficient condition of such improvements in the content of jobs. (Gershuny, 1978, pp. 116-26) Some writers have indeed visualized what are in essence leisure values – choosing for oneself and doing things for their own sake – invading work organizations. (see e.g. Dumazedier, 1974) There are clear tensions here with our first criterion of utility: while the two criteria may be compatible and even complementary to some extent – part of the potential satisfaction of work is the awareness of performing something of use to others – it is necessary in the end to decide which is ultimately superordinate.

A third possible caveat to the 'right to work' is that it can be transformed into an obligation to accept any employment that is offered in return for access to state benefits etc. In a few parts of the USA, for example, the 'workfare' system requires recipients of welfare to put in a certain number of hours per month on community work (Merritt, 1982, p. 170): some people reject it because of its compulsory and 'make-work' character, but others carry it out, however resentfully, because they need the money to live on. The same kind of proposal surfaces periodically in Britain: for example, the Economic Planning Council for Yorkshire and Humberside was reported as urging that there was no reason why any employable person should be financially supported by the state unless they made a contribution to community welfare (*Guardian,* 27 August 1979); again, Lord Gowrie, then a junior minister at the Department of Employment, was reported as suggesting that benefit should be cut for individuals who refused to participate in the government's special employment measures. (*New Society,* 24 July 1980) Even if employment is a right which the state must meet, unless individuals have a financial platform (in the form of the social wage) which enables them in effect to negotiate the terms in which it is met, the right may be perverted into an imposition and a curtailment of their freedoms.

As with the leisure scenario, the delivery of the 'right to work' in terms which are benign, and which gives those who are currently unemployed genuine access to the benefits associated with unemployment, requires a considerable act of political will. In particular, it requires a willingness on the part of those currently in employment – with the power and wealth which this provides – either to share the employment or to share some of its fruits so that additional employment can be created for those who are currently denied it. At the time of writing, there seems little significant evidence of such altruism, in either of these forms. Unions, despite intermittent declarations of concern for the unemployed, are basically preoccupied with the maintenance or improvement of their own members' standard of living: as Marsden (1982) puts it, 'workers' behaviour has had the appearance not of a co-ordinated resistance to government policies but of a highly fragmented pursuit of self-interest by the more powerful at the expense of the weak'. (p. 255) Incomes policies, which would seem an essential prerequisite for sharing communal resources more evenly, have been constantly undermined. At the same time, the 'tax revolt' has led to strong pressures to reduce the size of the redistribution economy. While the employment scenario remains a possibility, major social and political shifts would be required to achieve it.

Summary

Chapter eight has examined the possibility that measures might be taken to give access to employment to all who want it. As with the 'leisure ethic', there is a strong cultural tradition promoting the 'work ethic', and this has become closely associated with work as employment. Indeed, employment has become an important part of the contract between the individual and society. Viewed in this light, access to employment is a right. Two broad approaches to delivering this right have been identified. One is the notion of work-sharing, through encouraging part-time jobs, job-splitting, reducing the length of the working week, instituting longer holidays and sabbaticals, and banning overtime. The chief problem here is that work-sharing implies income-sharing. The alternative approach is to create new forms of employment. Some areas in which this might be done have been examined, and some of the issues which such measures confront have been noted. Among these is the question of the extent to which attention should be paid to the utility of the product of the work, and to the satisfaction which the work offers to the worker. Employment-creation measures also raise the issue of whether the right to employment implies an obligation to work. In the end, though, the main difficulty in delivering the 'right to work' is that it requires those currently in work to give up some of their power and wealth.

CHAPTER NINE

The Work Scenario

Self-employment

In the preceding chapters, the terms 'work' and 'employment' have at times been used interchangeably, in accordance with conventional usage. The point has however been made several times that the two are not synonymous, and that there are many forms of work outside employment. Even at times of full employment, there are some people who do not seek employment in the conventional sense of working for a wage, but instead seek their own definitions of work. They hold to the work ethic, but not to the employment ethic. Rising levels of unemployment have led to increased interest in these forms of work, in the hope that they might provide some constructive alternatives to the waste and negativeness of unemployment. It is with this that our fourth and final scenario is concerned.

Some of these forms of work operate outside the formal economy altogether: we shall come to these shortly. Within the formal economy, however, many people work not for others but for themselves. Such people fall into three main groups: first, those who are self-employed on their own; second, those who set up businesses employing other people; and third, those who set up workers' co-operatives which are owned by the workers themselves. Official statistics tend to be confined to the first two of these groups. In 1980, out of a total labour force of 26.3 million, 1.9 million were self-employed. They were concentrated in a narrow range of occupations and industries, and indeed 86 per cent were in five industrial groups: agriculture, forestry and fishing; construction; retail distribution; professional and scientific services; and miscellaneous services. Of these, construction accounted for 22 per cent, and retail distribution for 20 per cent. (Department of Employment, 1982) An analysis in 1974 showed that some three-fifths of the self-employed were workers on their own account, while two-fifths were employers of one or more other people. (Department of Employment, 1976, p. 1344). By contrast with these groups, the number working in workers' co-operatives is small indeed: the Co-operative Development Agency estimated that the 498 co-operatives listed in 1982 had a total of only 6,355 workers in all. (personal communication, June 1983)

Is the number of self-employed going up? Within a long-term context, the answer is 'no': whereas in 1921 10 per cent of the labour force were self-employed, by 1966 this had fallen to 6.4 per cent. (Royal Commission on the Distribution of Income and Wealth, 1979, table 2.11) There was a substantial increase between 1966 and 1973, during which the number of self-employed men increased by 255,000 while the male working population as a whole fell by one million (Department of Employment, 1976, p. 1344), but this was almost entirely due to the growth in the number of self-employed in the construction industry. Subsequent regulations to outlaw the 'lump' together with the slump in construction activity – plus a decline in self-employment in retail distribution owing to the closure of small shops – meant that the total went down in the late 1970s. (Department of Employment, 1982)

The early 1980s, however, saw another substantial increase: between 1979 and 1981 the number of self-employed went up by 12 per cent, the largest recorded biennial increase (Department of Employment, 1983b), largely, it would seem, in response to the business 'shake-out'. In broad historical terms, such increases are common at times of growing unemployment. (Newcomber, 1961, pp. 492-3) There has also been much public encouragement for people interested in setting up their own businesses. It has come partly from government, and partly also from large companies, which are now stating publicly that they are unlikely to recruit new employees at the levels they have done in the past. Such companies view the encouragement of entrepreneurial activity as a means simultaneously of communicating this message, of showing some social responsibility for its repercussions, but of doing so in a way which sustains an ideological climate congruent with their own activities.

Some large companies are indeed seeking to hive off some of their activities to small businesses and self-employed individuals, and to offer more work on a fee rather than a wage basis. As Handy (1980) points out *'fees* are paid for work done, for *output; wages* are paid for time spent, for *input'*. He argues that the 'contractual organization', in which as much work as possible is contracted out, is becoming more common, partly because of 'the costs in time, bureaucracy and legislation of employing anyone', and partly because of the increase in flexibility offered by 'new tools and machines which allow individuals to do what once needed shifts of work-forces'. (p. 432)

Some writers have accordingly suggested that in future there may be a major shift of paid work away from the factory and office and back into the home. The new technology makes it easier to work from home. Productive equipment is now often light and compact enough to be located there – an example quoted by Handy (1980) is the programmed sewing machine for £200 which, in effect, 'brings the rag-trade into the bedroom'. (p. 434) Moreover, advances in telecommunications systems, including 'teleconferencing', home terminals linked into distant word-processors, etc., mean that almost any white-collar work can be done at home. (Martin, 1978, p. 157) Toffler (1980) accordingly foresees the advent of what he calls 'the electronic cottage': 'a return to cottage industry on a new, higher, electronic basis, and with it a new emphasis on the home as the centre of society'. (p. 210) Certainly this would avoid the growing costs and discomfort of commuting for the individual, and the increasing overheads of work-places for the employer. Already there have been some moves in this direction in Britain: for instance, Rank Xerox announced that it was intending to disperse 150 of its executives to work from home. Although such moves do not necessarily imply a move from a wage to a fee relationship, it was perhaps significant that the first few executives dispersed in the Rank Xerox scheme reported that they were developing the freelance side of their work, as well as fulfilling their contractual obligations to their own company. *(New Society,* 26 August 1982)

The notion of the 'electronic cottage' does not inspire universal approval. Home-workers – most of them women – have traditionally been an exploited group, paid on a low, piece-rate basis. (see e.g. Hope *et al.,* 1976) Moreover, there are fears that basing office workers at home with their terminals will condemn them to the desolate social isolation from which many housewives, and indeed many unemployed people, suffer, and that this will undermine their sense of social belonging and so increase the already high anarchic tendencies in mature industrial societies. (Jahoda and Rush, 1980, p.40) Certainly, it would have major implications for housing policy: most modern homes have not been designed also to be work-stations, and if the rural cottage may be suited to home-based work, this is less likely to be true of, for example, the town maisonette or the flat in a high-rise block. Handy (1982, p. 22) has accordingly suggested that some form of community workplace may be needed, where space can be provided and social contact established and reinforced.

More widely, there is also concern about the implications of a general move towards employment being replaced by contract and fee work. It is one thing for Rank Xerox executives to earn additional income from such work, in much the way that academics and others have long done from lecturing, writing and consultancy work on top of their main employment. It is quite another to make one's living entirely from this kind of work. And while this may be feasible for some energetic professional workers in relatively affluent areas where a thriving economy is creating plenty of opportunities for such work, it will be a totally different proposition for depressed, unskilled and semi-skilled workers in run-down areas of the country.

This poses immediate problems in viewing self-employment as being any kind of significant response to unemployment. Interest in becoming self-employed is not of course confined to the unemployed: many in employment harbour longings to become independent. Nonetheless, the unemployed sometimes show a particular interest in self-employment, in view of the relative freedom and autonomy it would bring (see e.g. Economist Intelligence Unit, 1982, pp. 50-2; Marsden, 1982, p. 194): the experience of being made redundant by the acts or failings of others induces a desire in some to become masters (or mistresses) of their own fate. Few, however, seriously act upon it. This may be partly because the heavily corporatist structure of British society – big firms, extensive trade unionism, large public sector – has produced a collective social psychology which has limited the extent to which people have the skills and attitudes that would equip them for such action. Within such a culture, self-employment often remains a fantasy rather than being seen as a serious and practicable option.

Whatever the reasons, a careful analysis of the various studies of the redundant and unemployed by Johnson (1981) estimated that no more than five per cent of people affected by redundancies attempted to set up on their own. The figure tended to be much higher among professional and managerial workers than among clerical and manual workers, and among the latter to be higher among the skilled than among the unskilled. Johnson concluded that although policy initiatives to encourage self-employment might be worthwhile in cost-benefit terms, their absolute impact on the unemployment problem would be limited: the numbers of people who would attempt to set up on their own – and successfully sustain their effort – would not be likely in the foreseeable future to be sufficient to reduce the unemployment rate to any significant extent. Again, Bradley (1980) in his study of workers' co-operatives established in the early 1970s in Britain, France and Canada found that those set up as a means of saving jobs tended to experience growing tensions between the ideals of workers' control and the economic pressures posed by the workers' desire to hold on to their jobs, and that eventually they tended to have to choose between economic collapse and reversion to more traditional organizational structures. (for a more detailed case study, see Eccles, 1981)

For the fact is that those who are self-employed – whether in the sense of being on their own, of running their own small business, or of running a workers' co-operative – are at the mercy of short-term market forces. They do not have the protection which those employed in large organizations have in terms of contracts of employment and union support. Nor do they have the support and scope stemming from the capacity of large organizations to invest in long-term research, development, training, etc., to build expensive plant, and to survive bad times and individual disasters. If the main power and wealth are to remain within large organizations – and particularly, as seems likely, in large multi-national companies – then there will be a growing split between those securely protected by the plush frontage, the relatively secure salaries and the lavish fringe benefits of the big bureaucracies, and those fighting for survival in the entrepreneurial jungle outside. This is evident, for example, among those forming companies. Although the number of company formations increased in the early 1980s (DIT, 1983, p. 78), so did the bankruptcy and liquidation rate. (DIT, 1982, p. 715)

Yet it is clear that there are some forces which favour a growth in entrepreneurial activity. The self-employed tend to have much higher levels of job satisfaction than those who are working for other people. (Consumers Association, 1977, p. 490) As has already been suggested, the nature of the new technology is much more adaptable to decentralization and smaller-scale production than were the large machines characteristic of the Industrial Revolution. Account also needs to be taken, as Shanks (1981) points out, of 'the reviving taste for craftsmanship, the reaction against mass produced consumer products, the growing desire for individuality and self-expression among the peoples of the West ... When technology and public aspirations and values are pulling in the same direction, it is a powerful combination.' (pp. 26-7) The errors are to regard self-employment in its various forms as a ready-made solution to unemployment, or as a potential replacement for large organizations. The perpetration of such errors prevents attention being paid to the crucially important issue of how effective and socially equitable relationships can be established between the self-employed on the one hand and the large bureaucratic organizations on the other. Such relationships need to encourage the former and provide them with sufficient resources and support to prevent intolerable disparities between them and the main bastions of power and wealth, yet to do so without surrounding them with a level of regulatory control that will restrict their creativity and the satisfactions that they offer.

The informal economies

So far, our attention has been confined almost exclusively to work that takes place within the *formal* economy. It is however clear that a considerable and probably increasing amount of work is carried out in three *informal* economies. (Gershuny and Pahl, 1979/80; 1980; also Gershuny, 1979)

The first is the *'black'* economy, otherwise variously known as the 'underground' or 'hidden' economy. This covers work conducted wholly or partly for money which is concealed from taxation and regulatory authorities: it ranges from undeclared criminal and immoral earnings (e.g. prostitution, drug-trafficking), through office pilfering and perks, to undeclared income earned in particular by the self-employed, by 'moonlighters', and by the unemployed. Some of these activities are clearly illegal; some are more properly regarded as 'irregular'. (Ferman and Berndt, 1981) An estimate by Macafee (1980), based on the national accounts, suggested that the hidden economy accounted for 3.3 per cent of the national income in 1978, as opposed to 1.4 per cent in 1972; an estimate from the rather different perspective of the Inland Revenue, using different definitions of the term 'black economy', put the figure at 7½ per cent (quoted in *ibid*, p. 86); and another estimate has been as high as 15 per cent. (Feige, 1981) In Italy, the proportion has usually been estimated as being between 10 per cent and 25 per cent (de Grazia, 1980, p. 552), and some put it as high as 40 per cent (Hansen, 1979); moreover, it seems that parts of the black economy are officially tolerated as a matter of policy. As one former Italian minister put it:

> It is a bad thing to say, but these "deviations" are a positive thing, at least as far as employment is concerned. If the taxman were to intervene in this underground economy he would be acting in accordance with the principles of redistributive justice but would be ruining not only a host of small businessmen and their workers but perhaps the country's economy and social peace as well. (quoted in de Grazia, 1980, p. 558)

In Third World countries, too, official attitudes have been changing, following the report of the International Labour Organization (1972, chapter 13) on Kenya which argued that parts of the urban informal economies should be supported and promoted rather than being ignored and harrassed. Although in Britain the black economy is usually seen more in terms of additional earnings on the side rather than full-time occupation, similar arguments have begun to be advanced here as well: among the points made are that the hidden economy 'provides a safety valve, a means of anticipating official recognition of anomalies, or recognizing individual merit, and a channel for "unqualified ability", the opportunity for personal control of the work situation, and the sheer pleasure of beating the system'. (Outer Policy Research Circle, 1979, p. 3) Attitudes to the social morality of black-economy activity depend on whether the beneficiaries of tax regulations are seen to be the clients of the welfare state or its bureaucrats. On the one hand, it can be seen as undermining the public services on which all depend, and the benefits on which the poor rely for their livelihood. On the other hand, as Ward (1982) put it,

> Many of us, for a whole variety of reasons, do not accept the unspoken doctrine that the state is all-powerful and has an absolute right to provide its servants

with index-linked pensions at the expense of the poor, whose insurance contributions (in the fiction of national insurance) do not entitle them to have an income in old age which matches the rise in the cost of living. (p. 48)

Again, although there are dangers of social and political anarchy stemming fiom the fact that a significant economy is operating outside the law, note needs to be taken of the strong and spontaneously-evolved normative controls which operate among many participants in the hidden economy: Henry (1978, chapter 8) has suggested that policing can best be left largely to such controls.

The black economy is closely related to the formal economy, in the sense that it is still focused around a cash nexus. This is not however true of the other two informal economies. The first of these is the *communal* economy, which involves the production of goods or services that are consumed by people other than the producers, but are not sold on a monetary basis. This ranges from baby-sitting circles or car pools which operate on the basis of a formal exchange of tokens or credits, through exchanges of skills or of equipment which are part of a relationship of generalized reciprocity between friends, neighbours, etc., to pure gift activities for which no reciprocity is expected. The latter include voluntary work through voluntary organizations, and also some acts of friendship or neighbourliness. The central parts of this spectrum may blur into the black economy to some extent: Henry (1978, chapter 5) points out that what is important in hidden-economy trading is often not the monetary benefits it produces, but the relational ties and bonds of friendship which it generates and reinforces; payments are often made in kind rather than in money, and for many of the participants such trading is more moral than most legitimate business because it is concerned with helping other people. (*ibid*, p. 78) Certainly most stable working-class communities contain rich networks of reciprocal support which not only help to bind the community but also mean that less recourse has to be made to the formal economy outside (see e.g. Townsend, 1957; Young and Willmott, 1957); American studies have shown the same phenomenon among urban ghetto dwellers. (e.g. Stack, 1974) Thus such networks have economic as well as social value to the individual (see Pahl, 1980, pp. 6-7; Wallace, 1980, p. 7), and this is one reason why admonitions to the unemployed to 'get on their bikes' and move to new areas need to be treated with some caution: if such people subsequently fail to find a job in their new areas, they will be much less well off even in purely economic terms than if they had stayed where they were, because they will have cut themselves off from their existing networks and will almost inevitably find it more difficult to build up new ones.

The third informal economy is the *household* economy, which covers work within the home that involves the production for internal consumption of goods or services for which approximate substitutes might otherwise be purchased for money. These include cooking, decorating, laundry, child care, home repair, garden produce, etc. In the USA, Burns (1975, p. 6) has estimated that if all the work carried out within the household by men and (particularly) women were converted into monetary form, the total would be equal to the entire amount paid out in wages and salaries by every corporation in the country. In Britain, Gershuny (1979, p.3) has calculated on the basis of time-budget figures that by 1974/5 the total time devoted to household production (i.e. domestic work) in the UK amounted to about four-fifths of that devoted to formal economic activities.

To illustrate the distinction between these different economies, Pahl (1980, pp. 4-5) points to the various options open to someone wanting a particular job done – repairing a broken window, for example. He or she could:

(a) hire a glazier within the *formal* economy, paying the full cost including value-added taxes;
(b) find someone who is known to be able to mend windows, and pay cash for the job, possibly thereby entering the *black* economy, since it would not be clear whether such a person was declaring all his or her income, paying all his or her taxes, or working in time already paid for by another employer;
(c) ask a friend or neighbour to do it within the *communal* economy, either in exchange for specific goods or services now or in the future, or as part of a broader continuing relationship;
(d) do the job him/herself in his or her own time with his or her own tools, within the *household* economy.

A survey of 284 households in Detroit, USA, found that 60 per cent of the services which households reported using were secured through the communal and household economies, 10 per cent through the black economy, and only 30 per cent through the formal economy. (Ferman and Berndt, 1981, p. 27)

As we saw in chapter five, there are good economic grounds for supposing that the proportion of work being carried out within the informal economies is currently increasing, as the labour costs attached to services within the formal economy price more of these services out of the market. The implications of this argument are potentially profound. It suggests that employment within the formal economy is declining as a source of goods and services. It also suggests that, if this trend continues, the livelihood of many people will in future depend less on formal employment and more on the skills they have to deploy in their own households and communities.

At the same time, it is important to emphasize that there is not much evidence of the unemployed moving in a substantial way into the informal economies: much of the work within these economies is carried out by people who also are in formal employment, or by people outside the labour market altogether (notably housewives). In particular, it seems clear that the black economy is not significantly manned by the unemployed. Certainly some 'fiddling' goes on (Marsden, 1982, pp. 132-45), but the Economist Intelligence Unit (1982) found in a survey of over 1,000 unemployed people that 61 per cent said they had done no casual work at all, and only 8 per cent said they had received payment of some kind. (pp. 57-8) Broadly similar results were found by Roberts *et al.* (1981) in the case of young people: 'steady hustles' were more prevalent in neighbourhood gossip than in real life, and few of those involved in the black economy had discovered genuine long-term alternatives to orthodox employment. (pp. 21-4) As the Manpower Services Commission (1982c) points out, 'only those with marketable skills, for example in plumbing, electrical installation and car repairs, could earn enough in the hidden economy to justify the risk of detection'; since the majority of unemployed people do not have these kinds of skills, 'the opportunities to receive undeclared payments are limited to less well paid jobs, such as window cleaning or gardening, the rewards for which are unlikely to be sufficiently attractive to encourage systematic fraud'. (p. 21) Moreover, in the search for black-economy work the unemployed may be up against the competition of the employed, who because of their resource base in the formal economy are able to operate a low price structure which gives them a powerful market advantage. (Henry, 1982, pp. 467-8)

Even in the household economy, there is little sign that unemployed men are taking on more domestic responsibilities, even where their wives are the major income-earners. (see e.g. Pahl, 1982) The chief informal-economic arena in which the unemployed may be becoming more active is the communal economy: in the study by the Economist Intelligence Unit (1982, pp. 57-8) the majority of those who had done casual work had done it on an unpaid basis – gardening, painting, decorating, baby-sitting, etc. for friends and relatives. There have also been – as we saw in chapter four – some formal efforts to set up networks through which services can be exchanged among unemployed people.

It is also important to underline in more general terms the extent to which the informal economies are dependent on, and interact with, the formal economies. Perks and pilferages are linked to particular waged jobs; the offer of personal services for cash is often based on a knowledge of advanced industrial skills such as the workings of a motor car or television set; household production for one's own consumption uses capital equipment based on advanced technology, such as deep freezes. Even in Third World countries, artisans and traders in the informal sector are not part of a traditional subsistence economy but are heavily dependent upon the capitalist world economy. (Bryant, 1982) This is demonstrated graphically in Dore's (1976) description of typical Third World informal-sector workers:

> ... the roadside and empty-lot mechanics who will weld on a Bourneville cocoa tin to mend the exhaust pipe of the civil servant's Mercedes, the leather workers making hand-made bags for the tourist trade, the furniture-makers, the men who collect empty Essolube cans from the garages twice a day and have them processed into serviceable oil lamps by sunset. (p. 74)

As Santos (1979) puts it, 'there cannot, in reality, be a separate informal sector within an overall formal society.' (p. 225)

These interrelationships mean that any growth in the informal economies will offer benefits to the formal economies too. These may even apply to employment. For although the movement of services from the formal to the informal sector reduces employment in the production of services within the formal economy, it will increase employment in the 'intermediate' production and maintenance of the materials and infrastructures that are used in the production of services within the informal economies. (Gershuny, 1980b, p. 2) While the latter is unlikely to compensate the former, the additional time that individuals will be spending in informal production of services could also tend to reduce the time available for paid work – thus increasing opportunities for work-sharing. (*ibid*, p. 7)

Should then the shift towards the informal economies be permitted to continue, or even be given active encouragement? Certainly the informal economies offer a considerable degree of personal autonomy, and this seems to be a powerful attraction to those who participate in them. (Gershuny and Pahl, 1979/80, p. 126) Producing services for oneself or in reciprocal exchange with others is likely to be personally more satisfying and rewarding, reducing the alienation that results from the division and formalization of labour. (see Pahl, 1980) Moreover, from the consumer's point-of-view, the informal economies offer the possibility of making available personal services which, because they are not widely traded, are not constrained by the need to be hyperefficient in their use of labour. (Gershuny, 1979, p. 14)

On the other hand, since political and economic power remains vested in the formal economy, the growth of the informal economies could readily permit the development of a split society like that in many Third World countries, where policies of social protection are only extended to a small section of the economically active population, and the rest are too busy 'making out' to challenge the distribution of such social protection. (Bromley and Gerry, 1979) Morever, those who are outside formal employment are often those least well-equipped with the skills necessary for productive and rewarding informal activities. Similarly, the areas with the highest levels of unemployment are frequently those with a poor social infrastructure and limited markets for

work and included in the calculation of a revised GNP, and that housewives should be included in social security or other pension provision (or better still, one might add, in a National Dividend system of the kind proposed by Roberts (1982)). (see chapter seven above) The feminist 'wages for housework' movement has gone beyond this to advocate state-paid remuneration for women's household labour, thereby recognizing the value of this labour to society as a whole, not just to the husband. Through measures of these kinds:

> ... the choice confronting the ... mother would no longer be between taking a job or receiving no assistance (which is really no choice at all) but rather the choice between working at home, in her own house with her own children, or working outside the home. (O'Toole *et al.*, 1973, p. 180)

Such moves would integrate what Pym (1980) calls the 'free economy' in opposition to the 'institutional economy'. Pym argues that the growth of this 'free economy' – comprising self-employment and the informal economies – would make it possible to rescue the 'work ethic' from its perversion within employment:

> The work ethic is based on notional links between effort and reward; effort is goal-directed, reward tangible; striving for goals a question of individual responsibility, and environmental mastery and success matter ... The inability of employment to sustain its central value is evident from the most cursory of examinations. Typically more and more of us find the goals of our tasks complex and unclear; individual responsibility conceding to collective responsibility; and the link between effort and reward, at best tenuous. (p. 227)

The 'free economy', by contrast, establishes a direct relationship between the worker and the product of his or her work. It is more fully integrated in the life of the community, being focused around informal networks and contacts based on what Illich (1973) calls 'convivial' relations. It is less based on money, but it places a premium on skills which can be sold or, often, exchanged. Accordingly, says Pym, it offers more opportunities to women, to those with manual skills, and to those permanently resident, than to 'the mobile executive on the make'. (p. 234)

Much the same kind of scenario is sketched out by Robertson (1978) in what he terms 'the sane humane ecological (SHE) future'. In such a future:

> ... the acquisition of externally validated credentials, positions, possessions and qualifications which give one an advantage over one's less successful fellows will come to seem less important; the development of personal capacities to live one's life under one's own control, and also to help one's fellows to do the same, will come to seem more important. (p. 80)

Gorz (1982), too, argues that 'post-industrial socialism' should not seek to artificially sustain the 'relations of subordination, competition and discipline' that characterize the employment system, but rather to appropriate areas of autonomy outside this system (pp. 72-3):

> The priority task of a post-industrial left must therefore be to extend self-motivated, self-rewarding activity within, and above all, outside the family, and to limit as much as possible all waged or market-based activity carried out on behalf of third parties (even the state). (p. 87)

Such a scenario raises some problems. One is the issue of quality control. The formality of large organizations at least provides some protection for consumers, whereas in the free economy there would be more room for incompetence and even for fraudulence: Handy (1982, p. 19) notes that in Italy there are reported instances of medicines manufactured in the black economy which in no way contain what they purport to contain. If the 'free economy' were firmly located within stable networks, informal controls might be effective; but in view of the size of modern conurbations and the levels of geographical mobility (even if these were reduced somewhat), this seems unlikely to be sufficient.

A second problem in such scenarios is one that has already been mentioned earlier in this chapter, if in slightly different terms – the relationship between the 'free economy' and the 'institutional economy'. Pym (1980) and Gorz (1982) do not argue that the former can replace the latter: indeed, its prosperity will be significantly dependent on improvements in the effectiveness of the 'institutional economy', for instance through better use of technology. Their concern is rather that *employment* within the 'institutional economy' should be minimized rather than maximized. Yet the fact that much wealth and power will be located there will mean that mechanisms of intervention will be needed to redistribute some of the wealth and power to people within the 'free economy' – which in turn may imply some constraints on the 'freedom' of the latter.

A third and linked issue is whether the retreat of the state will enable adequate support to be provided for the poor and the weak. The intention presumably is that families in communities will assume responsibility for caring and welfare. But there would seem to be a contradiction in promoting the values of economic independence 'while at the same time advocating that social needs should be met through voluntary, unpaid and altruistic caring by something called the "community" '. (Marsden, 1982, p. 268)

The fact is that the work scenario, centred on the idea of a 'free economy', presents an alliance between two separate ethics. One is an entrepreneurial ethic, based on the notions of enterprise and self-sufficiency. The other is a communitarian ethic, based on the notions of co-operation and community. Crudely, the former is more readily evident at the moment in self-employment, small businesses, and the black economy; the latter is more readily evident in co-operatives and in the communal economy (the household economy would seem to have more equal elements of the two ethics). Even if the two are not incompatible, there are clearly tensions between them.

The cash nexus

A further division within the 'free economy' which can be fruitfully identified is that between forms of exchange built around a cash nexus and forms built around other kinds of relationships. Here the line of division is slightly different: it extends beyond the 'free economy' and lies between what are at present formal-economy (both 'institutional' and 'free') and black-economy activities on the one hand, and household-economy and communal-economy activities on the other. It could indeed be argued that the very concept of the household and communal economies represents an attempt to impose economic constructs on to activities which are basically not economic but social in nature.

Polanyi (1945) has described how the market, which was subordinated to the social and religio-cultural goals of early societies, came to set the goals of industrial societies. Commercial transactions became central, and economic growth (as measured by the size of the market) became the primary goal of governments. Marx and Engels (1967 ed.) attributed this specifically to capitalism, which

> ... has left no other nexus between man and man than naked self-interest, than callous "cash payment". (p. 82)

They further identified it particularly with employment:

> The bourgeoisie has stripped of its halo every occupation hitherto honoured and looked up to with reverent awe. It has converted the physician, the lawyer, the priest, the man of science, into its paid wage labourers. (p.82)

More widely, Marx saw money as the external substance on to which men had projected their humanity, and which they must supersede in order to return to this humanity in its fullness. They must accordingly get rid of bargaining, of buying and selling. (see Clayre, 1974, p. 47)

The critique of the 'cash nexus' was not original to Marx but was directly derived from Thomas Carlyle's affirmation:

> Cash payment is not the sole nexus of man with man – how far from it! (Carlyle, 1918 ed., p. 168)

Many other writers, too, have criticized the devaluation that occurs when human activities are turned over to the market-place, as when making love becomes prostitution. As Seabrook (1982) puts it:

> This mysterious alchemy transforms everything. Intangible things, moral, human and spiritual qualities are changed into commodities that can be bought and sold. (p. 8)

The result is to base services and gifts to others on an instrumental foundation in which self-interest is paramount. As Adam Smith reminded us, it is not out of regard for our welfare that the baker bakes our bread. (quoted in Anthony, 1977, p. 142)

The establishment of a welfare state in which services are made available freely to the public can be seen as an attempt to remove cash from service transactions. But here too, those offering such services have shown a growing concern with financial rewards in the form of salaries and wages, and a growing willingness to subordinate their clients' interests to strikes and other means of pressing for higher rewards where their present rewards are judged to be inadequate. Teachers, social workers, ambulance drivers, hospital workers: all are now willing to engage in 'industrial action'. In a society in which worth is judged in monetary terms, this is hardly surprising or reprehensible. Yet it encourages the view that such groups as well are ultimately more concerned with their own power and well-being than with the needs of their clients. Moreover, the growth of the bureaucratic structures of the welfare state produces a distance between service providers and clients which means that the services take on many of the impersonal characteristics of a commodity.

In addition, there are clear constraints on the extent to which the market economy can generate sufficient wealth to satisfy the economic demands of workers within the redistribution economy. Their rewards accordingly have to be based on some market criteria, even though their services are not directly subject to such criteria. The result is to limit the range of services they are able to offer. Thus, for example, the more income each teacher manages to secure, the fewer the number of teachers that can be afforded within a given education budget, and the larger the class sizes that pupils and students have to endure.

Thus moving activities into an economic sphere built around a cash nexus both devalues them in terms of their moral and social quality, and places artificial limits on their extent. Accordingly, some activities have been deliberately kept out of this sphere. A classic instance is blood donorship, which in the USA is treated as a commercial commodity but in Britain is donated anonymously and without gain (Titmuss, 1970); another is the lifeboat service, which is thus removed from the threat of industrial action. Moreover, every society is held together by activities for which payment is neither given nor expected – by activities motivated by love, caring, creativity, curiosity, energy. These include many personal services and also many voluntary activities in which people are able to express their interests and their social values – for example, through giving their time freely to causes for which they care.

Illich (1978) argues that unemployment makes possible an enormous release of activities of these kinds. He talks about the 'right to useful employment', in which use-value is substituted for exchange-value as the measure of the value of people's work. Indeed, he argues that public policy should be concerned with maintaining this right rather than with maintaining levels of consumption and/or trying artificially to generate more 'powerless' employment:

> Henceforth the quality of a society and of its culture will depend on the status of its unemployed: will they be the most representative productive citizens, or will they be dependants? (pp. 84-5)

This choice is however a false one. In a society in which access to essential goods requires money, the capacity to devote all one's time to working without monetary reward implies access to money without effort, which in turn – unless it takes the form of inherited wealth – implies a form of dependency. It could be based on a guaranteed minimum income, along the lines of the schemes discussed in chapter seven. Even here, however, as was pointed out towards the end of chapter eight, the expectation readily grows that some 'contribution' should be offered in return. Thus James Prior remarked to a House of Commons Select Committee that many young unemployed people would welcome the chance to 'earn' their benefit by doing 'voluntary work' (sic) in hospitals. (quoted in *New Society*, 29 June 1982) Again, a report prepared for the Church of England General Synod's Board for Social Responsibility argued that the narrow work ethic should be replaced by a broader 'contribution ethic', recognizing that 'a contribution to society can be made in many other ways than just by means of a conventional job'. The report then added:

> It may also be more satisfying, in the longer run, to receive an income, and a sense of worth, on the basis of one's contribution to society than as a result of a paid job itself. (Brett, 1981, pp. 14-5)

It failed to define what mechanism for distributing income was to be found, or how – if it was in *direct* exchange for the 'contribution' – it was to differ from a paid job.

Traditionally, it has been women who have been the chief sources of 'gift work' within households and within the community. Dependent on the incomes of their husbands, they have performed many of the unpaid caring and expressive roles, looking after young children and elderly parents, and carrying out the voluntary services for friends, neighbours and others – if only in giving time and attention – which are so crucial to the social cohesion of communities and to the quality of life within them. From the viewpoint of social status, and of access to power and wealth, such tasks are regarded as demeaning and entrapping; from the viewpoint of their social value and their moral quality, they must be regarded as superior to much if not all paid employment.

The rigid division of sex-roles has in the past tended to confine such roles to women, and to confine women to such roles: women have understandably begun to challenge the assumption that this should be so, and to point out that something is only truly a gift if it is offered from a position of choice. The result, however, is to intensify the tensions between cash-nexus work and 'purer' forms of work. While the former was largely identified with men, and the latter with women, the balance between the two was, in a sense, 'protected'. Now, both are more vulnerable to the other. And, since economic power and social status tend at present to be a stronger force than appeals to social and moral value, it is work outside the cash-nexus which appears to be particularly under threat. Feminism tends more readily to take the form of claims to male prerogatives and privileges than of affirmations of the superiority of traditionally female roles and values. (though cf. e.g. Friedan, 1982) Men, meanwhile, show little inclination to give up their power, status and wealth in the quest for social and moral virtue.

The future of work outside the cash-nexus is thus inextricably linked with the issue of what happens to the division of sex-roles in our society. The increased interest in such work, along with the attacks on the welfare state which often accompany it, are readily suspected of being camouflage for returning women to their traditional roles. In February 1983 the proposals of a committee of Cabinet ministers for the restructuring of the welfare state were leaked in the press: they included the suggestion that the committee should look at 'what more can be done to encourage families – in the widest sense – to reassume responsibility for the disabled, elderly, unemployed 16-year-olds'; they also included a proposal to 'encourage mothers (sic) to stay at home'. (*Guardian*, 17 February 1983)

Yet in principle the reduction in the need for employment could provide increased opportunities for work outside the cash-nexus on the part of men as well as women. Pressures in this direction are likely to have more credibility if they come not from people who are suggesting that others adopt the values and roles which they show no sign of adopting themselves, but from people who are prepared to preach by example. Again, they are likely to have more credibility if they are not aimed solely at relatively weak groups and if skills required and exercised voluntarily are given due recognition if and when the people concerned seek to enter or return to employment. They are further likely to have more credibility if the, are accompanied by hard-headed attention to how people are to be given a sufficient basic subsistence to be able to *afford* to offer their work without always needing to charge for it. Finally, they are likely to have more credibility if they recognize that voluntary work must be genuinely voluntary. If it is not, it becomes exploitation, and the victim is fully justified in saying 'Why should I do that when I'm not being paid for doing it?'

Conclusion

The work scenario has embraced a wider range of alternative concepts than the three earlier scenarios. It has brought into focus the distinctions between employment and non-employed work, between the formal economy and the informal economy, between the 'institutional economy' and the 'free economy', and between work built round a cash-nexus and work based on other principles. The boundaries between these different concepts are by no means coterminous. Nonetheless, it is clear that work can be seen in very much broader terms than employment, and that seeing it in this way enables us to explore in greater depth some of the basic value issues built into the notion of the 'work ethic'. Releasing the work ethic convincingly from its identification with employment will not be easy, and many value issues will still remain to be resolved. Nonetheless, such a separation provides a clear alternative to the notion of the 'right' (and obligation?) to enter employment, outlined in chapter eight.

Summary

Chapter nine has described a scenario in which more importance and value would be attached to the massive amount of work which takes place outside paid employment. These include various forms of self-employment within the formal economy. They also include work in three informal economies: the black economy, the communal economy, and the household economy. Together, they can be seen as comprising a 'free economy' in contrast to the 'institutional economy' of paid employment. This 'free economy', however, is heavily dependent on the 'institutional economy', and the relationship between the two is a matter of vital concern. Moreover, the 'free economy' represents an uneasy alliance between an entrepreneurial ethic and a communitarian ethic. It also consists of some activities built around a cash nexus, and some built around other kinds of relationships. Arguably, work built around a cash-nexus is inferior to 'gift work' in terms of its moral and social quality; on the other hand, the capacity to devote all one's time to working without monetary reward normally implies a form of dependency. The balance between the two forms of work has traditionally been largely 'protected' by the division of sex-roles. The future balance accordingly is closely related to the outcome of the current questioning of the way in which sex-roles are defined.

CHAPTER TEN

Probable and Preferable Futures

In the four preceding chapters, an attempt was made to outline four possible scenarios relating to the future of work. The aim has been to develop a framework within which the various possibilities which tend to be raised in discussions on this topic can be critically evaluated, and their implications explored. The hope is that this will have helped readers to clarify and review their own assumptions, and to relate them to alternatives which they may not have previously considered. In short, the intention has been to 'un-freeze' the attitudes to the future of work which the reader may hold.

In practice, of course, reality will be much more untidy than any scenario. Indeed, it is likely to combine elements of several scenarios, if not all of them. This is already the case: elements of all four scenarios are discernible in public attitudes and behaviour. The issue is one of balance. At present it is clearly the unemployment scenario that is dominant. It also seems likely to remain so while our society stays locked into its present range of assumptions. Yet of all the scenarios, the unemployment one is the least attractive and the least constructive. The question is whether society can galvanise its energy and creativity sufficiently to transform the negativeness and destructiveness of the unemployment scenario into something more positive.

The obstacles to such a transformation should not be underestimated. Schon (1971) pointed out that the resistance to change exhibited by social systems is not 'inertia' but is much more nearly a form of 'dynamic conservatism' – that is, a tendency to fight to remain the same. (p. 32) Social systems provide for their members not only sources of livelihood and protection against outside threat, but also a framework of theory and values which enables individuals to make sense of their lives. Challenges to the social system threaten this framework, and accordingly tend to be fiercely resisted. (*ibid*, p. 51)

One form which this resistance can take is the notion that it is not our basic concepts that need modifying but our efficiency in operating them: that 'when the economy gets moving again, the jobs will come back'. Powerful forces conspire to sustain this notion. Political parties feel compelled by popular pressure to promise to reduce unemployment substantially, yet are unable to question the centrality of employment, or credibly to challenge the vested interests of those who currently possess it. Trade unions support 'right to work' marches, but are basically concerned to protect and increase the incomes of their members, and so off-load the problem on to others – employers, the government and, if all else fails, foreigners. The parcel is passed from hand to hand, and the music never stops.

Yet the fact has to be asserted, firmly and powerfully, that the problem is not insoluble. In international terms and even more so in historical terms, Britain is an enormously affluent country. It does not *have* to continue to attach such crucial importance to a social construct like 'employment' to which it then denies access to large parts of its adult population. It *could* make a 'paradigm shift' of the kind which Kuhn (1970) described for scientific revolutions: a change in the basic beliefs or assumptions underlying people's perceptions and actions.

The four scenarios sketched in chapters six to nine are indeed basically paradigmatic, in the sense that they are concerned at root with different ways of *conceptualising* the nature and distribution of employment, work and leisure. Only in the case of the employment scenario (chapter eight) are major *structural* changes required, in order to make employment available to all who want it. In all of the other three scenarios, employment is restricted to certain groups: the difference between the scenarios is that the status attached to those who would otherwise have wanted employment but who are unable to to get it is variously defined as being 'unemployed' (chapter six), as being part of a 'leisure class' (chapter seven), and as being a worker outside employment (chapter nine). The differences have implications for tax systems and the other institutional mechanisms through which public attitudes are formally conveyed, but they are basically more conceptual than structural.

This being so, change is only likely to take place if scenarios such as those sketched in this book become matters for energetic public debate. The value of the scenarios is that they present some poles within which the debate can take place. At their theoretical extremes, they do so in stark terms. Thus of the three 'non-employment' scenarios, the 'pure' form of the unemployment scenario is one in which the unemployed are consigned to idleness, with all activity proscribed; the 'pure' form of the leisure scenario is one in which the role of the leisure class is limited to consumption; and the 'pure' form of the work scenario is one in which those outside employment are recognized as being engaged in various forms of informal but productive economic activity. In reality, of course, the unemployed already engage in 'leisure' activities and in informal economic activities. The point is that the dominant conceptual models incorporated in public attitudes and in tax systems etc. do not recognize or encourage these activities to the point where they can provide an extensive basis for alternative identities.

In evaluating the merits of the different scenarios from individual points of view, there are at least three issues of importance. The first is how people are to occupy their *time*. The second is the social *status* attached to their main social roles. And the third is their access to *income*. All three issues have traditionally for most adults been resolved, whether for better or for worse, by employment. All three are clearly *not* resolved in any satisfactory way by unemployment. The question is whether acceptable social arrangements could be made whereby they could be resolved by leisure or by work outside employment, or whether the only satisfactory solution is to find ways through acts of deliberate policy of returning to 'full employment'.

The different scenarios clearly contain elements of different political philosophies. In broad terms, the ideological tendency of the unemployment scenario could be regarded as capitalist, of the employment scenario as socialist, and of the work scenario as anarchist; the leisure scenario is less easy to categorize in this respect, though the fear was expressed in chapter seven that it could have totalitarian implications. Such categorization can easily, however, be over-emphasized. Thus one of the classic pleas for full employment (Beveridge, 1944) came not from a socialist but from a Liberal; while one of the strongest arguments for the work scenario in preference to the employment scenario has come from a socialist. (Gorz, 1982)

Certainly, though, the unemployment and (to a slightly lesser extent) leisure scenarios seem likely to be more intrinsically inegalitarian than the employment and work scenarios. This is largely because of the nature of the mechanisms for the distribution of wealth. At present wealth is effectively distributed by wages within the employment system or in kind through the services and facilities of the redistribution economy. If large numbers of adults are excluded from the employment system, then this ceases to be sufficient. In the unemployment scenario, however, this issue is barely addressed: the unemployed receive grudging and minimal benefits, and in doing so are made to feel guilty for being so dependent on others. In the leisure scenario, the benefits are at least regarded as a right rather than as a gift, with no stigma attached to them: their level is unlikely, however, to be high enough to avoid being identified with poverty in relative if not absolute terms. The employment and work scenarios are also capable of permitting considerable inequalities of wealth, but they make it more *possible* for such inequalities to be reduced, and at least can give people a real opportunity to influence the terms of their access to wealth and income.

Of course, the viability of all the options depends not just on the distribution but also on the generation of wealth. Jenkins and Sherman (1979) argue that there will be high levels of unemployment whether or not Britain's industrial capacity is modernized and regenerated. But:

> Although the projected unemployment rates are similar, there is a vital qualitative difference. Technological unemployment will be based on high growth, high profits and returns, a highly competitive manufacturing and service base and high incomes, and these enable constructive policies to be adequately funded. The low growth unemployment, on the other hand, is accompanied by low profits, low productivity, low income and is a desperate if not terminal situation. (p. 176)

Arguably, however, the fact that wealth under the high-growth strategy is created at the expense of jobs means that the issue of how it is to be distributed has to be tackled with special care and energy. If this is not done, then fears that the wealth is being generated solely for the benefit of a few are likely to lead to resistance to action (such as introduction of new technology) designed to achieve such growth, as well as – if the fears are subsequently born out – to reductions in demand. The latter point was well illustrated in an exchange in the USA between the President of General Motors, Charles Wilson, and the head of the Autoworkers Union, Walter Reuther. In a pay-bargaining row, Wilson threatened to automate the entire production line. 'And,' he warned, 'electrons don't pay union dues.' 'No,' said Reuther, 'but will the electrons buy your automobiles?' (quoted in Ritchie-Calder, 1982, p. 15)

Ultimately, the question of which scenarios are preferable to others depends on values. Do we work to live, or do we live to work? In Christian terms:

> Is work only a prelude to the Sabbath, the day in which we fully find ourselves and our Creator, or is the Sabbath a prelude to work, a way of re-charging ourselves for the main purpose? (Handy, n.d., pp. 14-15)

In Marxist terms, does the 'realm of freedom' begin after the 'realm of necessity' has been conquered, or does freedom consist in the humanization and diversification of the 'realm of necessity'? If the essence of the concept of leisure is the freedom to choose, as Entwistle (1978, pp. 173-4) maintains, then does the ultimate lie in achievement of such leisure, or in incorporating notions of freedom into one's work?

Then again, what is the purpose of work? O'Toole *et al.* (1973) suggest that work is 'an activity that produces something of value for others', and contrast it to activities in which people are productive only for themselves – which, O'Toole *et al.* suggest, is 'a possible definition of leisure'. (p. 3) This places work very firmly within a social context. Is paid employment, then, the only sound and socially equitable way of relating human energies to the needs of others, or is it a distorting force, a way of perverting work by depriving the worker of control over it, and of introducing a cash nexus which means that use-value is subordinated to exchange-value?

Compromises can be struck. A work-sharing approach to the employment scenario could readily be reconciled with a version of the leisure scenario in which increased leisure was made available to all rather than only to some, and this could also permit increased forms of non-employed work (the Aristotelian definition of leisure, indeed, has affinities with some of the forms of non-employed work discussed in chapter nine). Handy (1982) suggests that there are three kinds of work: *job-work,* i.e. conventional employment; *pocket-money work,* on a fee basis; and *gift-work,* given for free. If the job-work were shared more evenly, there would be opportunities for all to have time to do some pocket-money work and some gift-work too.

Again, if people felt they had a genuine choice between the extent to which they engaged in Handy's three forms of work, diverse patterns would become more viable. Scenarios in which particular groups are confined to one kind of work, with no opportunity to choose, are more likely to lead to recriminations, conflicts, and lack of mutual understanding between groups.

Roberts' (1982) proposals for a National Dividend also offer some compromises. By providing the right to income for subsistence, they enable the individual to cover his or her own 'realm of necessity', and open up their 'realm of freedom' in which they can choose either to work for income or to offer gift work or to engage in leisure. Moreover, 'instead of having the division into two classes, the employed and the unemployed, one would have a homogeneous adult population, any of whom might decide to work any number of hours/week from zero to no specific limit, and for any wage that they could obtain on the free market'. (p. 48)

There are however societal choices to be resolved, in terms of providing the framework within which the individual choices can be made. The issues are basically five-fold:

1 What relative value do we attach to work and to leisure?
2 What relative value do we attach to paid work and to unpaid work?
3 What are the forms of work we are prepared to pay for?
4 How are these forms of work to be distributed?
5 How is this distribution to be related to the generation and distribution of wealth?

There are profound questions, and profoundly political ones. The answers to which we have become accustomed since the Industrial Revolution are arguably not going to work any more. They lead into the social and economic whirlpool of the unemployment scenario. If, however, we could summon the courage and energy to find new answers and so to move towards one or more of the other scenarios, this might produce a society that would offer the chance of a fruitful and fulfilling life to more of its members than has been possible during the industrial phase of our history.

Summary

Chapter ten has argued that the unemployment scenario seems, at present, the most probable scenario but the least preferable. To move towards the leisure or work scenarios is mainly a conceptual change: what it requires is that the role of those currently regarded as 'employed' be conceived in a difficult and more positive way. To move towards the employment scenario would require more major structural changes. The merits of the different scenarios need to be evaluated in terms of at least three issues: how people are to occupy their time, the social status attached to their main social roles, and their access to income. The unemployment and leisure scenarios seem likely to be more intrinsically inegalitarian than the employment and work scenarios. The scenarios do not, of course, exhaust the range of alternatives: some possible compromises between them have been outlined. Nonetheless, if the negativism of sustained high unemployment is to be avoided, important societal choices have to be made, and they require re-evaluation of fundamental philosophical and political questions.

CHAPTER ELEVEN

Implications for Education

A map of the world that does not include Utopia is not worth even glancing at, for it leaves out the one country at which Humanity is always landing.

Oscar Wilde (1966 ed., p. 1089)

Implications of the employment and unemployment scenarios

What are the implications for education of the scenarios outlined and discussed in chapters six to ten? Arguably, it is only the employment scenario – in which the right to employment is recognized and, in general, delivered – which *permits* the satisfactory maintenance of current educational structures (based as they are on the close bonds between education and employment outlined in chapter one). And even this scenario, it should be noted, does not *require* such maintenance. It could, for example, lead to much closer and more direct links being established between learning and productive work, so enabling people to learn and work all their lives. (see e.g. Castles and Wüstenberg, 1979) The notion that education should *precede* employment is a static and conservative one, which emasculates education and inhibits it in responding to – and helping people to contribute creatively to – the dynamic pace of change within employment. Moreover, if the employment scenario is to pay attention, along the lines argued towards the end of chapters eight, to the social purposes of employment, and the satisfaction and fulfilment it offers to the worker, then this has radical implications for the process and structure of education. It means, for instance, that people need to be helped not only to acquire the technical skills to be employable, but also to develop the critical awareness which will enable them to participate in decision-making at and around the work-place. Nonetheless, the employment scenario makes less insistent demands for educational change than do the other scenarios.

In the unemployment scenario, in which unemployment continues at high levels, maintenance of the educational *status quo* is not a satisfactory option, for reasons which have been discussed in chapters two to four. Nonetheless, it is likely to be attempted, even though such attempts will come under increasing strain. As was illustrated in chapter two, the most evident effect of unemployment is to tighten the bonds between education and employment. If this continues into the unemployment scenario, it means that more investment will be made in promises which cannot be delivered. The basic dilemma – that education can improve the employability of a given individual in the labour market, but can do little or nothing to reduce unemployment at a collective level – will haunt and confuse teachers and students alike. There will be particular strains on the meritocratic ideals of the comprehensive school, the establishment of which was based on the expanding opportunities within a growing economy. (Hargreaves, 1982, pp. 68-70) The pressures to introduce tighter and earlier curricular divisions, so as to lower aspirations and expectations, will increase. Yet they will have to stop short of preparing particular groups of young people for unemployment. In a society where unemployment is defined negatively in order to maintain incentives to enter employment, the notion that certain young people should be conditioned to accept such a negative identity will be resisted by radicals and conservatives alike: by radicals because of its inegalitarian implications, by conservatives because of its challenge to the work ethic.

The result is that tensions within schools in particular will continue to grow. Schools in defence may feel under pressure to adopt a more repressive and restrictive curriculum. Yet, as one headmaster put it, 'the indignity of a bad school experience can no longer be bought off with a job at the end'. (Walker, 1982b) Some schools may accordingly summon the courage and energy to attempt more positive curricular and pedagogic reforms, of the kinds outlined in chapter three. But within the unemployment scenario, rigidly conceived, the scope for such reforms, and their capacity to provide a solution to pupil disaffection, must remain constrained by the restrictive pressures of societal forces and attitudes. The reforms only become truly viable if society moves towards the other, more positive scenarios. Meanwhile, one of their strengths is that they at least open the door to such alternatives.

Implications of the leisure scenario

With the final two scenarios – those of leisure and work – the problem of the pressure towards a divided curriculum remains, though at least both sides of the division are now more viable. The division is paricularly acute in the case of the leisure scenario, in which some work and others form a new leisure class, because of the gulf between the attitudes and skills required by the two groups. Put crudely, the task is likely to be seen as that of educating a minority to a high technical level, and finding effective ways of containing and distracting the others. In a sense, this would require a reversal of the present situation, where leisure values concerned with the intrinsic value of what is being learned and a disdain for vocational application tend to be more dominant in élite forms of education – as reflected, for example, in the low status traditionally given to technology in the universities (see Wiener, 1981, pp. 132-7) – while vocational values tend to be more dominant at lower levels. But how would the division occur? If, as was argued in chapter seven, it is essential that the decision to enter the leisure class is a matter of choice rather than an imposition, how is education to prepare people to be in a position to move in either of these two very different directions? And if, despite this, different curricular provision is to be made for different groups, when is the division to take place, and on what criteria is it to be based?

There are other problems in relating education to the notion of a leisure society. Hargreaves (1981, pp. 200-1) points out that educational solutions to the 'problem' of work and leisure are usually proposed in two forms: education *as* leisure, and education *for* leisure. The concept of education-as-leisure views education as a way of occupying people. It is currently reflected in the notion of using educational institutions as a way of 'mopping up' high youth unemployment, and in the alternative recurrent-education notion of responding to unemployment by enabling people to take sabbaticals at different points in their lives. It is strongly present, for example, in Stonier's (1983) argument that a sensible policy response to unemployment would be to launch a major expansion of the educational system; and also, paradoxically, in Fragnière's (1976, p. 181) suggestion that education should henceforth be viewed as a new form of 'employment'. The flaw in this kind of argument, as Hargreaves (1981) points out, is that 'the majority of people do not desire more formal education; and if education were to become an alternative to employment, rather than as now a means to it, they would want less of it than they have now, not more'. (p. 201) Certainly there would be considerable resistance if there was any sense of compulsion. And to base public policy on viewing *voluntary* educational participation as a major alternative to employment would require the educational system to be far more flexible and responsive to client demands than it is at present.

The other notion, of education-for-leisure, is also problematic. At the level of helping people to develop spare-time activities, it is ultimately, as Entwistle (1978, p. 178) puts it, 'trivial': valuable as such help may be, it hardly provides an adequate basis for an educational philosophy. The more important question is how education can help people to construct a satisfying life-style and social identity without work. This raises basic philosophical issues. Thompson (1967) argues that the notion that 'all time must be consumed, marketed, put to *use*', and that simply 'passing the time' is invalid and even offensive, is a product of industrial capitalism. (pp. 90–1) He continues:

> If we are to have enlarged leisure, in an automated future, the problem is not "how are men going to be able to *consume* all these additional time-units of leisure?" but "what will be the capacity for experience of the men who have this undirected time to live?" If we maintain a Puritan time-valuation, a commodity-valuation, then it is a question of how this time is put to *use,* or how it is exploited by the leisure industries. But if the purposive notation of time-use becomes less compulsive, then men might have to re-learn some of the arts of living lost in the industrial revolution: how to fill the interstices of their days with enriched, more leisurely, personal and social relations; how to break down once more the barriers between work and life. And hence would stem a novel dialectic in which some of the old aggressive energies and disciplines migrate to the newly-industrializing nations, while the old industrialized nations seek to rediscover modes of experience forgotten before written history begins. (p. 95)

What place is there in such a conception for an education system of the kind we have at present? Russell (1935, p. 19) maintains that 'the wise use of leisure ... is a product of civilization and education'. Whether, however, it is a product of extended *formal* and *compulsory* education is disputable. The essence of leisure is the freedom to choose how one uses one's time: the notion of preparing for it within a compulsory structure is accordingly, in some senses, a contradiction in terms. Similarly, leisure activities are performed essentially for the intrinsic satisfactions they offer, not for the extrinsic advantages they provide: learning methods which fail to respond to and sustain learner motivation are therefore totally inappropriate. Hargreaves (1981, p. 204) argues that at present it is often the case that 'the best way to kill young people's interest in an activity is for teachers to insert it in the formal curriculum'. He points out how teachers 'raid young people's natural leisure pursuits as potential curriculum fodder', but, by doing so, destroy much of the fun associated with them. Although there are many aspects of the formal curriculum which are relevant to leisure, the work-oriented nature of the pedagogy currently used for them tends to destroy learner interest and to lead to their being disliked and rejected.

A further problem with the notion of education-for-leisure is the value issues embedded in it. In principle it would seem to provide a much larger role than at present for the arts. (see Calouste Gulbenkian Foundation, 1982b) Should, however, such provision be based on high culture, or not? Does listening to Mozart have a higher value than poring over the racing results? Is reading Tolstoy intrinsically superior to passing the time with one's friends in the local or on the park bench? Is supporting one's local theatre 'better' than supporting the local football team? Hargreaves (1981, p. 206) argues strongly that to deny working-class children access to the best and richest of our culture it to reinforce their deprivation: what is needed is to divest such culture of any superfluous élitist trappings and to remove the artificial barriers which impede the learner's pleasurable access to it. This is, however, a demanding injunction, and though some teachers manage to achieve it, culture in general remains obstinately associated with class identities and pre-judices. If education for leisure is to be based on voluntary principles, it will have to respect and build upon people's existing cultural values, rather than starting from notions of cultural redemption.

It would seem, then, the leisure scenario raises a number of difficulties for education. Some of them are soluble. Some, however, stem from the struc-tural difficulties within the leisure scenario itself (see chapter seven) – notably the relationship between the notion of the leisure class and the working class.

Implications of the work scenario

Some of these latter difficulties are again present within the work scenario, in which more attention begins to be paid, and more value attached, to forms of work outside paid employment. Because the distinction between the notions of employment and of work is less marked than the distinction between the notions of employment and of leisure, the difficulties are less acute. Nonetheless, it is salutary to recognize the extent to which the education system has come to reflect a bureaucratized view of society oriented towards employment rather than towards other forms of work. In particular, as we saw in chapter one, the main emphasis in much educational provision is on the acquisition not of useful skills, but of paper qualifications which provide passports to enter the appropriate positions within the bureaucratic structure (where appropriate training will, if needed, be duly provided). This structure breeds dependency, based on the notion that so long as students learn certain bodies of knowledge and are able to reproduce them in examinations (and then, if they wish, immediately forget them), they will have appropriate opportunities made available to them. According to this view, jobs are created and shaped by impersonal, institutional structures: all the individual has to do is to find ways of gaining entry to them. Education is important largely because it controls many of the access points. This view of education reflects, and reproduces, a culture which is alien to, for example, entrepreneurial activity. It can be seen in the gulf that exists between being 'school-wise' and 'street-wise'. (Kushner and Logan, 1981)

In the work-outside-employment part of the work scenario, the place of education would need to be very different. Its primary attention would need to be not on educational qualifications but on, for example, the development of skills and knowledge in ways which emphasized their direct utility. Certification would still be needed, but it would be primarily concerned with certifying competence to perform particular tasks. Handy (1980, p. 440) has suggested that the process of certification might accordingly be less tied to educational institutions, and instead might be increasingly controlled by professions and craft unions. These would accredit people's competence not on a time-serving basis but at times when they were ready to have their competence tested – rather as with music examinations at present.

Within educational institutions, the main focus would need to be on the development of skills and knowledge within contexts which would make it possible to demonstrate their applicability to practical tasks. One interesting model for the implementation of such ideas is provided by the Tvind schools in Denmark. (see e.g. Castles and Wüstenburg, 1979, pp. 175-82; Thomas, 1979) Here theoretical education is linked with practical skills to enable the students to develop immediate working roles of direct use to the school community: printers to produce school materials, car mechanics to repair and suitably equip school buses, food technologists to secure the economic foundations of communal life, builders for the school buildings, and so on. Pupils have to decide in the light of comparative figures whether, for example, it would be more profitable and cheaper to purchase more cows and pigs than to buy meat. Wrong decisions mean a rise in living costs which reduces other possibilities and causes irritation: students experience directly, and have to live with, the consequences of their decisions. The schools thus model in microcosm a community which maximizes the degree to which it can be self-sufficient.

An alternative model is for schools to become much more closely integrated with the community around them. Handy (1980), for example, suggests that formal learning might be spread more thinly throughout life and dispersed more widely in the community. Schools would supplement families as the centres of learning networks, rather than as closed institutions. Teachers would release their monopolistic claims on education. Institutionalized learning, which suited the institutional society created by the Industrial Revolution, would become as unimportant in the post-industrial society as it had been in pre-industrial society. Costello and Richardson (1982) make the same point:

in particular, black-economy products. (Gershuny and Pahl, 1979/80, pp. 129-30) The dangers and difficulties, in short, would be especially acute if the encouragement of the informal economies were permitted to (or used as an excuse to) erode the basis of the welfare state, and/or if partial or total dependence on such economies were forced upon weak sections of the community rather than being freely chosen by relatively capable individuals.

An integrated 'free' economy?

It will have been noted that many similar points have been made about self-employment and about the informal economies. There is clearly a strong link between the two. Handy (1982), for instance, has suggested that the black economy might be Britain's latent entrepreneurial sector, and has asked whether we are right to outlaw it so indiscriminately or whether clever tax laws could preserve its good elements while continuing to condemn its fraudulent aspects. (p. 2) This leads to the argument that the informal economies should be given more legitimacy and recognition so that in effect they could be more closely merged with the concept of self-employment.

Two main proposals are made. One is that more of the black economy should be brought into the formal economy by, for instance, instituting a Negative Income Tax system of the kind discussed in chapter seven. This would make it possible for the unemployed and other groups legitimately to retain a fair amount of whatever income is earned, instead of being encouraged to enter the black economy by being locked into the poverty traps created by rigid benefit systems.

The second proposal is that ways should be found of measuring − and thereby attaching value to − work within the household and communal economies. As we saw in chapter five, the concept of the Gross National Product is concerned only with work which has exchange-value, and pays no attention to other work which has only use-value, even though the latter may at times be more satisfying to the worker and more valuable to the community. Yet the GNP is frequently regarded as a measure of national goals and achievement. As Wirtz (1975) has pointed out in the USA:

> If a dress is sold in a store, its price goes into the GNP; if one is made at home, that doesn't count. Collecting fees for pay at a hospital parking lot increases the GNP; a day spent in volunteer work at the hospital doesn't . . . One wonders how our national priorities might change if we were advised regularly not just of the Gross National Product but of the Net National Achievement. (p. 166)

O'Toole *et al.* (1973, p. 179) have accordingly argued that housewives should be included in the labour force, that a money value should be assigned to their

If the productive fabric of society is in effect being de-industrialized and traditional assumptions of bringing people together in large groups to work together begin to be challenged, is it not also true that the industrial models which have been applied to educational institutions come under a similar challenge? (p. 6)

These sets of ideas are all built around the two concepts which Handy (1980, p. 437) describes as the 'core constructs of the emerging scenario': 'self-sufficiency' and 'community'. There are some tensions between the two concepts, reflecting the tensions identified in chapter nine between the entrpreneurial ethic and the communitarian ethic, both of which are embedded within the work scenario. The former emphasizes independence; the latter, interdependence. The former tends to stress economic values – how to spot market gaps, how to read balance sheets, etc.; the latter tends to stress social values – how to work together, how to help others in the community, etc. Both are, however, brought together in the concept of the 'community school' as envisaged, for example, by Peacock *et al.* (1982) and also by Hargreaves (1981). Hargreaves indeed refers to the need for community schools to foster simultaneously 'the productive orientation' and 'skills that are important to community participation and control'. (p. 204) What both ethics share is a hostility to the dependency generated by much of the present educational system. They also share a hostility to the fact that, in order to distinguish some young people as 'successes', this system by definition and design labels large numbers of others as 'failures', and does so in relation to narrow criteria which have little if any relevance to capability. The essence of the community school as conceived by Hargreaves and by Peacock *et al.* is that it seeks to value and develop pupils' self-confidence, their capacity to take initiatives, and their willingness to take responsibility for their actions. Grounded in the realities of the contexts in which people live, it seeks to draw learning out of their personal experiences, to develop skills and knowledge which will enable them to take more control over their lives, and to affirm their sense of their own value and their own potency. It also seeks to involve others in the community as active partners in the learning process.

The difficulty with such objectives is that they are difficult to attain unless they are implemented throughout the educational system. While educational provision based on these objectives sits side by side with formal examination courses leading towards the more élite jobs, the aims built into its content and process tend to be undermined by its structural position. *What* is done is outweighed by the impact of the 'label' attached to it. This is certainly often the case within schools at present. For instance, Woods (cited in Hargreaves, 1982, pp. 117-8) quotes a pupil on an examination course talking about those on a community studies course as saying:

They can't learn in Maths and English, and that sort of thing, but they learn about the community.

A number of the community studies course students recognized the same message:

> I think the community service was just to get us out of school so that other kids could have a lesson, just to let other people look after us for a bit so other children could have the teachers.

The effects of such perceptions are often stronger than, and therefore effectively undermine, the benign intentions of community studies and other attempts at more 'relevant' learning.

This problem again reflects the wider structural issue, discussed in chapter nine, of the relationship in the work scenario between work outside the formal economy and work within, in particular, the institutional monoliths where much wealth and power are likely to continue to be concentrated. If the gulf is large, it will make educational reforms difficult. If the élite jobs remain firmly entrenched within the bureaucratic sector of the formal economy, accessible only to those who acquire the appropriate credentials, there is a danger that those educated in accordance with an alternative model will be rigidly excluded from such jobs. Accordingly, many students (and their parents) will resist the alternative, much as they might be attracted to it in terms of what it is trying to achieve.

We are back here to the choice within a hierarchically divided society between what Turner (1960) calls a 'contest' system and a 'sponsored' system. (see the dicussion of this in chapter one) The continuing dilemma is that a 'contest' system which aims to give all youngsters a chance to enter high-status jobs is likely to adopt an educational structure and curriculum that is at best relevant only to the needs of the 'winners' and leaves the 'losers' high and dry; whereas a 'sponsored' system which attempts to serve the future needs of different groups tends to entrench further the existing socio-economic divisions in society. In the end, the only ways out of this dilemma are for the inequalities to be reduced to a point where alternatives are less likely to be evaluated in terms of their positions in the hierarchy, and/or for the recognition to take place that the structural and curricular changes proposed in response to work outside employment will also be appropriate for the more traditional forms of employment. In the latter respect, the growing recognition among some employers that the qualities they have long demanded are ill-served by the examination system and by the dominance of the academic tradition (see e.g. the quotation in chapter two from Marsden, 1983) is at least a small, hopeful sign.

There are two further points that need to be made. The first is to recognize the extent of the pressures to develop new formal institutional structures in response to youth unemployment, rather than to permit the loosening of such structures, as implied by the work scenario. The solutions posed vary: extended education and training, work experience, national service, national community service. All, though, tend to have a strong custodial character, and because of this, to encourage dependency. Some of the structures have more capacity for 'informality' than others: the decentralized nature of YOP, for example, permitted some schemes to develop more expressive and creative structures. (see chapter four) If, however, a youth opportunities programme were to be devised for the work scenario, it would have to permit and encourage not only work experience and training in useful skills, but also opportunities to develop projects based on self-employment, co-operatives, community business ventures, skill exchanges, etc. Rather than simply presenting work tasks to young people, it would need to encourage them to take an active role in identifying needs in the local community, and in developing ways of meeting those needs.

The second point is that if tolerable and acceptable relationships are to be established within the work scenario between the formal economy and the informal economies, or – more pertinently, perhaps – between the 'institutional' economy and the 'free' economy (see chapter nine), this will require a strong element of political education. A danger with the notion of encouraging self-sufficiency and entrepreneurship is that it focuses people's attention on immediate ways in which they can 'make out' within their own particular situations, and distracts them from attending to the larger social structures of which they are part. Yet these structures determine the terms on which the exercise of their efforts is based and the resources to which they have access. The energies required to construct one's own local ways of survival can easily leave the continuing power and wealth of the large institutional structures unquestioned and therefore reinforced. A 'work scenario' society that claimed to be democratic would need in its educational provision to seek to enable all its citizens not only to take more control over their own lives but also to play their part in determining the nature of the social structures within which their lives would be lived.

It would thus seem that the work scenario implies major changes within education. At least six such changes can be identified (these are adapted slightly from a list suggested to me by Elliot Stern of the Tavistock Institute of Human Relations):

1 *From* education as narrowly preparing for vocational and other 'slots' with little concern for developing a critical social awareness

To education as a broad preparation for life, including social understanding and awareness and social criticism

2 *From* education as a discrete experience, probably within and end-on to schooling

To education as a continuous lifelong process of learning

3 *From* education as based on limited access, involving selection of, rather than choice by, individuals

To education as based on open access, widely available in varied forms within which choices can be made

4 *From* education as a determinant of life-chances from an early age, on a basis which largely reproduces existing differentials and inequalities

To education as a catalyst for social mobility throughout life

5 *From* education as the prerogative of professionals based within the formal educational institutions

To education as a task shared by and sometimes led by nonprofessional educators

6 *From* education as a centralized activity based on 'core curricula' and centrally controlled standards

To education as a decentralized activity with curricula which are negotiated and evaluated locally

Where from here?

It is clear, then, that all of the scenarios can imply different educational structures from those which we have at present, and that the differences are particularly marked in the case of the leisure and work scenarios. The work scenario has been dwelt upon at more length than the others, partly because it offers particularly sharp contrasts to current educational provision, and partly because, of the three positive alternatives to the negativeness of the unemployment scenario, it is the one that seems most tangible and accessible at present.

There are limits to the extent to which educational providers can afford to base their provision on any particular scenario in advance of the societal changes necessary to *create* that scenario. At present the uncertainties about the likely directions of these changes tend to cloud the vision and constrain the creativity of people working in education. The result is a mixture of conservatism and confusion, reflecting the conservatism and confusion in society at large. It seems to stem from a sense that we are moving into a postindustrial society, but that we do not yet have a clear idea of what this means, and that we are having to make the move at a time of sustained recession

when the constraints on economic growth are much more evident than the
opportunities offered by the productive power of advanced technology.

Accordingly, it is unclear whether – in terms of Maslow's (1954) hierarchy
of needs – the future in advanced industrial societies is likely to permit
increased attention to be paid to the need for 'self-actualization' (i.e. people's
need to fulfil the potential that lies within them) or whether it is going to
require, for example, regression to the primacy of basic psychological and
safety needs. This is an important issue for educators. In principle,
technological developments could mean that robots could be used to do the
kind of work to which many people have been condemned in the past – work
requiring no skills, and no training. Accordingly, there could be increased
scope for education to release and develop the full range of people's talents,
creativity and energies. This cannot be done, however, unless societal
structures are developed which enable these attributes to be expressed and
harnessed. At present, the status of the unemployed tends to be defined in
ways which actively inhibit such expression. (see chapter six) And
educational expenditure, far from being greatly expanded – as proposed, for
example, by Stonier (1983) – has been cut.

In this situation, educators tend to talk about the need to develop people's
'flexibility', 'adaptability' and 'coping skills'; and about the need to develop
within each individual a sense of self-confidence or personal worth that is not
dependent on external measures like examination certificates or securing a
job. The notion that personal development can be abstracted from social
contexts in this way is a delusion. People's sense of themselves is crucially
affected by the messages that are fed back to them about their place in their
immediate community and the wider society. Unless 'flexibility' and
'adaptability' are related to this kind of awareness, they become mere
pliability and acquiescence.

The delusion is, moreover, dangerous in its effects. As Hargreaves (1982)
points out:

> It leaves teachers with the false impression that they do not need to ask the two
> key questions – what kind of society do we want, and how is education to help
> us to realize that society – and can ask only – what kind of individuals do we
> want and how can education help to create such individuals? (p. 92)

In doing so, it reinforces the *status quo*. To claim to be apolitical is itself a
political position, of an essentially conservative nature.

Education, therefore, needs to have a view of the future. If it does not, it
will be likely to be 'framed' by a view of the present, or (more probably) a
view of the past, or (more probably still) a view of an idealized past that
never existed. Waller (1932, p. 34) pointed out how communities tend to use

schools in particular as a 'museum of virtue': as repositories for certain ideals which they wish to keep alive, even though these ideals have less and less accordance with the realities adults perceive in their own lives. Schools and other educational institutions could thus in practice become shrines for the continued veneration of idealized forms of employment – worshipped not directly but through the graven images of educational qualifications – without making any contribution to generating the social changes required to make such employment available to those who want it, or to create other positive alternatives.

To break out of this, schools need alternative visions to respond to. They must also resist pressures to tighten their boundaries, and instead should seek to establish more active links with the communities of which they are part. These links need to go far beyond the fund-raising activities to which they are often confined at present. They should involved, for example, people in the community being used as resources for learning, adults learning alongside children, and possibly the restructuring of school time. This will both expose schools to the realities of what is happening around them, and will enable the school alongside other educational institutions to play a more active role in helping communities to develop constructive responses to the problems they face.

Not only do educational institutions themselves need to have a view of the future, but perhaps they should devote at least some attention to exploring *possible, probable* and *preferable* societal futures with their students. (Toffler, 1974) At present, schools in particular do very little to help students think about what the future may be like, and what its implications are for them: the curriculum tends to look backwards rather than forwards, and so to be constantly in danger of perpetuating redundant images, attitudes and values. Yet for individuals to be autonomous, they need to have the capacity to conceive of possible selves in possible futures. (Law, 1981a) Perhaps, therefore, some space should be found within the curriculum for 'future studies', as was done in one of the schools described in chapter three.

The notion of teaching for the future presents obvious pedagogic problems. Many teachers may feel uncomfortable about a curriculum which, by definition, will not be based on a fixed body of knowledge over which they can claim mastery. There may also be difficulties in achieving credibility with students whose sense of 'relevance' may be firmly grounded in the present. A careful balance will need to be sought between fantasy and creative thinking (e.g. use of science fiction) on the one hand, and well-grounded realism (e.g. looking at changes in the recent past as a basis for understanding the concept of 'change') on the other. The aim should be, as Toffler (1974) puts it, 'not to create elegantly complex, well-ordered, accurate images of the future, but to help learners cope with real-life crises, opportunities and perils'; and to strengthen their ability to participate in shaping the direction of change, 'whether through invention, informed acquiescence, or through intelligent resistance'. (p. 13) For example, a futures approach implies that, in teaching science and technology, attention should be paid to social and ethical implications. In such ways, the curriculum can provide a social context for the aim of developing adaptability and flexibility, in a way which makes this aim tenable. Moreover, a curriculum that is focused towards the future – and explicitly so at some points – may be a more appropriate basis for reacting creatively to the present than a curriculum focused towards the past.

Not the least of the potential merits of future studies is that it helps students to establish some understanding of the relationship between personal and political levels of action. The capacity for political theorizing is no substitute for practical capability. On its own, it can easily become arid and sterile. Political change comes as much from the personal action of living – from people responding in practical ways to the situations with which they are confronted – as from political rhetoric. As Gorz (1982, p. 11) puts it, 'no new liberties can be granted from above, by institutionalized power, unless they have already been taken and put into practice by people themselves'. At the same time, however, the ability to understand the wider context for one's actions means that one is able to take fuller responsibility for the broader effects of these actions, and to consider the possibility of acting to change the context where this seems necessary or appropriate.

This is particularly important in relation to the future of work. We have pointed out that to exclude political discussion is a political standpoint, but one that entrenches the *status quo* by preventing if from being subjected to criticism. Yet we have also argued in chapter ten that, of the four scenarios we have presented, the one that is closest to the *status quo* – the unemployment scenario – is much the least desirable.

The underlying question here is whether the role of education is to reproduce the *status quo* or to transform it. The notion that education can be a significant *agent* of social change is now somewhat discredited. Nonetheless, it is clear that education can be a *catalyst* of change, or can be an *obstacle* to change. The importance of the initiatives described in chapters three and four, modest as many of them are, is that they represent a potential for catalysing change. This potential could be especially strong if such responses and initiatives could be linked to a framework which would enable teachers and students to explore their wider implications. My main hope for this book is that it may help them to develop innovation within such a framework.

Summary

Chapter eleven has explored the implications for education of the scenarios presented in part II of the book. Only the employment scenario permits the satisfactory maintenance of current educational structures (and even this scenario does not require it). The unemployment scenario makes it likely that attempts to defend the *status quo* will become increasingly frenzied and increasingly ineffective. The leisure scenario presents problems because of the gulf between the attitudes and skills that would be required by the 'new working class' and the 'new leisure class'; moreover, there are difficulties both in the concept of education-as-leisure and in the concept of education-for-leisure. Some of these difficulties recur in the work scenario, but in a less acute form; to attach increased attention and value to work outside employment would, however, challenge the present bureaucratic structure of the educational system, and the practices within it which tend to foster the dependency characteristic of bureaucratized employment. It has been argued that education needs a view of the future: that to talk of 'flexibility', 'adaptability' etc. as if they can be abstracted from social contexts is delusory. It has also been suggested that 'future studies' should be incorporated into the curriculum. Educational institutions should not allow themselves by design or default to reinforce the negative *status quo* of the unemployment scenario, but should seek to act as catalysts of change towards more positive scenarios of the future.

References

Advisory Council for Adult and Continuing Education: *Education for Unemployed Adults*. Leicester: ACACE, 1982

Allen, R.: *The Economic Effects of a Shorter Working Week*. Government Economic Service Working Paper No. 33. London: HM Treasury, 1980 (mimeo)

Annett, J., Wilson, J., and Piech, J.: 'Skill Loss, Part 1: Opinion and Experiment'. *Journal of European Industrial Training*, Volume 5 No. 7, 1981

Anthony, P.D.: *The Ideology of Work*. London: Tavistock, 1977

Arendt, H.: *The Human Condition*. Chicago: University of Chicago Press, 1958

Aristotle: *Politics*. Edited and translated by John Warrington. London: Dent, 1959 ed. (written 4th century BC)

Arnold, E., Huggett, C., Senker, P., Swords-Isherwood, N., and Shannon, C.Z.: *Microelectronics and Women's Employment in Britain*. Falmer: Science Policy Research Unit, University of Sussex, 1982

Ashton, D.N., and Field, D.: *Young Workers*. London: Hutchinson, 1976

Ashton, D.N., Maguire, M.A., and Garland, V.: *Youth in the Labour-Market*. London: Department of Employment, 1982

Association for Adult and Continuing Education: 'More than an Alternative to Work'. *NATFHE Journal*, Volume 7 No. 3, April-May 1982

Atkinson, A.B.: 'Unemployment Benefits and Incentives'. In Creedy, J.: *The Economics of Unemployment in Britain*. London: Butterworths, 1981

Atkinson, P., Rees, T.L., Shone, D., and Williamson, H.: 'Social and Life Skills: the Latest Case of Compensatory Education'. In Rees, T.L., and Atkinson, P. (eds.): *Youth Unemployment and State Intervention*. London: Routledge & Kegan Paul, 1982

Bacon, R., and Eltis, W.: *Britain's Economic Problems: Too Few Producers*. London: Macmillan, 1976

Bakke, E.W.: *The Unemployed Man*. London: Nisbet, 1933

Bakke, E.W.: 'The Cycle of Adjustment to Unemployment'. In Bell, N.W., and Vogel, E.F. (eds.): *A Modern Introduction to the Family*. London: Routledge & Kegan Paul, 1960

Balogh, J.: *Profile Reports for School-Leavers*. London: Longman Resources Unit/Schools Council, 1982

Banks, M.H., Mullings, C., and Jackson, E.J.: 'A Bench-Mark for Youth Opportunities'. *Employment Gazette*, Volume 91 No. 3, March 1983

Banks, O.: *The Sociology of Education* (3rd edition). London: Batsford, 1976

Barron, I., and Curnow, R.: *The Future of Microelectronics: Forecasting the Effects of Information Technology*. London: Frances Pinter, 1979

Barron, R.D., and Norris, G.M.: 'Sexual Divisions and the Dual Labour Market'. In Barker, D.L., and Allen, S. (eds.): *Dependence and Exploitation in Work and Marriage*. London: Longman, 1976

Barry, J., and O'Connor, D.: 'Costs and Benefits of Sponsoring the Unemployed'. *Employment Gazette*, Volume 90 No. 3, March 1982

Bayly, L.P.: *The Work Experience Programme.* London: Manpower Services Commission, 1978 (mimeo)

Bazalgette, J.: *School Life and Work Life.* London: Hutchinson, 1978(a)

Bazalgette, J.: 'Freedom and Authority in the Relations Between Teachers and Taught'. In Blackham, J. (ed.): *Education for Autonomy.* London: Bedford Square Press, 1978(b)

Beck, J.: 'Education, Industry and the Needs of the Economy'. *Cambridge Journal of Education,* Volume 11 No. 2, 1981

Becker, G.S.: *Human Capital: a Theoretical and Empirical Analysis, with Special Reference to Education.* New York: National Bureau of Economic Research, 1964

Bedeman, T., and Courtenay, G.: *One in Three.* Special Programmes Research and Development Series No. 13. Sheffield: Manpower Services Commission, 1983

Bedeman, T., and Harvey, J.: *Young People on YOP.* Special Programmes Research and Development Series No. 3. London: Manpower Services Commission, 1981

Bell, D.: *The Coming of Post Industrial Society.* London: Heinemann, 1974

Berg, I.: *Education and Jobs: the Great Training Robbery.* Harmondsworth: Penguin, 1970

Beveridge, W.H.: *Full Employment in a Free Society.* London: Allen & Unwin, 1944

Beynon, H.: *Working for Ford.* Wakefield: EP Publishing, 1975

Boor, M.: 'Relationship Between Unemployment Rates and Suicide Rates in Eight Countries, 1962-1976'. *Psychological Reports,* Volume 47, 1980

Bosanquet, N., and Doeringer, P.B.: 'Is There a Dual Labour Market in Great Britain?' *Economic Journal,* Volume 83 No. 330, 1973

Bourdieu, P., and Passeron, J.C.: *Reproduction in Education, Society and Culture.* London: Sage, 1977

Bowles, S., and Gintis, H.: *Schooling in Capitalist America.* London: Routledge & Kegan Paul, 1976

Box, S., and Hale, C.: 'Economic Crisis and the Rising Prisoner Population in England and Wales'. *Crime and Social Justice,* Volume 17, Summer 1982

Bradley, K.: 'A Comparative Analysis of Producer Co-operatives: Some Theoretical and Empirical Implications'. *British Journal of Industrial Relations,* Volume 18 No. 2, July 1980

Brandt, W., *et al.*: *North-South: a Programme for Survival.* London: Pan, 1980

Brandt, W., *et al.*: *Common Crisis.* London: Pan, 1983

Braverman, H.: *Labor and Monopoly Capital.* New York: Monthly Review Press, 1974

Bray, E.: 'Mini-Co's in Schools'. In Watts, A.G. (ed.): *Work Experience and Schools.* London: Heinemann, 1983

Brenner, M.H.: *Estimating the Social Costs of National Economic Policy: Implications for Mental and Physical Health, and Criminal Aggression.* Joint Economic Committee of Congress, Employment Paper No. 5. Washington, DC: US Government Printing Office, 1976 (mimeo)

Brenner, M.H.: 'Health Costs and Benefits of Economic Policy'. *International Journal of Health Services,* Volume 7 No. 4, 1977(a)

Brenner, M.H.: 'Personal Stability and Economic Security'. *Social Policy,* Volume 8 No. 1, May/June 1977(b)

Brenner, M.H.: 'Unemployment, Economic Growth, and Mortality'. *The Lancet,* No. 8117, 24 March 1979(a)

Brenner, M.H.: 'Mortality and the National Economy: a Review, and the Experience of England and Wales, 1936–76'. *The Lancet*, No. 8142, 15 September 1979(b)

Brenner, M.H.: 'Unemployment and Health'. *The Lancet*, No. 8251, 17 October 1981

Brett, P.: 'Unemployment – What Can Be Done?' Industrial Committee Working Paper 11. London: Church of England General Synod Board for Social Responsibility, 1981 (mimeo)

Bridges, D.: 'Teachers and "the World of Work" '. In Elliott, J., Bridges, D., Ebbutt, D., Gibson, R., and Nias, J.: *School Accountability*. London: Grant McIntyre, 1981

Briggs, A. (ed.): *William Morris: Selected Writings and Designs*. Harmondsworth: Penguin, 1962

Bromley, R., and Gerry, C. (eds.): *Casual Work and Poverty in Third World Cities*. Chichester: Wiley, 1979

Brown, R.: 'The Price of Special Measures'. *Management Today*, March 1979

Bryant, J.: 'An Introductory Bibliography to Work in the Informal Economy in Third World Literature'. In Laite, J. (ed.): *Bibliographies on Local Labour Markets and the Informal Economy*. London: Social Science Research Council, 1982 (mimeo)

Burgess, E.W.: *Aging in Western Societies*. Chicago: University of Chicago Press, 1960

Burns, S.: *The Household Economy*. Boston: Beacon, 1975

Calouste Gulbenkian Foundation: *Community Business Works*. London: Calouste Gulbenkian Foundation, 1982(a)

Calouste Gulbenkian Foundation: *The Arts in Schools*. London: Calouste Gulbenkian Foundation, 1982(b)

Carlyle, T.: *Past and Present*. Oxford: Clarendon Press, 1918 (first published 1843)

Castles, S., and Wüstenberg, W.: *The Education of the Future*. London: Pluto Press, 1979

Central Policy Review Staff: *Education, Training and Industrial Performance*. London: HMSO, 1980

Central Statistical Office: *Social Trends 12*. London: HMSO, 1981

Centre for Contemporary Cultural Studies: *Unpopular Education: Schooling and Social Democracy in England since 1944*. London: Hutchinson, 1981

Chanan, G.: 'To Sustain Life – Schools' Concepts of Adult Work'. *New Universities Quarterly*, Volume 31 No. 1, Winter 1976/7

Clark, C.: *The Conditions of Economic Progress*. London: Macmillan, 1940

Clayre, A.: *Work and Play*. London: Weidenfeld & Nicolson, 1974

Clemitson, I., and Rodgers, G.: *A Life to Live: Beyond Full Employment*. London: Junction Books, 1981

Cohen, S.: *Folk Devils and Moral Panics*. London: MacGibbon & Kee, 1972

Collins, R.: *The Credential Society*. New York: Academic Press, 1979

Colombatto, A.: *A Nationwide Social Service: a Proposal for the 1980s*. Centre for Labour Economics Discussion Paper No. 84. London: London School of Economics and Political Science, 1980 (mimeo)

Community Business Ventures Unit: *Whose Business is Business?* London: Calouste Gulbenkian Foundation, 1981

Confederation of British Industry: *Unemployment – a Challenge for Us All*. Report of CBI Steering Group on Unemployment. London: CBI, 1982

Consumers Association: 'How You Rate Your Job'. *Money Which?* September 1977

Cooper, N.: *School-Industry Link Schemes: a Study and Recommendations*. London:

Department of Education and Science, 1981 (mimeo)

Costello, N., and Richardson, M. (eds.): *Continuing Education for the Post-Industrial Society*. Milton Keynes: Open University Press, 1982

Daniel, W.W.: *The Unemployed Flow: Stage 1 Interim Report*. London: Policy Studies Institute, 1981 (mimeo)

Dauncey, G.: *Facing Unemployment*. Cambridge: CRAC/Hobsons, 1983

Davies, B.: *From Social Education to Social and Life Skills Training: In Whose Interests?* Occasional Paper 19. Leicester: National Youth Bureau, 1979

Davies, R., Hamill, L., Moylan, S., and Slee, C.H.: 'Incomes In and Out of Work'. *Employment Gazette*, Volume 90 No. 6, June 1982

Daws, P.P.: 'Are Careers Education Programmes in Schools a Waste of Time? – a Reply to Roberts'. *British Journal of Guidance and Counselling*, Volume 5 No. 1, January 1977

Daws, P.P.: 'The Socialization/Opportunity-Structure Theory of the Occupational Location of School Leavers: a Critical Appraisal'. In Watts, A.G., Super, D.E., and Kidd, J.M. (eds.): *Career Development in Britain*. Cambridge: CRAC/Hobsons, 1981

de Grazia, R.: 'Clandestine Employment: a Problem of our Times'. *International Labour Review*, Volume 119 No. 5, September–October 1980

Deacon, A.: 'The Scrounging Controversy: Public Attitudes Towards the Unemployed in Contemporary Britain'. *Social and Economic Administration*, Volume 12 No. 2, Summer 1978

Deacon, A.: 'Unemployment and Politics in Britain since 1945'. In Showler, B., and Sinfield, A. (eds.): *The Workless State*. Oxford: Martin Robertson, 1981

Department of Education and Science: *Careers Education in Secondary Schools*. Education Survey 18. London: HMSO, 1973

Department of Education and Science: *Educating Our Children*. London: HMSO, 1977(a)

Department of Education and Science: *Education in Schools: a Consultative Document*. London: HMSO, 1977(b)

Department of Education and Science: *Aspects of Secondary Education in England: a Survey by HM Inspectors of Schools*. London: HMSO, 1979(a)

Department of Education and Science: *Local Authority Arrangements for the School Curriculum*. London: HMSO, 1979(b)

Department of Education and Science: *Proposals for a Certificate of Extended Education* (Keohane Report). London: HMSO, 1979(c)

Department of Education and Science: *A Framework for the School Curriculum*. London: HMSO, 1980(a)

Department of Education and Science: *A View of the Curriculum*. HMI Matters for Discussion Series No. 11. London: HMSO, 1980(b)

Department of Education and Science: *The School Curriculum*. London: HMSO, 1981

Department of Education and Science: *17+: a New Qualification*. London: HMSO, 1982(a)

Department of Education and Science: *English School Leavers 1980-81*. Statistical Bulletin 10/82. London: DES, 1982(b)

Department of Education and Science: *Projections of School Leavers to 1990-91 with an Estimate for 1995-96*. Statistical Bulletin 6/83. London: DES, 1983

Department of Employment: 'New Estimates of Employment on a Continuous Basis: Employers and the Self-Employed 1961-1974'. *Department of Employment Gazette,* Volume 84 No. 12, December 1976

Department of Employment: 'Measures to Alleviate Unemployment in the Medium Term: Work-Sharing'. *Department of Employment Gazette,* Volume 86 No. 4, April 1978

Department of Employment: 'An Increase in Earlier Retirement for Men'. *Employment Gazette,* Volume 88 No. 4, April 1980

Department of Employment: 'Numbers of Self-Employed People 1971-1979'. *Employment Gazette,* Volume 90 No. 1, January 1982

Department of Employment: 'Statistical Series'. *Employment Gazette,* Volume 91 No. 1, January 1983(a)

Department of Employment: 'How Many Self-Employed?' *Employment Gazette,* Volume 91 No. 2, February 1983(b)

Department of Employment: 'Statistical Series'. *Employment Gazette,* Volume 91 No. 4, April 1983(c)

Department of Employment/Department of Health and Social Security: *Payment of Benefits to Unemployed People.* London: HMSO, 1981

Departmental Committee on Juvenile Education in Relation to Employment After the War: *Final Report.* London: HMSO, 1917

Departments of Industry and Trade: 'Insolvencies in England and Wales: November'. *British Business,* Volume 9 No. 15, 17 December 1982

Departments of Industry and Trade: 'New Companies Registered in Britain: November'. *British Business,* Volume 10 No. 2, 14-20 January 1983

Dilnot, A.W., and Morris, C.N.: 'The Exchequer Costs of Unemployment'. *Fiscal Studies,* Volume 2 No. 3, November 1981

Doeringer, P.B., and Piore, M.J.: *Internal Labor Markets and Manpower Analysis.* Lexington, Massachusetts: Heath, 1971

Donovan, A., and Oddy, M.: 'Psychological Aspects of Unemployment: an Investigation into the Emotional and Social Adjustments of School Leavers'. *Journal of Adolescence,* Volume 5 No. 1, March 1982

Dore, R.: *The Diploma Disease.* London: Allen & Unwin, 1976

Douglas, C.H.: *Economic Democracy.* London: Palmer, 1920

Drucker, P.: *The Age of Discontinuity.* London: Heinemann, 1969

Dumazedier, J.: *Toward a Society of Leisure* (translated by S.E. McClure). New York: Free Press, 1967

Dumazedier, J.: *Sociology of Leisure.* Amsterdam: Elsevier, 1974

Durkheim, E.: *Suicide.* London: Routledge & Kegan Paul, 1952 (first published 1897)

Eccles, T.: *Under New Management.* London: Pan, 1981

Ecology Party: *Working for a Future.* London: Ecology Party, 1980

Economist Intelligence Unit: *Coping with Unemployment: the Effects on the Unemployed Themselves.* London: EIU, 1982

Edgley, R.: 'Education for Industry'. *Educational Research,* Volume 20 No. 1, November 1977

Eisenberg, P., and Lazarsfeld, P.F.: 'The Psychological Effects of Unemployment'. *Psychological Bulletin,* Volume 35 No. 8, June 1938

Entwistle, H.: *Education, Work and Leisure.* London: Routledge & Kegan Paul, 1970

Entwistle, H.: *Class, Culture and Education.* London: Methuen, 1978

Equal Opportunities Commission: *Job-Sharing: Improving the Quality and Availability of Part-Time Work.* Manchester: EOC, 1981

Eyer, J.: 'Prosperity as a Cause of Death'. *International Journal of Health Services,* Volume 7 No. 1, 1977(a)

Eyer, J.: 'Does Unemployment Cause the Death Rate Peak in Each Business Cycle?: a Multifactor Model of Death Rate Change'. *International Journal of Health Services,* Volume 7 No. 4, 1977(b)

Fagin, L.: *Unemployment and Health in Families.* London: Department of Health and Social Security, 1981 (mimeo)

Feige, E.: 'The UK's Unobserved Economy: a Preliminary Assessment'. *Journal of Economic Affairs,* Volume 1 No. 4, July 1981

Ferman, L.A., and Berndt, L.E.: 'The Irregular Economy'. In Henry, S. (ed.): *Can I Have It In Cash?* London: Astragal, 1981

Field, F.: 'Unhappy Returns'. *New Society,* No. 909, 6 March 1980

Finn, D.: 'Whose Needs? Schooling and the "Needs" of Industry'. In Rees, T.L., and Atkinson, P. (eds.): *Youth Unemployment and State Intervention.* London: Routledge & Kegan Paul, 1982

Fisher, J.: 'Popular Planning and Educational Aspects'. Paper delivered at a Foundation for Education with Production conference on 'Has Work a Future?' held at University College, Cardiff, April 1983 (mimeo)

Fleisher, B.M.: 'The Effect of Unemployment on Juvenile Delinquency'. *Journal of Political Economy,* Volume 71 No. 6, December 1963

Fleming, D., and Lavercombe, S.: *Ready for the Real World?* Summary Report. Sheffield: Department of Education Studies, Sheffield City Polytechnic, 1979 (mimeo)

Fleming, D., and Lavercombe, S.: 'Talking About Unemployment with School-Leavers'. *British Journal of Guidance and Counselling,* Volume 10 No. 1, January 1982

Floud, J., Halsey, A.H., and Martin, F.M.: *Social Class and Educational Opportunity.* London: Heinemann, 1956

Flude, R., and Parrott, A.: *Education and the Challenge of Change.* Milton Keynes: Open University Press, 1979

Fragnière, G.: *Education without Frontiers.* London: Duckworth, 1976

Franey, R.: *Poor Law.* London: CHAR/CPAG/CDC/NAPO/NCCL, 1983

Freud, S.: *Civilization and its Discontents.* London: Hogarth, 1930

Friedan, B.: *The Second Stage.* London: Michael Joseph, 1982

Friedman, M., and Friedman, R.: *Free to Choose.* London: Secker & Warburg, 1980

Frith, S.: 'Dancing in the Streets'. *Time Out,* 20 March 1981

Further Education Curriculum Review and Development Unit: *A Basis for Choice* (Mansell Report). London: FEU, 1979

Further Education Curriculum Review and Development Unit: *Developing Social and Life Skills.* London: FEU, 1980

Gabor, D.: *Inventing the Future.* Harmondsworth: Penguin, 1964

Galbraith, J.K.: *The Affluent Society* (2nd edition). Harmondsworth: Penguin, 1970

Gallacher, J., Ohri, A., and Roberts, L.: 'Unemployment and Community Action'.

Community Development Journal, Volume 18 No. 1, January 1983

Galland, O., and Louis, M.-V.: 'Chômage et Action Collective'. *Sociologie du Travail,* No. 2/81, April-June 1981

Garraty, J.A.: *Unemployment in History.* New York: Harper & Row, 1978

Gershuny, J.I.: *After Industrial Society?: the Emerging Self-Service Economy.* London: Macmillan, 1978

Gershuny, J.I.: 'The Informal Economy: its Role in Post-Industrial Society'. *Futures,* Volume 11 No. 1, February 1979

Gershuny, J.I.: 'The Social Division of Labour: Working Time and Economic Development'. Falmer: Social Policy Research Unit, University of Sussex, 1980(a) (mimeo)

Gershuny, J.I.: 'The Prospects for "the Alternative Programme": Time-Budget Evidence on the Future of Work'. Falmer: Social Policy Research Unit, University of Sussex, 1980(b) (mimeo)

Gershuny, J.I., and Pahl, R.E.: 'Work Outside Employment: Some Preliminary Speculations'. *New Universities Quarterly,* Volume 34 No. 1, Winter 1979/80

Gershuny, J.I., and Pahl, R.E.: 'Britain in the Decade of the Three Economies'. *New Society,* No 900, 3 January 1980

Ginsburg, M.B., Meyenn, R.J., and Miller, H.D.R.: 'Teachers, the "Great Debate" and Education Cuts'. *Westminster Studies in Education,* Volume 2, 1979

Gladstone, F.: 'Crime and the Crystal Ball'. *Home Office Research Unit Bulletin,* No. 7, 1979

Goacher, B.: *Recording Achievement at 16+.* York: Longman Resources Unit/Schools Council, 1983

Golding, P., and Middleton, S.: *Images of Welfare: Press and Public Attitudes to Poverty.* Oxford: Martin Robertson, 1982

Goodson, I.F.: *School Subjects and Curriculum Change.* London: Croom Helm, 1983

Gorz, A.: *Farewell to the Working Class.* London: Pluto Press, 1982

Gravelle, H.S.E., Hutchinson, G., and Stern, J.: 'Mortality and Unemployment: a Critique of Brenner's Time-Series Analysis'. *The Lancet,* No. 8248, 26 September 1981

Gray, J., McPherson, A.F., and Raffe, D.: *Reconstructions of Secondary Education.* London: Routledge & Kegan Paul, 1983

Greaves, K., Gostyn, P., and Bonsall, C.: *Off the Job Training on YOP.* Special Programmes Research and Development Series No. 12. Sheffield: Manpower Services Commission, 1982

Green, V.H.H.: *Renaissance and Reformation.* London: Arnold, 1952

Grubb, W.N., and Lazerson, M.: 'Vocational Solutions to Youth Problems: the Persistent Frustrations of the American Experience'. *Educational Analysis,* Volume 3 No. 2, 1981

Gurney, R.M.: 'The Effects of Unemployment on the Psycho-Social Development of Young People'. *Journal of Occupational Psychology,* Volume 53, 1980

Gurney, R.M.: 'Leaving School, Facing Unemployment, and Making Attributions about the Causes of Unemployment'. *Journal of Vocational Behavior,* Volume 18 No. 1, February 1981

Halsey, A.H.: 'Sociology and the Equality Debate'. *Oxford Review of Education,*

Volume 1 No. 1, 1975

Hammermesh, D.S., and Soss, N.M.: 'An Economic Theory of Suicide'. *Journal of Political Economy*, Volume 82 No. 1, January/February 1974

Handy, C.: 'The Challenge of Industrial Society'. In Reedy, S., and Woodhead, M. (eds.): *Family, Work and Education*. London: Hodder & Stoughton/Open University Press, 1980

Handy, C.: *The Informal Economy*. Wivenhoe, Essex: Association of Researchers in Voluntary Action and Community Involvement, 1982

Handy, C.: *The Future of Work: a View of the Problems and Possibilities*. Windsor: St George's House, n.d. .

Hansen, J.: 'The Real Black Economy'. *New Society*, No. 884, 13 September 1979

Hargreaves, D.: 'Unemployment, Leisure and Education'. *Oxford Review of Education*, Volume 7 No. 3, 1981

Hargreaves, D.: *The Challenge for the Comprehensive School*. London: Routledge & Kegan Paul, 1982

Harris, K.: *Teachers and Classes: a Marxist Analysis*. London: Routledge & Kegan Paul, 1982

Harrison, R.: 'The Demoralizing Experience of Prolonged Unemployment'. *Department of Employment Gazette*, Volume 84 No. 4, April 1976

Hatch, S.: 'Change and Dissent in the Universities: an Examination of the Sources of Protest'. In Butcher, H.J., and Rudd, E. (eds.): *Contemporary Problems in Higher Education*. London: McGraw-Hill, 1972

Hawkins, K.: *Unemployment*. Harmondsworth: Penguin, 1979

Hayes, C.: 'Evaluation of Some Policy Options – the Contribution of Training'. In *Unemployment*. IMS Manpower Studies No. 7. Falmer: Institute of Manpower Studies, University of Sussex, 1983

Hayes, C., Fonda, N., Pope, M., Stuart, R., and Townsend, K.: *Training for Skill Ownership – Learning To Take It With You*. IMS Report No. 68. Falmer: Institute of Manpower Studies, University of Sussex, 1983

Hayes, C., Izatt, A., Morrison, J., Smith, H. and Townsend, C.: *Foundation Training Issues*. Falmer: Institute of Manpower Studies, University of Sussex, 1982

Hayes, J., and Nutman, P.: *Understanding the Unemployed*. London: Tavistock, 1981

Henry, S.: *The Hidden Economy: the Context and Control of Borderline Crime*. London: Robertson, 1978

Henry, S.: 'The Working Unemployed: Perspectives on the Informal Economy and Unemployment'. *Sociological Review*, Volume 30 No. 3, August 1982

Hepworth, S.J.: 'Moderating Factors of the Psychological Impact of Unemployment'. *Journal of Occupational Psychology*, Volume 53, 1980

Hilgendorf, L., and Welchman, R.: *Learning at Work*. Special Programmes Research and Development Series No. 9. London: Manpower Services Commission, 1982(a)

Hilgendorf, L., and Welchman, R.: 'Organizational and Social Issues in the Transfer and Use of Learning'. Learning at Work Development Project Working Paper No. 7. London: Tavistock Institute of Human Relations, 1982(b) (mimeo)

Hill, J.M.M.: 'The Psychological Impact of Unemployment'. *New Society*, No. 798, 19 January 1978

Hirsch, F.: *Social Limits to Growth*. London: Routledge & Kegan Paul, 1977

Holmes, S., and Lightfoot, M.: 'The World in the Classroom'. *Times Educational Supplement*, 30 January 1981

Hope, E., Kennedy, M., and de Winter, A.: 'Homeworkers in North London'. In Barker, D.L., and Allen, S. (eds.): *Dependence and Exploitation in Work and Marriage*. London: Longman, 1976

House of Commons Education, Science and Arts Committee: *The Secondary School Curriculum and Examinations: with Special Reference to the 14 to 16-Year-Old Age Group*, Volume 1. London: HMSO, 1981

House of Commons Expenditure Committee: *Thirteenth Report, Session 1977-78: People and Work, Volume 1*. London: HMSO, 1978

Hoyt, D.P.: 'The Relationship Between College Grades and Adult Achievement: a Review of the Literature'. Iowa City: American College Testing Program, 1965 (mimeo)

Huizinga, J.: *Homo Ludens*. London: Routledge & Kegan Paul, 1949

Hunt, A.: *The Elderly at Home*. London: HMSO, 1978

Illich, I.: *Tools for Conviviality*. London: Calder & Boyars, 1973

Illich, I.: *The Right to Useful Employment*. London: Marion Boyars, 1978

Incomes Data Services: *Cutting the Working Week*. Study 264. London: IDS, 1982

International Facts and Forecasting Ltd.: 'WEP Sponsors Survey'. London: IFF, 1978 (mimeo). (Not formally published, but reported in MSC house journal *Network*, August 1979)

International Labour Organization: *Employment, Incomes and Equality: a Strategy for Increasing Productive Employment in Kenya*. Geneva: ILO, 1972

Jackson, M.: 'Youth Opportunities . . . Pressure of Numbers'. *Times Educational Supplement*, 8 April 1983

Jaco, E.G.: *The Social Epidemiology of Mental Disorders – a Psychiatric Survey of Texas*. New York: Russell Sage Foundation, 1960

Jacobs, E., Orwell, S., Paterson, P., and Weltz, F.: *The Approach to Industrial Change in Britain and West Germany*. London: Anglo-German Foundation for the Study of Industrial Society, 1978

Jahoda, M.: 'The Impact of Unemployment in the 1930s and 1970s'. *Bulletin of the British Psychological Society*, Volume 32, August 1979

Jahoda. M.: *Employment and Unemployment: a Social-Psychological Analysis*. Cambridge: Cambridge University Press, 1982

Jahoda, M., and Rush, H.: *Work, Employment and Unemployment*. Falmer: Science Policy Research Unit, University of Sussex, 1980 (mimeo)

Jahoda, M., Lazarsfeld, P.F., and Zeisel, H..: *Marienthal: the Sociography of an Unemployed Community*. London: Tavistock, 1972 (first published 1933)

Jamieson, I., and Lightfoot, M.: *Schools and Industry*. London: Methuen, 1982

Jeffs, T.: *Youth Conscription: a Discussion of the Arguments against National Community Service for the Young Unemployed*. London: Youthaid, 1982 (mimeo)

Jenkins, C., and Sherman, B.: *The Collapse of Work*. London: Eyre Methuen, 1979

Johnson, P.: 'Unemployment and Self-Employment: a Survey'. *Industrial Relations Journal*, Volume 12 No. 5, September/October 1981

Jordan, B.: 'The Dole Volunteers'. *New Society*, No. 926, 14 August 1980

Jordan, B., and Drakeford, M.: 'Major Douglas, Money and the New Technology'.

New Society, No. 903, 24 January 1980

Joshi, H.E.: 'Secondary Workers in the Employment Cycle: Great Britain 1961-1974'. *Economica,* Volume 48 No. 189, 1981

Kahn, H., and Wiener, A.J.: *The Year 2000.* London: Macmillan, 1967

Kaplan, H.R., and Tausky, C.: 'Work and the Welfare Cadillac: the Function of and Commitment to Work among the Hard-Core Unemployed'. *Social Problems,* Volume 19 No. 4, Spring 1972

Kasl, S.V.: 'Changes in Mental Health Status Associated with Job Loss and Retirement'. In Barrett, J.E. (ed.): *Stress and Mental Disorder.* New York: Raven Press, 1979

Kasl, S.V., and Cobb, S.: 'Blood Pressure Changes in Men Undergoing Job Loss: a Preliminary Report'. *Psychosomatic Medicine,* Volume 32 No. 1, January-February 1970

Kasl, S.V., Gore, S., and Cobb, S.: 'The Experience of Losing a Job: Reported Changes in Health, Symptoms and Illness Behaviour'. *Psychosomatic Medicine,* Volume 37 No. 2, March-April 1975

Kellner, P.: 'Maggie's Missing Million'. *New Statesman,* No. 2610, 27 March 1981

Kelvin, P.: 'Social Psychology 2001: the Social Psychological Bases and Implications of Structural Unemployment'. In Gilmour, R., and Duck, S. (eds.): *The Development of Social Psychology.* London: Academic Press, 1980

Kelvin, P.: 'Work as a Source of Identity: the Implications of Unemployment'. *British Journal of Guidance and Counselling,* Volume 9 No. 1, January 1981

Keynes, J.M.: 'Economic Possibilities for our Grandchildren'. In *Essays in Persuasion.* London: Macmillan, 1931

Keynes, J.M.: *The General Theory of Employment, Interest, and Money.* London: Macmillan, 1936

Killeen, J., and Bird, M.: *Education and Work: a Study of Paid Educational Leave in England and Wales (1976/77).* Leicester: National Institute of Adult Education, 1981

Knasel, E.G., Kidd, J.M., and Watts, A.G.: *The Benefit of Experience: Individual Guidance and Support within the Youth Opportunities Programme.* Special Programmes Research and Development Series No. 5. London: Manpower Services Commission, 1982

Kuhn, T.S.: *The Structure of Scientific Revolutions* (2nd edition). Chicago: University of Chicago Press, 1970

Kumar, K.: *Prophecy and Progress.* Harmondsworth: Penguin, 1978

Kushner, S., and Logan, T.: 'Street-Wise or School-Wise'. *Times Educational Supplement,* 25 September 1981

Lavercombe, S., and Fleming, D.: 'Attitudes and Duration of Unemployment among 16-Year-Old School-Leavers'. *British Journal of Guidance and Counselling,* Volume 9 No. 1, January 1981

Law, B.: 'Careers Theory: a Third Dimension?' In Watts, A.G., Super, D.E., and Kidd, J.M. (eds.): *Career Development in Britain.* Cambridge: CRAC/Hobsons, 1981(a)

Law, B.: 'Community Interaction: a "Mid-Range" Focus for Theories of Career Development in Young Adults'. *British Journal of Guidance and Counselling,* Volume 9 No. 2, July 1981(b)

Law, B., and Watts, A.G.: *Schools, Careers and Community.* London: Church Information Office, 1977

Lee, R.: *Beyond Coping: Some Approaches to Social Education*. London: Further Education Curriculum Review and Development Unit, 1980

Loney, M.: 'The Politics of Job Creation'. In Craig, G., Mayo, M., and Sharman, N. (eds.): *Jobs and Community Action*. London: Routledge & Kegan Paul, 1979

Macafee, K.: 'A Glimpse of the Hidden Economy in the National Accounts'. *Economic Trends*, No. 316, February 1980

Maguire, M.J., and Ashton, D.N.: 'Employers' Perceptions and Use of Educational Qualifications'. *Educational Analysis*, Volume 3 No. 2, 1981

Main, B.G.M., and Raffe, D.: 'Determinants of Employment and Unemployment among School Leavers: Evidence from the 1979 Survey of Scottish School Leavers'. *Scottish Journal of Political Economy*, Volume 30 No. 1, February 1983

Makeham, D., and Morgan, P.: *Evaluation of the Job Release Scheme*. London: Department of Employment, 1980

Manpower Services Commission: *Vocational Preparation for Young People: a Discussion Paper*. Training Services Agency. London: HMSO, 1975

Manpower Services Commission: *Young People and Work* (Holland Report). London: MSC, 1977

Manpower Services Commission: *Long-Term Unemployment*. Manpower Paper 1. Sheffield: MSC, 1982(a)

Manpower Services Commission: *Labour Market Quarterly Report*, November 1982(b)

Manpower Services Commission: *Manpower Review 1982*. Sheffield: MSC, 1982(c)

Manpower Services Commission: *Annual Report 1981/82*. Sheffield: MSC, 1982(d)

Manpower Services Commission: 'Review of Fourth Year of Special Programmes'. *MSC Special Programmes News*, October 1982(e)

Manpower Services Commission: *Youth Task Group Report*. London: MSC, 1982(f)

Manpower Services Commission: *Labour Market Quarterly Report*, February 1983

Manpower Services Commission: *Instructional Guide to Social and Life Skills*. London: MSC, n.d.

Marcuse, H.: *Eros and Civilization*. New York: Beacon, 1955

Marcuse, H.: *One Dimensional Man*. London: Routledge & Kegan Paul, 1964

Markall, G.: 'The Job Creation Programme: Some Reflections on its Passing'. In Rees, T.L., and Atkinson, P. (eds.): *Youth Unemployment and State Intervention*. London: Routledge & Kegan Paul, 1982

Markall, G., and Gregory, D.: 'Who Cares? The MSC Interventions: Full of Easter Promise'. In Rees, T.L., and Atkinson, P. (eds.): *Youth Unemployment and State Intervention*. London: Routledge & Kegan Paul, 1982

Marris, P., and Rein, M.: *Dilemmas of Social Reform*. London: Routledge & Kegan Paul, 1967

Marsden, C.T.: 'Youth Employment and Unemployment: Implications for Education and Training'. London: British Petroleum Company, 1983 (mimeo)

Marsden, D.: *Workless* (revised edition). London: Croom Helm, 1982

Martin, A.: 'Helping the Unemployed'. *Initiatives*, No. 1, May 1982

Martin, J.: *The Wired Society*. Englewood Cliffs, New Jersey: Prentice-Hall, 1978

Martin, J.P., and Webster, D.: *The Social Consequences of Conviction*. London: Heinemann, 1971

Marx, K.: *Selected Writings in Sociology and Social Philosophy* (ed. T.B. Bottomore and

M. Rubel). Harmondsworth: Penguin, 1963

Marx, K.: *Capital: a Critique of Political Economy* (translated by B. Fowkes). Harmondsworth: Penguin, 1976 (first published 1867)

Marx, K., and Engels, F.: *The Communist Manifesto* (translated by S. Moore). Harmondsworth: Penguin, 1967 (first published 1848)

Maslow, A.: *Motivation and Personality*. New York: Harper, 1954

McLellan, D.: *The Thought of Karl Marx: an Introduction*. London: Macmillan, 1971

McIntosh, N., and Smith, D.J.: *The Extent of Racial Discrimination*. London: PEP, 1974

Meadows, D.H., Meadows, D.L., Randers, J., and Behrens, W.W.: *The Limits to Growth*. New York: Universe, 1972

Merritt, G.: *World Out of Work*. London: Collins, 1982

Mills, C.W.: *White Collar*. New York: Oxford University Press, 1951

Minford, P.: *Unemployment: Cause and Cure*. Oxford: Martin Robertson, 1983

Ministry of Education: *Statistics of Education 1962, Part Three*. London: HMSO, 1964

Mishan, E.J.: *The Economic Growth Debate: an Assessment*. London: Allen & Unwin, 1977

Moorhouse, G.: *Against All Reason*. London: Weidenfeld & Nicolson, 1969

Morgan, R., and Cheadle, A.J.: 'Unemployment Impedes Resettlement'. *Social Psychiatry*, Volume 10, 1975

Morris, W.: *Signs of Change*. London: Reeves & Turner, 1888

Morse, N.C., and Weiss, R.S.: 'The Function and Meaning of Work and the Job'. *American Sociological Review*, Volume 20 No. 2, April 1955

Morton-Williams, R., and Finch, S.: *Young School Leavers*. Schools Council Enquiry One. London: HMSO, 1968

Mouly, J.: 'Employment: a Concept in Need of Renovation'. In Freedman, D.H. (ed.): *Employment Outlook and Insights*. Geneva: International Labour Organization, 1979

Moylan, S., and Davies, B.: 'The Disadvantages of the Unemployed'. *Employment Gazette*, Volume 88 No. 8, August 1980

Moylan, S., and Davies, B.: 'The Flexibility of the Unemployed'. *Employment Gazette*, Volume 89 No. 1, January 1981

Mukherjee, S.: *There's Work to be Done*. London: HMSO, 1974

Mukherjee, S.: *Unemployment Costs* ... London: PEP, 1976

Mungham, G.: 'Workless Youth as a "Moral Panic" '. In Rees, T.L., and Atkinson, P. (eds.): *Youth Unemployment and State Intervention*. London: Routledge & Kegan Paul, 1982

National Joint Advisory Council: *Training for Skill* (Carr Report). London: HMSO, 1958

National Youth Bureau: 'Alternatives to Unemployment: Some Options for Youth Workers'. Leicester: NYB, 1982 (mimeo)

Newcastle City Council: 'The Direct Costs and Immediate Effects of the Closure of the Scotswood Works of Vickers on the Newcastle Area'. Joint report of the City Planning Department, Management Services Department and Welfare Rights Service. Newcastle-upon-Tyne: Newcastle City Council, 1979 (mimeo)

Newcomber, M.: 'The Little Businessman: a Study of Business Proprietors in Poughkeepsie, New York'. *Business History Review*, Volume XXXV No. 4, Winter 1961

Newland, K.: *Productivity: the New Economic Context*. Worldwatch Paper 49. Washington, DC: Worldwatch Institute, 1982

Northcott, J., and Rogers, P.: *Microelectronics in Industry: What's Happening in Britain*. London: Policy Studies Institute, 1982

Oakley, A.: *The Sociology of Housework*. London: Martin Robertson, 1974

O'Connor, D.: 'Probabilities of Employment after Work Experience'. *Employment Gazette*, Volume 90 No. 1, January 1982

Office of Population Censuses and Surveys: *Census 1981 County Monitor: Merseyside Supplement, Liverpool Special Area*. London: OPCS, 1981

Office of Population Censuses and Surveys: *General Household Survey 1980*. London: HMSO, 1982(a)

Office of Population Censuses and Surveys: *Labour Force Survey 1981*. London: HMSO, 1982(b)

Orwell, G.: *The Road to Wigan Pier*. London: Gollancz, 1937

O'Toole, J., *et al.: Work in America*. Cambridge, Massachusetts: MIT Press, 1973

Outer Policy Research Circle: *Policing the Hidden Economy*. London: OPRC, 1979 (mimeo)

Pahl, R.E.: 'Employment, Work and the Domestic Division of Labour'. *International Journal of Urban and Regional Research*, Volume 4 No. 1, March 1980

Pahl, R.E.: 'Family, Community and Unemployment'. *New Society*, No. 1001, 21 January 1982

Parker, S.: *The Sociology of Leisure*. London: Allen & Unwin, 1976

Peacock, A., Crowther, J., and Vallely, M.: 'The Potential of Community Schools for Building Up Alternative Responses to the Threat of Unemployment'. Edinburgh: Scottish Council for Research in Education, 1982 (mimeo)

Pearce, B., Varney, E., Flegg, D., and Waldman, P.: *Trainee Centred Reviewing*. Special Programmes Research and Development Series No. 2. London: Manpower Services Commission, 1981

Pemberton, A.: 'Doing Something about Nothing: a Note on the Australian Government's Response to Dole Fraud'. *Australian and New Zealand Journal of Sociology*, Volume 16 No. 3, November 1980

Peterson, A.D.C.: 'Education for Work or for Leisure?' In Haworth, J.T., and Smith, M.A. (eds.): *Work and Leisure*. London: Lepus, 1975

Phares, E.J.: *Locus of Control in Personality*. Morristown, New Jersey: General Learning Press, 1976

Phillips, A.W.: 'The Relation Between Unemployment and the Rate of Change of Money Wage Rates in the United Kingdom, 1861-1957'. *Economica*, Volume 25 No. 100, November 1958

Phillips, L., Votey, H.L., and Maxwell, D.; 'Crime, Youth and the Labor Market'. *Journal of Political Economy*, Volume 80 No. 3, May/June 1972

Polanyi, K.: *Origins of Our Time: the Great Transformation*. London: Gollancz, 1945

Poole, H.: 'The Psychological Effects of Unemployment on Young People'. Paper presented to the British Association for the Advancement of Science, York, September 1981 (mimeo)

Public Accounts Committee: *Ninth Report from the Committee of Public Accounts – Session 1976-77*. HC 532. London: HMSO, 1977

Pym, D.: 'Towards the Dual Economy and Emancipation from Employment'. *Futures*, Volume 12 No. 3, June 1980

Radloff, L.S., and Cox, S.: 'Sex Differences in Depression in Relation to Learned Susceptibility'. In Cox, S. (ed.): *Female Psychology: the Emerging Self*. New York: St Martin's Press, 1981

Raffe, D.: 'Education, Employment and the Youth Opportunities Programme: Some Sociological Perspectives'. *Oxford Review of Education*, Volume 7 No. 3, 1981(a)

Raffe, D.: 'Special Programmes in Scotland: the First Year of YOP'. *Policy and Politics*, Volume 9 No. 4, 1981(b)

Ramsden, S., and Smee, C.: 'The Health of Unemployed Men: DHSS Cohort Study'. *Employment Gazette*, Volume 89 No. 9, September 1981

Raven, J.: *Education, Values and Society*. London: Lewis, 1977

Rees, T.L., and Gregory, D.: 'Youth Employment and Unemployment: a Decade of Decline'. *Educational Analysis*, Volume 3 No. 2, 1981

Reich, C.A.: *The Greening of America*. New York: Random House, 1970

Ridley, F.F.: 'View from a Disaster Area: Unemployed Youth in Merseyside'. *Political Quarterly*, Volume 52 No. 1, January-March 1981

Rigby, A.: *Alternative Realities: a Study of Communes and their Members*. London: Routledge & Kegan Paul, 1974

Ritchie-Calder, Lord: 'A Case for Non-Work'. *The Nevis Quarterly*, No. 2, January 1979

Ritchie-Calder, Lord: 'Education for the Post-Industrial Society'. In Costello, N., and Richardson, M.: *Continuing Education for the Post-Industrial Society*. Milton Keynes: Open University Press, 1982

Roberts, Keith: *Automation, Unemployment and the Distribution of Income*. Maastricht, Netherlands: European Centre for Work and Society, 1982

Roberts, Kenneth: 'The Social Conditions, Consequences and Limitations of Careers Guidance'. *British Journal of Guidance and Counselling*, Volume 5 No. 1, January 1977

Roberts, Kenneth: 'The Sociology of Work Entry and Occupational Choice'. In Watts, A.G., Super, D.E., and Kidd, J.M. (eds,): *Career Development in Britain*. Cambridge: CRAC/Hobsons, 1981

Roberts, Kenneth, Duggan, J., and Noble, M.: *Unregistered Youth Unemployment and Outreach Careers Work, Final Report, Part One: Non-Registration*. Research Paper No. 31. London: Department of Employment, 1981

Roberts, Kenneth, Duggan, J., and Noble, M.: 'Out-of-School Youth in High-Unemployment Areas: an Empirical Investigation'. *British Journal of Guidance and Counselling*, Volume 10 No. 1, January 1982

Robertson, J.: *The Sane Alternative*. London: James Robertson, 1978

Robin, A.A., Brooke, E.M., and Freeman-Browne, D.L.: 'Some Aspects of Suicide in Psychiatric Patients in Southend'. *British Journal of Psychiatry*, Volume 114 No. 511, June 1968

Rothwell, R.: 'Technology, Structural Change and Manufacturing Employment'. *Omega*, Volume 9 No. 3, 1981

Rotter, J.B.: 'Generalized Expectancies for Internal versus External Control of Reinforcement'. *Psychological Monographs*, Volume 80 No. 1, 1966

Royal Commission on the Distribution of Income and Wealth: *Report No. 8: Fifth*

Report on the Standing Reference. Cmnd. 7679. London: HMSO, 1979

Rubber and Plastics Processing Industry Training Board: *Work and Learning.* Brentford: RPPITB, 1978

Russell, B.: *In Place of Idleness, and Other Essays.* London: Allen & Unwin, 1935

Russell, B., and Russell, D.: *The Prospects of Industrial Civilization.* London: Allen & Unwin, 1923

Sainsbury, P.: *Suicide in London.* London: Chapman & Hall, 1955

Santos, M.: 'Circuits of Work'. In Wallman, S. (ed.): *Ethnicity at Work.* London: Macmillan, 1979

Sawdon, A., and Tucker, S.: *CEP is Working.* Special Programmes Research and Development Series No. 7. London: Manpower Services Commission, 1982

Sawdon, A., Tucker, S., and Pelican, J.: *Study of the Transition from School to Working Life.* London: Youthaid, 1979 (mimeo)

Scase, R.: 'Images of Progress, 1: Sweden'. *New Society,* No. 742/743, 23/30 December 1976

Scharff, D.E.: 'Aspects of the Transition from School to Work'. In Hill, J.M.M., and Scharff, D.E.: *Between Two Worlds.* London: Careers Consultants, 1976

Schon, D.A.: *Beyond the Stable State.* London: Temple Smith, 1971

Schools Council: *Careers Education in the 1970s.* Working Paper 40. London: Evans/Methuen, 1972

Schools Council: *The Practical Curriculum.* Working Paper 70. London: Methuen, 1981

Schumacher, E.F.: *Small is Beautiful.* London: Blond & Briggs, 1973

Scottish Education Department: *From School to Further Education* (Brunton Report). Edinburgh: HMSO, 1963

Seabrook, J.: 'Have We Reached the End of the Working Class Epic?' *New Society,* No. 949, 22 January 1981(a)

Seabrook, J.: 'Unemployment Now and in the 1930s'. *Political Quarterly,* Volume 52 No. 1, January–March 1981(b)

Seabrook, J.: *Unemployment.* London: Quartet, 1982

Senior, B.: 'Evaluation of Member Satisfaction in a Skills Exchange for Unemployed People'. *The New Psychologist,* January 1983(a)

Senior, B.: 'Adult Educational Responses to Unemployment: a Critique and Proposal'. Milton Keynes: The Open University, 1983(b) (mimeo)

Shanks, M.: *Work and Employment in Post-Manufacturing Society.* Maastricht, Netherlands: European Centre for Work and Society, 1981

Shepherd, D.M., and Barraclough, B.M.: 'Work and Suicide: an Empirical Investigation'. *British Journal of Psychiatry,* Volume 136, May 1980

Short, C., and Taylor, D.: 'Unemployment: Causes and Palliatives'. *Youth and Policy,* Volume 1 No. 2, 1982

Showler, B.: 'Racial Minority Group Unemployment: Trends and Characteristics'. *International Journal of Social Economics,* Volume 7 No. 4, 1980

Showler, B.: 'Political Economy and Unemployment'. In Showler, B., and Sinfield, A.: *The Workless State.* Oxford: Martin Robertson, 1981

Showler, B., and Sinfield, A.: 'A Most Unequal Tax'. In Showler, B., and Sinfield, A.: *The Workless State.* Oxford: Martin Robertson, 1981

Silver, H.: 'Salaries for Students'. *Universities Quarterly,* Volume 19 No. 4, September

1965

Simon, B.: *Studies in the History of Education 1780-1870*. London: Lawrence & Wishart, 1960

Singer, E.J., and Johnson, R.: *Helping Young People to Learn*. London: Institute of Personnel Management/Manpower Services Commission, 1983 (mimeo)

Sleigh, J., and Boatwright, B.: 'New Technology: the Japanese Approach'. *Department of Employment Gazette*, Volume 87 No. 7, July 1979

Sleigh, J., Boatwright, B., Irwin, P., and Stanyon, R.: *Manpower Implications of Micro-Electronic Technology*. London: HMSO, 1979

Smith, D.J.: *Racial Disadvantage in Employment*. London: PEP, 1974

Smith, D.J.: *The Facts of Racial Disadvantage*. London: PEP, 1976

Smith, D.J.: *Unemployment and Racial Minorities*. London: Policy Studies Institute, 1981

Smith, S.D.: 'Young People and Employment (2): Employers' Use of Work Experience'. *Education Policy Bulletin*, Volume 8 No. 1, Spring 1980

Southgate, P.: 'The Disturbances of July 1981 in Handsworth, Birmingham: a Survey of the Views and Experiences of Male Residents'. In *Public Disorder*. Home Office Research Study No. 72. London: HMSO, 1982

Stack, C.B.: *All Our Kin: Strategies for Survival in a Black Community*. New York: Harper & Row, 1974

Stafford, E.M.: 'The Impact of the Youth Opportunities Programme on Young People's Employment Prospects and Psychological Well-Being'. *British Journal of Guidance and Counselling*, Volume 10 No. 1, January 1982

Stafford, E.M., Jackson, P.R., and Banks, M.H.: 'Employment, Work Involvement and Mental Health in Less Qualified Young People'. *Journal of Occupational Psychology*, Volume 53 No. 4, December 1980

Stern, E.: 'Youth, Work and Changing Cultures: Some Considerations of the Context of Youth Opportunities'. MSC Learning at Work Development Project Working Note 5. London: Tavistock Institute of Human Relations, 1980 (mimeo)

Stonier, T.: *The Wealth of Information*. London: Methuen, 1983

Stretton, H.: *Housing and Government*. Sydney: Australian Broadcasting Corporation, 1974

Stronach, I., and Weir, A.D.: *Once Upon a Timetable: Final Evaluation Report on the Strathclyde EEC Project*. Glasgow: Jordanhill College of Education, 1983 (mimeo)

Swain, G.: 'The Youth Worker as Initiator and Provider'. In *Information Pack: The Youth Worker as Initiator and Provider*. Leicester: National Youth Bureau, 1982 (mimeo)

Swift, B.: 'Job Orientations and the Transition from School to Work: a Longitudinal Study'. *British Journal of Guidance and Counselling*, Volume 1 No. 1, January 1973

Swinscow, D.: 'Some Suicide Statistics'. *British Medical Journal*, 23 June 1951

Tawney, R.H.: *Religion and the Rise of Capitalism*. London: Murray, 1926

Tawney, R.H.: *Equality*. London: Allen & Unwin, 1964 (first published 1931)

Taylor, R.: 'Is Britain Over-Manned?' *New Society*, No. 712, 27 May 1976

Taylor, R.: 'Quarter of Work Force Lost Jobs'. *Observer*, 5 September 1982

Theobald, R.: *Free Men and Free Markets*. New York: Potter, 1963

Thomas, H.: 'Schools, Teacher Training and the Working World: Reflections on Case Studies'. *European Journal of Education*, Volume 14 No. 4, 1979

Thompson, E.P.: 'Time, Work-Discipline and Industrial Capitalism'. *Past and Present*, No. 38, 1967

Thornton, P., and Wheelock, V.: 'What Future for Employment?' *Employee Relations*, Volume 1 No. 1, 1979

Titmuss, R.: *The Gift Relationship*. London: Allen & Unwin, 1970

Tobin, J.: 'On Improving the Economic Status of the Negro'. *Daedalus*, Volume 94 No. 4, Fall 1965

Toffler, A. (ed.): *Learning for Tomorrow: the Role of the Future in Education*. New York: Vintage Books, 1974

Toffler, A.: *The Third Wave*. London: Collins, 1980

Touraine, A.: *The Post-Industrial Society*. New York: Random House, 1971

Townsend, C., and Devereux, C.: 'Skill Development and the Curriculum'. *Educational Analysis*, Volume 3 No. 2, 1981

Townsend, P.: *The Family Life of Old People*. London: Routledge & Kegan Paul, 1957

Trades Union Congress: *Economic Review 1978*. London: TUC, 1978

Turner, G.: *The Social World of the Comprehensive School*. London: Croom Helm, 1983

Turner, R.H.: 'Sponsored and Contest Mobility and the School System'. *American Sociological Review*, Volume XXV No. 5, December 1960

University Grants Committee: *University Statistics 1980, Volume 2: First Destinations of University Graduates 1980-81*. Cheltenham: Universities' Statistical Record, 1982

University of Warwick Institute of Employment Research: *Review of the Economy and Employment*. Coventry: Institute for Employment Research, 1982 (mimeo)

Veblen, T.: *The Theory of the Leisure Class*. New York: Macmillan, 1899

Vecchio, R.P.: 'The Function and Meaning of Work and the Job: Morse and Weiss (1955) Revisited'. *Academy of Management Journal*, Volume 23 No. 2, June 1980

Vigderhous, G., and Fishman, G.: 'The Impact of Unemployment and Familial Integration on Changing Suicide Rates in the USA, 1920-1969'. *Social Psychiatry*, Volume 13 No. 4, 1978

Vonnegut, K.: *Player Piano*. London: Macmillan, 1953

Wainwright, W., and Elliott, D.: *The Lucas Plan: a New Trade Unionism in the Making?* London: Allison & Busby, 1982

Walker, A.: 'The Social Consequences of Early Retirement'. *Political Quarterly*, Volume 53 No. 1, January-March 1982 (a)

Walker, A., Ormerod, P., and Whitty, L.: *Abandoning Social Priorities*. Poverty Pamphlet 44. London: Child Poverty Action Group, 1979

Walker, G.: 'Mending the Fuse'. *Education*, 30 April 1982 (b)

Wallace, C.: 'Adapting to Unemployment'. *Youth in Society*, No. 40, March 1980

Waller, W.: *The Sociology of Teaching*. New York: Wiley, 1932

Ward, B.: *Progress for a Small Planet*. Harmondsworth: Penguin, 1979

Ward, C.: 'Workers of the World Disperse'. *Careers Journal*, Volume 2 No. 3, 1982

Ward, R.: *Evaluating the Effects of Careers Education*. Unpublished MPhil thesis, The Hatfield Polytechnic, 1981

Warr, P.: 'A National Study of Non-Financial Employment Commitment'. *Journal of Occupational Psychology*, Volume 55, 1982

Watts, A.G.: 'A Structure for Careers Education'. In Jackson, R. (ed.): *Careers Guidance: Practice and Problems*. London: Arnold, 1973(a)

Watts, A.G.: 'The Qualifications Spiral'. *Sunday Times Magazine*, 7 October 1973(b)

Watts, A.G.: 'A Policy for Youth?' *The Ditchley Journal*, Volume IV No. 1, Spring 1977(a)

Watts, A.G.: 'Careers Education in Higher Education: Principles and Practice'. *British Journal of Guidance and Counselling*, Volume 5 No. 2, July 1977(b)

Watts, A.G.: 'The Implications of School-Leaver Unemployment for Careers Education in Schools'. *Journal of Curriculum Studies*, Volume 10 No. 3, September 1978

Watts, A.G.: 'Educational and Careers Guidance Services for Adults: II. A Review of Current Provision'. *British Journal of Guidance and Counselling*, Volume 8 No. 2, July 1980

Watts, A.G.: 'Careers Education and the Informal Economies'. *British Journal of Guidance and Counselling*, Volume 9 No. 1, January 1981

Watts, A.G. (ed.): *Schools, YOP and the New Training Initiative*. Cambridge: CRAC/Hobsons, 1982

Watts, A.G. (ed.): *Work Experience and Schools*. London: Heinemann, 1983(a)

Watts, A.G.: 'Skill Transfer and Post-YTS Realities'. *Lifeskills Teaching Magazine*, Volume 2 No. 2, April 1983(b)

Waugh, C.: 'Youth Training Scheme: In Whose Interests?' *Socialism and Education*, Volume 10 No. 1, 1983

Weber, M.: *The Protestant Ethic and the Spirit of Capitalism* (translated by T. Parsons). London: Allen & Unwin, 1930 (first published 1904-5)

Weisbrod, B.A.: *The Voluntary Nonprofit Sector*. Lexington, Massachusetts: Heath, 1977

Westergaard, J., and Resler, H.: *Class in a Capitalist Society*. London: Heinemann, 1975

White, M.: *Shorter Working Time*. London: Policy Studies Institute, 1980

Wiener, M.J.: *English Culture and the Decline of the Industrial Spirit, 1850-1980*. Cambridge: Cambridge University Press, 1981

Wilby, P.: 'The Classes of '83'. *Sunday Times*, 22 May 1983

Wilde, O.: 'The Soul of Man Under Socialism' (first published 1890). In *Complete Works of Oscar Wilde*. London: Collins, 1966

Williams, R.: *The Long Revolution*. London: Chatto & Windus, 1961

Williams, R.: *Keywords*. London: Fontana/Croom Helm, 1976

Williamson, H.: 'Client Response to the Youth Opportunities Programme'. In Rees, T.L., and Atkinson, P. (eds.): *Youth Unemployment and State Intervention*. London: Routledge & Kegan Paul, 1982

Willis, P.: *Learning to Labour*. Farnborough: Saxon House, 1977

Windschuttle, K.: *Unemployment*. Ringwood, Australia: Penguin, 1979

Wirtz, W.: *The Boundless Resource*. Washington, DC.: New Republic, 1975

Woods, P.: *The Divided School*. London: Routledge & Kegan Paul, 1979

Young, M., and Willmott, P.: *Family and Kinship in East London*. London: Routledge & Kegan Paul, 1957

Young, S., and Hood, N.: *Chrysler UK: a Corporation in Transition*. New York: Praeger, 1977

Subject Index

Name Index

The help of Sandra Greenhall of NICEC in compiling this index is gratefully acknowledged.